A COMPREHENSIVE GUIDE TO THE

FAIR LABOR STANDARDS ACT

FOR PUBLIC EMPLOYERS

DIANE M. JUFFRAS

The School of Government at the University of North Carolina at Chapel Hill works to improve the lives of North Carolinians by engaging in practical scholarship that helps public officials and citizens understand and improve state and local government. Established in 1931 as the Institute of Government, the School provides educational, advisory, and research services for state and local governments. The School of Government is also home to a nationally ranked Master of Public Administration program, the North Carolina Judicial College, and specialized centers focused on community and economic development, information technology, and environmental finance.

As the largest university-based local government training, advisory, and research organization in the United States, the School of Government offers up to 200 courses, webinars, and specialized conferences for more than 12,000 public officials each year. In addition, faculty members annually publish approximately 50 books, manuals, reports, articles, bulletins, and other print and online content related to state and local government. The School also produces the *Daily Bulletin Online* each day the General Assembly is in session, reporting on activities for members of the legislature and others who need to follow the course of legislation.

Operating support for the School of Government's programs and activities comes from many sources, including state appropriations, local government membership dues, private contributions, publication sales, course fees, and service contracts.

Visit sog.unc.edu or call 919.966.5381 for more information on the School's courses, publications, programs, and services.

Michael R. Smith, Dean
Thomas H. Thornburg, Senior Associate Dean
Jen Willis, Associate Dean for Development
Michael Vollmer, Associate Dean for Administration

FACULTY

Whitney Afonso	James M. Markham
Trey Allen	Christopher B. McLaughlin
Gregory S. Allison	Kara A. Millonzi
David N. Ammons	Jill D. Moore
Ann M. Anderson	Jonathan Q. Morgan
Maureen Berner	Ricardo S. Morse
Frayda S. Bluestein	C. Tyler Mulligan
Mark F. Botts	Kimberly L. Nelson
Anita R. Brown-Graham	David W. Owens
Peg Carlson	William C. Rivenbark
Connor Crews	Dale J. Roenigk
Leisha DeHart-Davis	John Rubin
Shea Riggsbee Denning	Jessica Smith
Sara DePasquale	Meredith Smith
Jacquelyn Greene	Carl W. Stenberg III
Norma Houston	John B. Stephens
Cheryl Daniels Howell	Charles Szypszak
Willow S. Jacobson	Shannon H. Tufts
Robert P. Joyce	Aimee N. Wall
Diane M. Juffras	Jeffrey B. Welty (on leave)
Dona G. Lewandowski	Richard B. Whisnant
Adam Lovelady	

Printed in the United States of America
24 23 22 21 20   1 2 3 4 5
ISBN 978-1-56011-973-9

UNC | **SCHOOL OF GOVERNMENT**

Contents

Chapter 3
Compensable Time 59

Introduction

The Fair Labor Standards Act (FLSA) was the first—and remains one of the most—important worker protection laws. Since 1938, the FLSA has required employers to pay employees at least the federal minimum wage (currently $7.25 per hour) and to pay a premium rate of one-and-one-half times an employee's regular rate of pay for every hour over forty hours that the employee works in a seven-day workweek. Congress had two primary reasons for adopting the overtime requirement in 1938. First, it wanted to encourage employers to hire more workers instead of simply requiring current employees to work longer hours. This would create additional jobs at a time of widespread unemployment. The second was to prevent workers from being overworked and to ensure that they were being compensated—and compensated fairly—for long hours of work, frequently in arduous conditions in coal mines, factories, and textile mills. Before employers were required to compensate workers with overtime pay, it was not uncommon in some industries and geographical areas for employees to work as many as sixty to eighty hours per week, sometimes for as little as $1.00 per day. A sixty-to-eighty-hour workweek necessarily translated to ten-to-eleven-hour workdays and seven-day workweeks. Before the passage of the FLSA, child labor under these conditions was common.[1]

The Application of the FLSA to Public Employers

Initially and for a period of almost forty years, the FLSA applied only to private employers. In 1966, Congress amended the Act to include some governmental employees within its protections. In 1974, Congress expanded coverage of the FLSA to include all public employees. In a confusing 1976 decision, the United States Supreme Court held that the FLSA applied only to state and local governmental employees engaged in "traditional governmental functions."[2] The Court overturned that decision in 1985 in *Garcia v. San Antonio Metropolitan Transit Authority*,[3] holding that the FLSA applied to all public employees regardless of the functions they performed. Later that year, Congress passed a series of amendments to the FLSA that recognized the unique situation of public employers in being funded by and accountable to their taxpayers. It was these amendments that established the general rules applicable to, for example, governmental employers' use of compensatory time off, volunteers, and

---

1. For a brief overview of labor practices in the early twentieth century, see Peter Cole, *The Law That Changed the American Workplace*, Time.com (June 24, 2016), http://time.com/4376857/flsa-history/. For a more-detailed discussion, see Robert H. Zieger, Timothy J. Minchin, & Gilbert J. Gali, American Workers, American Unions: The Twentieth and Early Twenty-First Centuries ch. 1 (2014).

2. *See* Nat'l League of Cities v. Usery, 426 U.S. 833 (1976).

3. 469 U.S. 528 (1985) (Court overruled its decision in *Usery*).

the 207(k) twenty-eight-day scheduling exemption for law enforcement officers and firefighters. The U.S. Department of Labor (DOL) then promulgated Part 553 of its FLSA regulations, "Application of the Fair Labor Standards Act to Employees of State and Local Governments."

Exemption from the Overtime Requirement: A Short History

In the Beginning

Certain employees are exempt from the overtime requirement of the FLSA. The Act exempts from this requirement workers "employed in a bona fide executive, administrative, or professional capacity."[4] The statute does not define the terms "executive," "administrative," and "professional." Instead, it delegates authority to define these concepts with the binding power of law to the Secretary of Labor.[5] In 1938, DOL issued its first set of regulations defining the type of job duties required for a position to be exempt under one of the executive, administrative, or professional categories. Evaluation of a position based on these regulations (and subsequent amendments to and interpretations of them) has come to be known as the *duties test*. Two years later, in 1940, DOL introduced two additional requirements to the test for exemption from the FLSA's overtime rule. The first was that an employee had to be paid a predetermined amount each pay period without any reductions due to the quality or quantity of the employee's work. This has come to be known as the *salary test*, and it is currently set out at Section 541.602 of title 29 of the Code of Federal Regulations (C.F.R.). The second requirement was that an employee's salary had to meet a specific minimum amount. This has come to be known as the *salary threshold test*, and it is currently set out at Section 541.600 of the same C.F.R. title. When the FLSA was enacted in 1938, the minimum salary threshold was $30 per week.[6] In 2004, it was increased to $455 per week ($23,660 annualized), and on January 1, 2020, that figure rose to $684 per week ($35,568 annualized).

Between 1938 and 1975, the salary threshold was increased and the duties tests were revised numerous times. Between 1975 and 2004, however, the regulations were only revised twice—both times in 1992 on separate occasions. The first 1992 revision created an exemption to the salary basis test limited to public employees. This revision created the provision currently found at Section 541.710(a) of C.F.R. Title 29 that allows public employers to dock the salary of their exempt employees who are absent from work when they have no accrued paid leave, have asked for but been denied permission to use accrued paid leave, or choose to use unpaid leave. The second 1992 revision introduced a new computer-related duties test for determining exemption following an amendment to the FLSA in 1990.

---

4. *See* 29 U.S.C. § 213(a)(1).
5. *See* 29 U.S.C. § 213(a)(1); Batterton v. Francis, 432 U.S. 416, 425 n.9 (1977).
6. *See* 3 Fed. Reg. 2518 (Oct. 20, 1938).

The 2004 Regulations

In 2004, DOL issued a substantial revision of the overtime regulations, including an increase to the salary threshold from $250 per week to $455 per week. The 2004 Final Rule also created a new exemption for so-called "highly-compensated employees," which exempted employees from overtime if they were paid a total annual salary of at least $100,000 and customarily and regularly performed at least one of the exempt responsibilities of the executive, administrative, or professional duties tests.[7]

The 2016 Regulations

In 2016, DOL issued a new rule raising the minimum salary an employee must make to be exempt from overtime from $455 per week ($23,660 annualized) to $913 per week ($47,476 annualized)—an increase of just over 100 percent.[8] The new salary minimum was to take effect December 1, 2016. Also part of the 2016 Rule and scheduled to take effect at the same time were (1) an increase in the minimum salary necessary for an employee to be exempt from overtime as a highly-compensated employee (from $100,000 annually to $134,004 annually), (2) a provision for automatic updating of the salary thresholds every three years, and (3) a new provision allowing employers to include nondiscretionary bonuses in an amount of up to 10 percent of the minimum salary level. The 2016 Rule made no changes to the duties tests and no changes to any of the other rules regarding compensable time and overtime.

Because DOL anticipated that the unprecedented increase in the salary threshold would meet resistance, it went to great pains to explain the reasoning behind the increase in its preamble to the rule. DOL explained that the threshold was designed to provide a clear, bright-line test for determining the exempt status of most positions. In other words, if an employee made above a certain amount, he or she was probably doing work that should be exempt. In 1975, 65 percent of the nation's workers fell below the then-threshold of $250 per week and were eligible for overtime. The 2004 salary threshold of $455 per week was below the poverty line for a family of four. Only 12 percent of salaried workers nationwide fell below it, which meant that the salary threshold no longer provided a bright-line test. Instead, for 88 percent of the country's workforce, a duties test analysis had to be undertaken to determine exempt status. In the introductory comments to the 2016 Rule, DOL said that it made a mistake in setting the salary threshold at $455 per week in 2004. The 2016 Rule's threshold of $913 per week represented the 40th percentile of earnings for a full-time (thirty-five hours per week), full-year, salaried worker in the fourth quarter of 2015. In the preamble to the 2016 Final Rule, DOL reiterated its conviction that a standard salary level at the 40th percentile would be a "bright line" that adequately distinguishes between employees whose positions are likely to meet the duties test requirements and those whose positions are likely not to do so.

---

7. The exemption for highly-compensated employees may be found at 29 C.F.R. § 541.601.
8. *See* 81 Fed. Reg. 32,391 (May 23, 2106).

The Litigation over the 2016 Regulations

In September 2016, a little more than two months before it was to go into effect, twenty-one states joined together in a lawsuit challenging the 2016 Rule in federal district court in Texas. They challenged not only the specific salary level set by DOL—$913 per week—but also DOL's very authority to include any salary level as part of the text for FLSA exemption. As part of that lawsuit, the plaintiffs filed a motion for a nationwide emergency preliminary injunction, citing the irreparable harm that the states (and particularly their budgets) would suffer if the new rule were allowed to go into effect on December 1. The motion was granted less than two weeks before the rule would have gone into effect. The Obama administration appealed the injunction to the federal Fifth Circuit Court of Appeals, which has jurisdiction over federal courts in Texas.

After a number of delays owing to the transition in administrations and the relatively late confirmation of President Trump's second nominee to head DOL, Alexander Acosta, DOL finally filed its reply brief in its appeal of the preliminary injunction on June 30, 2016. There, DOL revealed that it had decided "not to advocate for the specific salary level ($913 per week) set in the final rule." It asked that the Fifth Circuit address only the question of whether DOL had authority to set a salary level at all. DOL went on to say that instead of issuing a new proposed rule setting forth a specific salary level (in testimony before Congress, Secretary Acosta indicated that he favored a salary level between $30,000 and $35,000), it would instead seek information from stakeholders and issue a proposed rule later when the question of DOL's authority to set a salary level was settled. Oral argument before the Fifth Circuit was then set for October 2017.

In the meantime, some of the plaintiffs in the case asked the trial judge for summary judgment. A judge may grant summary judgment in a case, without holding a trial, when the parties agree on all of the relevant material facts in the case and the only thing left to do is to apply the law to the facts. The judge granted the plaintiffs' motion and declared the 2016 Rule invalid. The judge further found that DOL did have the authority to set a salary threshold as part of the test for determining overtime exemption. But he also found that DOL did not have the authority to set a salary threshold so high that it effectively eliminated the duties tests. The salary threshold of $913 per week, he concluded, did just that. At a level of $913 per week, the salary threshold became the effective and sole test of exempt status.[9] The judge also found the automatic updating of the salary threshold to be unlawful, based as it was on the $913 minimum salary.[10] Given that the trial judge's final ruling was in accord with DOL's position as set forth in its brief for the Fifth Circuit appeal, DOL was not expected to, and did not, appeal that decision. Instead, it asked the Fifth Circuit to dismiss its appeal, which it accordingly did.

---

9. *See* Nevada v. U.S. Dep't of Labor, 275 F. Supp. 3d 795, 807–08 (E.D. Tex. 2017).
10. *Id.* at 808.

The 2019 Change to the Salary Threshold Test

Fast forward to 2019. Recognizing that the salary level test's usefulness diminishes as the wages of employees entitled to overtime increases and the real value of the salary threshold falls, DOL issued a new rule raising the salary threshold effective January 1, 2020, to $684 per week ($35,568 annualized). This time, however, DOL used the same methodology it had used in 2004 and pegged the new salary threshold at the 20th percentile of earnings of full-time salaried workers in the lowest-wage census region (in 2004 and in 2019, the South) and in the retail sector based on the most recent data available from DOL.[11] DOL has changed the methodology used in the 2016 Rule to set the salary threshold for the highly-compensated employee exemption: it is now set at the 80th percentile of full-time salaried workers nationally.[12] For 2020 and beyond, this is an annual salary of $107,432. Instead of proposing automatic increases to the salary threshold, as the 2016 Rule had, DOL now says that it will increase the salary threshold on a regular basis using the federal government's standard notice-and-comment procedure.[13] Like the 2016 Rule, the 2019 Rule contains a new provision allowing employers to include nondiscretionary bonuses in an amount of up to 10 percent of the minimum salary level. The 2019 salary threshold rule made no changes to the duties tests and no changes to any of the other rules regarding compensable time and overtime.

Interpreting the FLSA

An employer bears the burden of proof in establishing that an exemption from the FLSA's overtime rules applies.[14] And for most of the FLSA's existence, the exemptions from overtime for employees performing executive, administrative, and professional duties have been narrowly construed.[15] In its 2018 decision in *Encino Motorcars, LLC v. Navarro*,[16] however, the U.S. Supreme Court expressly rejected that practice. Reasoning that the FLSA's exemptions are as much a part of its purpose as is its overtime requirement, the Court held that because the FLSA does not anywhere say that its

---

11. *See* 84 Fed. Reg. 51,230, 51,238 (Sept. 27, 2019).

12. *See id.* at 51,250.

13. *See id.* at 51,252.

14. *See* Corning Glass Works v. Brennan, 417 U.S. 188, 195 (1974) (employer did not sustain burden of proof in establishing that bona fide factor other than sex accounted for wage differentials between men and women in case brought under Equal Pay Act provisions of the FLSA); Darveau v. Detecon, Inc., 515 F.3d 334, 337 (4th Cir. 2008) (employer established that vice president of sales job duties satisfied the administrative exemption).

15. *See* Arnold v. Ben Kanowsky, Inc., 361 U.S. 388, 392 (1960) (employer did not fall within FLSA exemption for retail sales establishments); A.H. Phillips, Inc. v. Walling, 324 U.S. 490, 493 (1945) (same); Morrison v. Cty. of Fairfax, 826 F.3d 758, 761 (4th Cir. 2016) (fire captains not exempt under executive or administrative duties test); Williams v. Genex Servs., LLC, 809 F.3d 103, 105 (4th Cir. 2015) (holding that registered nurse was employed in professional capacity).

16. 138 S. Ct. 1134 (2018) (car-dealer service advisers are exempt from overtime).

exemptions should be construed narrowly, the proper approach is to give them a "fair (rather than a 'narrow') interpretation."[17] The decision did not change the burden of proof for establishing that an exception applies; that remains with the employer.

It is unclear what practical effect the *Encino Motorcars* decision will have going forward. Several defendants in FLSA cases have asked for reconsideration of decisions in light of *Encino Motorcars*, but the courts in question found that the High Court's decision did not change the outcomes in any of the defendants' cases.[18] Elsewhere, courts cite *Encino Motorcars* for the proposition that exemption must be given a fair reading and then proceed to make their analyses without further comment.[19] It isn't clear that the *Encino Motorcars* decision is going to change the way the U.S. Department of Labor handles investigations and enforcement actions for overtime violations or that it will make much of a difference in the outcomes in exemption cases, except possibly in a few cases where the correct classification is a close call.

The FLSA Going Forward into the Future

A thorough understanding of the Fair Labor Standards Act continues to be essential for all employers, both public and private. Paying employees correctly is necessary both because it helps attract and keep good employees and because mistakes may cause an employer to find itself on the hook for as much as two years of back overtime for each employee who has not been paid correctly. This book lays out the rules governing exempt status, the kinds of activities for which employees must be paid (compensable time), and overtime, with special attention paid to the issues and problems with which North Carolina public employers routinely grapple. The book would not, therefore, be possible without the questions and hypotheticals posed by School of Government clients who participate in our classes and advising services.

---

17. *Id.* at 1142.

18. *See* Wilkins v. Just Energy Grp. Inc., No. 13-CV-5806, 2019 WL 1317756, at *3 (N.D. Ill. Mar. 22, 2019) (court's summary judgment ruling did not turn on any general principle of statutory construction that called for reading FLSA exemptions narrowly); Berry v. Best Transp., Inc., No. 4:16-cv-00473-JAR, 2018 WL 6830097, at *8 (E.D. Mo. Dec. 27, 2018) (court gave a fair reading to the Motor Carrier Act exemption in the first place).

19. *See* Flood v. Just Energy Mktg. Corp., 904 F.3d 219, 228, 234–35 (2d Cir. 2018) (interpreting outside sales exemption); McKinnon v. City of Merced, No. 1:18-cv-001124-LJO-SAB, 2018 WL 6601900, at *3–4 (E.D. Cal. Dec. 17, 2018) (examining whether holiday pay should be included in the regular rate).

Chapter 1

Who Is Exempt from Overtime? The Salary Tests and the Duties Tests

When talking about employees, the most common distinction made is that between "exempt" and "nonexempt" employees. These terms mean, respectively, either exempt from the overtime rules of the Fair Labor Standards Act (FLSA)[1] or not exempt and subject to the FLSA's overtime rules. The practical difference between an employee's classification as exempt or nonexempt is that an exempt employee may be required to work more than his or her scheduled workweek without receiving any additional compensation beyond their fixed weekly salary. In contrast, nonexempt employees must always be paid overtime at a rate of time-and-one-half their regular rate of pay for every hour worked over forty hours in a given workweek.

How does an employer determine whether a position is exempt under the Fair Labor Standards Act? A position is exempt from the FLSA's overtime rules if it meets three requirements:

1. the position is paid a minimum of $684 per week;
2. the position is paid on a salary basis; and
3. the duties of the position satisfy either the executive duties test, the administrative duties test, or a professional duties test.[2]

These requirements are discussed in more detail in the sections below.

Salary Threshold Test

The requirement that the employee be paid a minimum of $684 per week is known as the *salary threshold test*. A minimum salary of $684 per week amounts to an annualized salary of $35,568, and employers frequently make reference to the salary threshold using the annualized salary figure. But to qualify for exempt status an employee must

---

1. 29 U.S.C. Ch. 8.
2. *See* 29 C.F.R. §§ 541.100, .200, .204, .300, .400, .602.

be paid $684 **each week**, unless the employer elects to apply discretionary bonuses or incentives of up to 10 percent of the minimum salary, in which case the minimum salary exclusive of bonuses and incentives must be no less than $615.60 per week.[3]

The inclusion of nondiscretionary bonuses and incentives in calculating the minimum salary is a fairly recent practice. In 2020, the United States Department of Labor (DOL) began allowing up to 10 percent of the minimum salary (now $684 per week) to be satisfied by nondiscretionary bonuses, incentives, and commissions. These payments must be made annually or more frequently. If by the last pay period of a year the sum of an employee's weekly salary plus nondiscretionary bonus, incentive, and commission payments received does not equal fifty-two times the minimum salary threshold of $684 per week, the employer may make one final payment sufficient to reach the required level no later than the next pay period after the end of the year. The year may be measured by any fifty-two-week period, but unless a period other than the calendar year is identified in advance in the employer's records, DOL will assume that the measurement period is the calendar year.[4] Any such final payment made after the end of the year may count only toward the prior year's salary amount and not toward the salary amount in the year it was paid.[5]

Salary Basis Test

In addition to earning a minimum of $684 per week, an employee must be paid that $684 on a "salary basis." What does it mean when we say that an employee is paid on a salary basis? Consider the following hypothetical.

> *Susan is a salaried employee and does not receive overtime or any additional compensation, no matter how many hours she works in a given workweek. Robert is a salaried employee and is paid overtime whenever he works more than the forty hours per week that his job description and schedule require. Both are paid in accordance with the requirements of the federal Fair Labor Standards Act.*

How can that last statement be correct? Salaried employees do not have to be paid overtime, do they? The answer to these questions requires an understanding of the difference between the concepts of "salaried" and "exempt".

---

3. *See* 29 C.F.R. § 541.602(a)(3).

4. *Id.*

5. *See id.*

What Does It Mean to Be Salaried?

The relevant Fair Labor Standards Act (FLSA) regulation issued by the U.S. Department of Labor (DOL) defines an employee paid on a "salary basis" as one who is paid a predetermined amount each pay period without any reductions due to the quality or quantity of the employee's work.[6] In other words, the employee must receive his or her full salary for any week in which he or she performs *any* work—regardless of the total number of days or hours worked in that week.[7] That is all that salary basis means in this context.

The definition of salary basis, though, doesn't explain how one employee can be paid on a salary basis and not be entitled to additional compensation for any extra time he or she has put into the job, while another employee paid on a salary basis can have a legally enforceable right to overtime compensation. That is because the right to overtime does not depend upon salary basis. It depends upon a position's *exempt* status, which includes, *among other requirements*, that the employee be paid on a salary basis. So, it is possible to have two employees each working forty-eight hours within the same week with one earning overtime while the other does not.

Do Leave Policies Affect Being Paid on a Salary Basis?

What happens when an employee paid on a salary basis takes off a few days because he or she is ill or wants to take a vacation? Almost all—if not all—local governments provide their employees with some minimal amount of paid sick, vacation, or personal leave. Federal appeals courts from around the country have long held that substitution of paid leave for salary does not affect salary basis or exempt status. Salary basis and exempt status are "only affected by monetary deductions for work absences and **not** by non-monetary deductions from fringe benefits such as personal or sick time."[8]

When a salaried **nonexempt** employee has used all of his or her accrued paid leave and takes time off nonetheless, the employer is free to deduct from the employee's paycheck a pro-rata amount of the weekly salary—in effect, to treat the employee like an hourly employee. The primary reason for paying a nonexempt employee on a salary basis is convenience, both for the employer and the employee. The FLSA requires an employer to pay a nonexempt employee only for the time actually worked, so a deduction from wages for absences from work does not violate the law. The employee can be paid on a salary basis again the following week.

When an **exempt** employee (salaried by definition) has used all of his or her accrued paid leave and needs time off, things get a little hairier—but only in the private sector, not in the public sector. In the private sector, an employer who pays an exempt employee less than the agreed-upon weekly salary because that employee

---

6. *See* 29 C.F.R § 541.602(a).

7. *See* 29 C.F.R. § 541.602(a)(1).

8. *See, e.g.,* Schaefer v. Ind. Mich. Power Co., 358 F.3d 394, 400 (6th Cir. 2004) (emphasis added). *See also* Haywood v. N. Am. Van Lines, Inc., 121 F.3d 1066, 1070 (7th Cir. 1997).

has worked fewer than the agreed-upon number of days violates the FLSA and may potentially destroy the exempt status of the position. In this scenario, the exempt position becomes a nonexempt position not only for that workweek but, potentially, for past and future workweeks as well. This is known as the *no-docking rule*.

The FLSA provides an exception from this formidable rule for employees of a government agency. Under Section 541.710(a) of Title 29 of the Code of Federal Regulations,

> [a]n employee of a public agency who otherwise meets the salary basis requirements of § 541.602 shall not be disqualified from exemption . . . on the basis that such employee is paid according to a pay system established by statute, ordinance or regulation, or by a policy or practice established pursuant to principles of public accountability, under which the employee accrues personal leave and sick leave and which requires the public agency employee's pay to be reduced or such employee to be placed on leave without pay for absences for personal reasons or because of illness or injury of less than one work-day when accrued leave is not used by an employee because:
>
> 1. Permission for its use has not been sought or has been sought and denied;
> 2. Accrued leave has been exhausted; or
> 3. The employee chooses to use leave without pay.

In other words, public employers are free to treat salaried exempt employees the same way they treat salaried or hourly nonexempt employees for the purposes of paid leave policies.

There are no specific requirements that a local government employer must follow to avail itself of what is sometimes called the "public accountability exception to the no-docking rule," and there is no definition of "public accountability." The courts have interpreted the concept broadly, finding government employers to have established pay practices based on principles of public accountability where the government organization was required to regularly open its books to outside auditors,[9] where provisions of state or local law allowed for the payment of government funds only where services have actually been rendered,[10] or where the practice was merely consistent with such a principle.[11] That is the case in North Carolina, where the state constitution requires that all units of state and local government be accountable for their use of taxpayer funds and prohibits the payment of state or local government

---

9. *See* Worley v. City of Cincinnati, No. C-990506, 2000 WL 1209989 (Ohio Ct. App. Aug. 25, 2000).

10. *See* Demos v. City of Indianapolis, 302 F.3d 698, 702–03 (7th Cir. 2002).

11. *See* Conroy v. City of Chicago, 644 F. Supp. 2d 1061, 1066–67 (N.D. Ill. 2009).

funds unless services have actually been rendered. Article I, Section 32 of the North Carolina Constitution provides,

> No person or set of persons is entitled to exclusive or separate emoluments or privileges from the community but in consideration of public services.

North Carolina public employers that have enacted pay practices that provide paid sick, vacation, or personal days and allow for deductions from pay when no paid leave is available do so in accordance with state law and, thus, satisfy the principle of public accountability. The bottom line? Public employers may make deductions from the pay of exempt employees who do not report for work and who either do not have accrued paid leave or do not satisfy the requirements for the use of accrued paid leave, just as they may from the salaries of salaried nonexempt employees.

Other Allowable Deductions

There are other deductions that may be made from the salary of an exempt employee without losing exempt status for that position. For example, an employer may suspend an employee without pay for violating a safety rule of major significance or for violations of rules governing workplace conduct. Also, deductions from an exempt employee's salary are permitted to account for the employee's partial first or last weeks of work, or partial weeks or days of work taken in accordance with Family and Medical Leave Act leave, and to offset any amounts received by an employee for jury duty, testimony as a witness, or as military pay where the employee is also receiving payment from their local government employer for that day. These exceptions will be discussed in Chapter 2, as will those deductions that cannot be made from the wages of either exempt or nonexempt employees.

The fact that an employee is paid on a salary basis does not by itself make that employee an exempt employee. The position also must meet the other two requirements for exemption, including one of the duties tests. Each of the duties tests in the third requirement is distinct and independent; a position need only satisfy one of them to be considered exempt. The *executive duties test* evaluates whether the position is a management position with significant authority over other employees. The *administrative duties test* evaluates whether the position is an office position that supports management and has significant decision-making authority in areas other than supervision of employees. The *professional duties tests* evaluate whether the position is one that requires an advanced academic degree or other high-level training. For each of these categories, it is the specific duties and responsibilities of the individual position—not the job title or job description—that determine whether or not the position is exempt from overtime.

Duties Tests: The Executive, Administrative, and Professional Tests

As noted above, in addition to being paid a minimum of $684 each week on a regular basis, an employee must have significant responsibilities, specialized skills, or both, to qualify for exemption from overtime. The U.S. Department of Labor (DOL) has organized these requirements into three separate areas: executive, administrative, and professional. For a position to be exempt from overtime, it must satisfy one of the corresponding duties tests.

The Executive Exemption from Overtime Pay

The executive duties test evaluates whether a position is a management position with significant authority over other employees. This test is relatively straightforward. For an employee to be in an exempt executive position, he or she must

1. have a primary duty of management of the organization or one of its recognized departments or subdivisions; **and**
2. customarily and regularly direct the work of two or more employees; **and**
3. have the authority to hire or fire other employees, or have his or her recommendations as to hiring, firing, promotion, or other change of status be given particular weight.

The regulations require that the position meet *all three* of these requirements to be exempt.[12]

Primary Duties

Most jobs have multiple duties. What does the term "primary duty" mean in the context of the FLSA overtime exemptions? DOL's FLSA regulations define the phrase "primary duty" as meaning the "principal, main, major or most important duty that the employee performs."[13] There is no minimum amount of time that an employee must spend performing the primary duty, although the regulation defining primary duty notes that employees who spend more than 50 percent of their time on exempt work are likely to be exempt.[14] Still, employees who spend less than 50 percent of their time on exempt work may still qualify for an exemption. The determining factor is "the character of the employee's job as a whole."[15]

The Primary Duty of Management

In assessing whether a position has a primary duty of management, the regulations direct employers to consider

- the relative importance of the employee's management duties compared with his or her other duties;
- the amount of time spent performing management work;

---

12. *See* 29 C.F.R. § 541.100.
13. *See* 29 C.F.R. § 541.700(a).
14. *See* 29 C.F.R. § 541.700(b).
15. *See* 29 C.F.R. § 541.700(a).

- the employee's relative freedom from direct supervision; and
- the relationship between the employee's salary and the wages paid to other employees for the kind of nonexempt work, if any, performed by the employee.

The regulations also give examples of the particular kinds of duties that DOL considers to be "management" duties. The list includes

- interviewing, training, and selecting employees;
- setting and adjusting pay and hours;
- planning, apportioning, and directing the work of other employees;
- evaluating the productivity and efficiency of other employees;
- recommending promotions for other employees;
- handling complaints and grievances;
- planning and controlling the budget;
- monitoring legal compliance;
- imposing penalties for violations of rules;
- implementing training programs; and
- handling community complaints.[16]

Supervising the Work of Two or More Employees

The FLSA regulations require that an employee direct the work of two or more full-time employees "or their equivalent" to qualify for the executive exemption. Therefore, supervision of four half-time employees satisfies this requirement.[17] DOL has said that in this context, it considers a full-time employee to be an employee who works forty hours each week. Where the normal full-time workweek of an individual employer is fewer than forty hours, however—thirty-seven hours, for example—DOL will consider that to constitute full-time employment.[18]

Authority to Hire or Fire

The final requirement for the executive exemption is that the position have actual hiring or firing authority, or at least significant influence over such decisions. The regulations require authority to hire *or* fire, not both. An employee who has authority to make new hires and promotions but is not a decision maker with respect to dismissals may still qualify as an executive employee. Similarly, an employee who has authority to terminate another employee but who is not involved in hiring decisions would also qualify for the executive exemption.[19]

---

16. *See* 29 C.F.R. § 541.102.
17. *See* 29 C.F.R. § 541.104.
18. *See* 69 Fed. Reg. 22,122, 22,135 (Apr. 23, 2004).
19. *See* 29 C.F.R. § 541.100(a)(4).

Under the North Carolina General Statutes, the only local government employees who have final hiring and firing authority are city and county managers, the county sheriff and register of deeds, and the directors of county social services and health departments (except in counties that have consolidated these departments) and area mental health authorities (local management entities-managed care organizations, or LME-MCOs). In all cases, the persons holding these positions will have management as a primary duty and will have the requisite supervisory authority to qualify for the executive exemption. These positions would therefore be the exception to the rule that it is job duties, not job title, that determines exempt status. *These particular positions—and only these—may be considered to qualify for the executive exemption automatically.*

Recommendations about Hiring or Firing Given Particular Weight

If a position has a primary duty of management and supervises two or more full-time employees, does not have legal hiring or firing authority, but *does* have significant influence ("particular weight") over hiring or firing, that position will also qualify for the executive exemption. What does "particular weight" mean in this context? In the regulation explaining "particular weight," DOL identifies three key factors: (1) whether making such recommendations is actually part of the employee's job duties, (2) the frequency with which the employee makes these recommendations and/or the frequency with which the employer requests recommendations from the employee, and (3) the frequency with which the employer adopts the employee's recommendations. Merely making suggestions about hiring, terminations, or promotions is not enough. If an employee's recommendations are not solicited or are not followed very often, the employee will not meet the requirements of the executive duties test.[20]

Which positions are likely to make recommendations about hiring or firing that are accorded "particular weight?" In many jurisdictions, assistant city and county managers, town administrators, and department and division heads will have such influence. In cities and counties of relatively larger size, it is usually a direct supervisor without final decision-making authority who evaluates an employee's performance or conduct and makes the initial, detailed recommendation to terminate, with the final decision being made by the city or county manager or a county department head with statutory authority to hire and fire.

Employees Who Perform Both Exempt Management and Nonexempt Duties: Which Are the Primary Duties?

Many departments and divisions are headed by employees who perform both managerial and nonexempt duties. The regulations provide that employers may still classify such employees as exempt executives provided that their *primary* duty is management. Employees who have both exempt and nonexempt duties should not be confused with "working supervisors" or "working foremen," whose primary duty

---

20. *See* 29 C.F.R. § 541.105.

consists of the regular work of the department or division, not management, while supervising those who are working alongside them. The regulations expressly state that working supervisors are not to be considered exempt employees.[21]

Consider the example of an electrician whose primary duty is to perform electrical work but who also directs the work of other electricians working in the same unit or at the same site, orders parts and materials for the job, and receives requests for electrical work. This electrician is nonexempt even though he carries out some management-related duties. Similarly, an otherwise nonexempt electrician who substitutes for an exempt supervisor when the supervisor is absent does not become an exempt executive by having the occasional responsibility to supervise others.

In contrast, true exempt executives who also perform nonexempt tasks perform their managerial responsibilities on a regular basis. They themselves decide when and for how long to perform managerial duties and when and for how long to perform nonexempt tasks—no supervisor determines this. Exempt executives typically remain responsible for the operations and personnel under their supervision even while they perform nonexempt tasks. Consistent with the definition of primary duty as discussed above, there is no limit on the amount of time that an executive may spend on nonexempt tasks to qualify as exempt.

Case Law on Positions with Exempt Executive and Nonexempt Duties

Most of the court decisions that address the proper application of the executive exemption to positions with concurrent exempt and nonexempt duties involve the position of store manager. Although "store manager" is a quintessentially private-sector position, the reasoning the courts adopt in these cases is applicable to local government positions.

Consider *Jones v. Virginia Oil Co.*, a Fourth Circuit Court of Appeals case from 2003. In that case, the court held that an assistant manager who spent 75 to 80 percent of her time performing nonexempt work could still be classified as an exempt executive because she could perform many of her management duties while she performed the nonexempt work.[22] Both Terri Jones, the plaintiff, and her employer agreed that Jones supervised two full-time employees and that she performed both managerial and nonexempt work. At issue was whether her primary duty was management when she spent the majority of her time flipping burgers, working the registers, and cleaning the bathrooms and parking lot.[23]

The court reached the conclusion that Jones was exempt after considering the factors set forth by DOL for determining whether a duty is primary. The court found with respect to the first factor—the relative importance of the managerial tasks—that Jones was responsible for hiring, scheduling, training, and disciplining employees and for checking inventory and ordering supplies, handling customer complaints,

---

21. *See* 29 C.F.R. § 541.106.
22. *See* Jones v. Va. Oil Co., 69 F. App'x 633, 639 (4th Cir. 2003).
23. *See id.* at 636.

counting daily receipts, and making bank deposits. These responsibilities, and Jones' own testimony that she was "in charge of everything," convinced the court that the success of the store depended on Jones' performing her managerial tasks.[24]

As for the second factor—the amount of time spent on management—the court noted that while Jones was doing nonexempt tasks she was simultaneously supervising employees, handling customer complaints, dealing with vendors, and completing daily paperwork. The court concluded that time, while important, could not be determinative in this case.[25]

With respect to the extent of Jones' discretion, the court found that this factor also weighed in favor of finding management as her primary duty: Jones had the discretion to hire, supervise, and fire employees; to handle customer complaints; and to run the day-to-day operations of the store as she saw fit.[26] Finally, Jones earned significantly more than other employees performing the same nonexempt duties as she.[27]

The court rejected Jones' claim that she was a "working supervisor" entitled to overtime, holding that "where an individual's responsibilities extend 'to the evaluation of . . . subordinates' and include 'the exercise of considerable discretion,' the working foreman exception does not apply."[28]

The Fourth Circuit reached a similar conclusion in a more recent case, *In re Family Dollar FLSA Litigation*.[29] Plaintiff Irene Grace was the store manager of a Family Dollar chain store. Grace claimed that a full 99 percent of her time was spent on nonexempt duties such as "putting out freight," working a cash register, "doing schematics," and performing janitorial work. The court, however, was not persuaded that this made her a nonexempt employee, noting that even while Grace performed these nonexempt tasks, she remained the person responsible for running the store and that she performed her managerial duties at the same time. Grace herself had testified that while running the cash register, she simultaneously considered the condition of the front of the store and kept an eye out for theft. The success and profitability of the store (and the size of the bonus she received) depended on her decision making and good judgment alone, which she exercised at the same time as she performed nonexempt duties.[30]

The Fourth Circuit emphasized the fact that her managerial duties were of greater importance than her nonexempt duties, given that the district manager visited the store only every two to three weeks. It was Grace who decided how to handle customer or employee complaints, made and revised schedules, arranged the stock display, and decided when to sweep the floor, restock the shelves, or fill out required

---

24. *See id.* at 637–38.
25. *See id.* at 637.
26. *See id.* at 638.
27. *See id.* at 638–39.
28. *See id.* at 639.
29. *See In re* Family Dollar FLSA Litig., 637 F.3d 508 (4th Cir. 2011).
30. *See id.* at 514–17.

paperwork. There was no other person making those decisions at the store.[31] Finally, the court noted that Grace was paid significantly more than other store employees in absolute terms and that she had the ability to influence the amount of her own compensation, a component of which was a bonus based on the profitability of the store she managed.[32] For all of these reasons, the Fourth Circuit found that Grace's position as store manager was exempt from overtime.[33]

How would the Fourth Circuit's analysis in *Jones* and *Family Dollar* apply to a public-sector position with both exempt and nonexempt duties? Consider the following hypothetical.

> *The city of Paradise, N.C., needs to determine whether its chief code enforcement officer is an exempt executive or a non-exempt position. The position's duties include assigning the daily work of five code enforcement officers, supervising and evaluating the officers and other staff of the division, resolving disputes, preparing information in support of budget requests and administering the division's budget, and reviewing and maintaining enforcement records prepared by other officers. The demands on the code enforcement division are such that it cannot afford to have one position devoted solely to management. Thus, in addition to managing the division, the chief also goes into the field on a daily basis to conduct inspections for compliance with applicable codes and standards, to identify violations and notify property owners of the violations and necessary corrective actions, and to conduct follow-up investigations.*
>
> *The city's human resources director determines that the chief spends only 40 percent of his time on management duties and a full 60 percent doing enforcement work in the field.*

The *Jones* and *Family Dollar* cases say that the actual time spent on exempt duties is not determinative of exempt status, so in this hypothetical the human resources director has considered the relative importance of the managerial tasks themselves. The position's exempt duties are much more important than its nonexempt duties: it seems fair to say that without the chief's supervision of the other officers and assignment of their work in accordance with their individual skills and expertise, and without the chief's maintenance of records and budget work, the Paradise code enforcement division could not function effectively. Were the chief not to perform the nonexempt inspection work, on the other hand, the division might perhaps take longer to respond to complaints and might fall behind in its inspections, but it would continue to perform its core functions.

---

31. *See id.* at 517.
32. *See id.* at 517–18.
33. *See id.* at 518.

Does the chief code enforcement officer exercise discretion in performing his management duties? This is one of the other factors the Fourth Circuit considered in determining whether a store manager was a true executive or merely a working supervisor. The human resources director correctly concluded that the position's scheduling duties; role in hiring, evaluating, and firing of workers; preparation of budget requests; and review of enforcement records requires significant exercise of judgment. The final factor also weighs in favor of classifying the chief position as exempt: the chief makes about $8,500 more than the highest-paid of the other code enforcement officers.

Numerous positions in local government involve the concurrent performance of both exempt and nonexempt duties, particularly positions in law enforcement above the rank of patrol officer or patrol deputy. These will be discussed in more detail below in the section on the administrative duties test.

The Administrative Exemption from Overtime Pay

While the executive duties test evaluates whether a position is a management position with significant authority over other employees, the administrative duties test evaluates whether a position is an office position that supports management and has significant decision-making authority in areas other than supervision of employees. To satisfy the administrative duties test, a position must meet two requirements in addition to being paid on a salary basis and earning a minimum of $684 per week. The position must

1. have a primary duty of office or nonmanual work directly related to management or the general business operations of the employer **and**
2. perform work requiring the exercise of discretion and independent judgment on matters of significance to the employer.[34]

These two requirements are anything but straightforward.

Primary Duty

Here, as in the executive duties test, "primary duty" means the "principal, main, major or most important duty that the employee performs." There is no set minimum amount of time that must be spent on administrative tasks for such work to be an employee's primary duty. The same factors applicable to executive employees—the relative importance of exempt tasks and the time spent on exempt tasks—are used to evaluate whether an employee is an exempt administrator.[35]

---

34. *See* 29 C.F.R. §§ 541.200(a)(1), (2).
35. *See* 29 C.F.R. § 541.700.

Work Related to Management or General Business Operations

The FLSA regulations define "work related to management or general business operations" as meaning to "perform work directly related to assisting with the running or servicing of the business, as distinguished, for example, from working on a manufacturing production line or selling a product in a retail or service establishment."[36] The regulations give the following as examples of work related to "the running or servicing of the business":

- finance, accounting, or auditing;
- purchasing and procurement;
- personnel management, human resources, and employee benefits;
- safety and health;
- insurance and quality control;
- public relations, advertising, and marketing;
- computer network, Internet, and database administration; and
- legal and regulatory compliance.[37]

Of course, local government employment encompasses a great deal more non-manual and office work than just those associated with the fields in this list. What about the position of city or county clerk or the work done in the register of deeds office? City and county planners? Lieutenants and captains in a public safety agency and 911 telecommunicators? Social workers? To understand whether positions like these qualify for the administrative exemption, we must return to the regulations' definition of administrative exempt work as "work directly related to assisting with the running or servicing of the business, *as distinguished, for example, from working on a manufacturing production line or selling a product in a retail or service establishment*" (emphasis added). In contrasting administrative duties with production or sales work, the regulations distinguish the basic work, purpose, or mission of an organization from the other kinds of work necessary to allow the organization to do its basic work.

Think of the mission of a governmental department or agency as the equivalent of the regulation's reference to production work. What is the basic work, or mission, of a fire department, for example? Firefighting and fire prevention. The work done to hire and pay firefighters and to outfit the firefighters and their trucks is not the mission work of local government but is, instead, the management and general business operations work that supports the mission. What is the mission of a public health department? To educate the public and to provide health services. Why does the register of deeds office exist? To record deeds and other documents in the public record. Thus, a firefighter, a public health nurse who staffs a clinic, and an employee of the register of deeds office who records mortgages on the land records are each engaged in the equivalent of the production work of their employer. None of these

---

36. *See* 29 C.F.R. 541.201(a).
37. *See* 29 C.F.R. § 541.201(b).

positions would qualify for the administrative exemption, even if the job duties of the position required the exercise of discretion and independent judgment in matters of significance, as the positions of firefighter, nurse, and assistant register surely do.

Other employees of the fire department, public health department, and register of deeds office whose work supports the fighting of fires, provision of health services, and recording of documents may well qualify for the administrative exemption. For example, the primary duties of a fire battalion chief may not be the fighting of fires (one of the purposes or the mission of local government). Instead, the battalion chief's primary duties may be the administrative work that she does in coordination with human resources and with the jurisdiction's purchasing officer that allows her unit to be scheduled, outfitted, trained, and ready to fight fires. If the person in this position exercises discretion and independent judgment on matters of significance, she may be administratively exempt. The office manager who runs the day-to-day operation of the clinic where the public health nurse practices may also be so exempt. The assistant register of deeds who implements the policies adopted by the elected register and oversees operations of the office may also qualify as an administrative employee, even if another assistant register does not.

Discretion and Independent Judgment

If a position's primary duties qualify as office work directly related to management or general business operations, that is still not the end of the exemption inquiry. To be exempt, the position must involve work that requires discretion and independent judgment in matters of significance to the employer. Fundamental to the concept of "discretion and independent judgment" is the question of whether the employee has options from which to make a decision or choice. The FLSA regulations contain a non-exhaustive list of factors to consider in determining whether a position satisfies the criteria for discretion and independent judgment. Many of the factors focus on *the extent of the employee's authority either to act in the employer's name without prior approval or to take action that may deviate from established policy.* The list includes looking at whether the employee

- formulates, interprets, or implements management policies or operating practices;
- makes or recommends decisions that have a significant impact on general business operations or finances—this includes work that relates to the operation of a particular segment or department of the organization that nonetheless affects general business operations to a significant degree;
- is involved in planning long- or short-term objectives for the organization;
- handles complaints, arbitrates disputes, or resolves grievances;
- represents the organization during important contract negotiations;

- has the authority to commit the employer in matters that have significant financial impact; and
- has the authority to waive or deviate from employer policies and procedures without prior approval.[38]

In addition to these factors set forth in the FLSA regulations, in determining whether a position requires discretion and independent judgment, courts have also considered whether the position has

- freedom from direct supervision,
- personnel responsibilities,
- trouble-shooting or problem-solving responsibilities,
- authority to set budgets,
- a degree of public contact, or
- responsibility for advertising and promotion work.[39]

Employers frequently make the mistake of assuming that an employee must have final decision-making authority in order for a position to qualify for the administrative exemption. The regulations, however, recognize that many organizations require that significant decisions must receive multiple layers of review or approval. The regulations therefore allow a position to satisfy the discretion and independent judgment requirement even if the employee's decisions or recommendations are subject to review.[40] This is an important allowance for local governments where, for example, department or division heads may make the preliminary decisions about which candidate to hire or which model of expensive equipment to purchase, but final authority for the decision rests with the city or county manager. Similarly, an employee might narrow down purchasing choices to two competing products and provide an explanation of the pros and cons of each but may be required to leave the final choice to a department head or the manager. Where the cost of a purchase is large and the expenditure subject to the pre-audit requirement of the North Carolina General Statutes, the decision to purchase the specific item may be made by an administrative exempt employee, even if the purchase must receive final approval from the finance director.

Matters of Significance

Unfortunately for employers, the FLSA regulations do not define the term "matters of significance" other than to say what they are not. Case in point: The fact that poor job performance by an employee could have significant financial consequences for the employer does not, in and of itself, mean that the employee exercises discretion and independent judgment with respect to matters of significance. For example, the primary job duty of an employee working in accounts receivable may be processing incoming checks for deposit into the employer's account. The employee is supposed to double-check the amount of the check against the amount due. Suppose

---

38. *See* 29 C.F.R. § 541.202(c).
39. *See* 69 Fed. Reg. 22,122, 22,144 (Apr. 23, 2004).
40. *See* 29 C.F.R. § 541.202(e).

the employee processes a check bearing the notation "paid in full" but is distracted and neglects to check the amount due. The check is for substantially less—tens of thousands of dollars less—than the amount actually owed. Even though the mistake causes the employer to lose thousands of dollars, the employee's job duties are clerical and routine and do not involve the exercise of discretion and independent judgment in matters of significance. That employee is nonexempt. The potential for such an error cannot form the basis for classifying this position as exempt under the administrative duties test.[41]

Examples of Positions Satisfying the Administrative Duties Test

The regulations set forth examples of positions that would satisfy both the requirement that work be directly related to management or general business operations and the mandate that the work involve discretion and independent judgment. They include a human resources manager who formulates employment policies even though the decision to adopt the policies is made by others. The regulations contrast the position of human resources manager with that of a personnel clerk who collects information about job applicants and rejects those who do not meet basic qualifications but is not involved in further evaluation of qualifying applicants.[42] DOL offers as another example a purchasing agent who makes major purchases but is required to consult with top management before finalizing any major purchase. This position may well be exempt. Finally, an executive or administrative assistant to a city or county manager may be administratively exempt if the manager has delegated to the assistant the authority to arrange meetings, handle callers, and answer correspondence without having to follow specific instructions or procedures.[43] In contrast, an employee who operates an expensive piece of equipment is not performing work involving the exercise of discretion and independent judgment on a matter of significance.[44]

Examples of Positions Not Satisfying the Administrative Duties Test

The regulations contain specific examples of government employees who will not qualify for the administrative exemption, namely, "inspectors and investigators of various types, such as fire prevention or safety, building or construction, health or sanitation, environmental or soils specialists and similar employees."[45] The regulations explain that the work of such employees does not meet the first element of the administrative duties test as it does not relate to management or general business operations. Their work also does not generally require the exercise of discretion and independent judgment but instead involves the gathering of information and the application of established techniques, procedures, or standards.[46] The regulations

---

41. *See* 29 C.F.R. § 541.202(f).
42. *See* 29 C.F.R. § 541.203(e).
43. *See* 29 C.F.R. § 541.203(d).
44. *See* 29 C.F.R. § 541.203(g).
45. *Id.*
46. *See* 29 C.F.R. §§ 541.203(g), (j).

make clear that clerical or secretarial tasks, recording or tabulating data, or doing other kinds of routine work does not qualify as work requiring the exercise of discretion and independent judgment on matters of significance.[47]

Positions That Are Hard to Classify

Whether or not a position meets the requirements of the administrative duties test is the subject of much litigation. In the public sector, one of the most frequent issues arising in contested FLSA classifications is whether the position satisfies the requirement that its duties be directly related to management or general business operations or whether those duties are better characterized as core government or mission work. When the job is one that exists in both the public and private sectors, the issue that comes up most often is whether the employee in the position exercises discretion and independent judgment in matters of significance to the employer. To better understand these issues, let's look at three positions found in the imaginary city of Paradise, North Carolina: city planner, accountant, and management analyst.

The City Planner

City and county planners are one of the linchpins of local government. The U.S. Department of Labor's (DOL) Bureau of Labor Statistics' occupational dictionary describes urban and regional planners as positions that "develop land use plans and programs that help create communities, accommodate population growth, and revitalize physical facilities in towns, cities, counties, and metropolitan areas."[48] In the city of Paradise, the city planner position performs the following duties:

- handles the subdivision process;
- conducts site-plan reviews for compliance with setback uses, zoning, landscaping, and parking codes;
- recommends approval or disapproval of plans or site-plan modifications;
- administers zoning, subdivision, open space, and other planning regulations;
- works with applicants, citizens, and industrial and commercial representatives in preparing development applications; and
- appears before planning boards and governing boards.

Paradise had long classified the non-supervisory positions in its planning departments as exempt. The city's human resources director and attorney have recently concluded that this classification is incorrect and that the positions of City Planner I, City Planner II, and Senior Planner should all be classified as nonexempt and that employees in these positions should be paid overtime when they work in excess of forty hours in a workweek. How did they reach this conclusion?

---

47. *See* 29 C.F.R. §§ 541.202(d), (e).

48. U.S. Dep't of Labor, Bureau of Labor Statistics, *Occupational Outlook Handbook*, "Urban and Regional Planners: What Urban and regional Planners Do," https://www.bls.gov/ooh/life-physical-and-social-science/urban-and-regional-planners.htm#tab-2 (last visited Aug. 16, 2019).

The first prong of the administrative duties test asks whether the position has a primary duty of office or nonmanual work directly related to management or general business operations of the employer. The duties of city (and county) planners clearly qualify as nonmanual work and take place, for the most part, within an office setting. So far, so good. But the work of local government planners is **not related** to the management or general business operations of the employing government unit. Recall the discussion of the meaning of management in the section on the executive duties test, *supra*. Examples of the particular kinds of duties that DOL considers to be "management" duties include

- interviewing, training, and selecting employees;
- setting and adjusting pay and hours;
- planning, apportioning, and directing the work of other employees;
- evaluating the productivity and efficiency of other employees;
- recommending promotions for other employees;
- handling complaints and grievances;
- planning and controlling the budget;
- monitoring compliance with laws regulating the operation of the government unit;
- imposing penalties for violations of workplace rules;
- implementing training programs; and
- handling community complaints about employees and the overall operation of the organization.[49]

The duties of the Paradise planners (and of most local government planners) do not directly relate to any of the items on DOL's list of management duties.

The planner's duties fall squarely within the boundaries of what is local government's mission work. Recall the distinction between the basic work or mission of an organization and the other kinds of work that is necessary for the organization to be able to do its basic work. The mission work of local government is to provide those services that only local government provides: public safety, roads, utilities, and the like. What is the basic or mission work of the Paradise planning department? When asked, the Paradise planning director replies that it is to develop and implement land use plans within the jurisdiction and to develop plans related to the need and placement of community facilities, parks, and open spaces; to coordinate land use plans with transportation and transit plans; to work with the jurisdiction's economic development team and to review development proposals; to coordinate rezoning and approve subdivision plans; and, sometimes, to facilitate the annexation process.

As the planning director's answer makes clear, the work of the Paradise planning department is the basic work of local government, as core a form of mission work as is law enforcement and firefighting. It is what local government exists to do. As such, it is not work related to the management or business operations of the city. Rather,

---

49. *See* 29 C.F.R. § 541.102.

the management and business operations of the city exist to facilitate the work of planners, as well as that of police, firefighters, emergency medical crews, sanitation workers, road crews, and economic development teams, to name just a few examples of local governments' mission work. The position of city planner does not satisfy the first prong of the administrative duties test. It is, as the Paradise human resources director and attorney conclude, a nonexempt position.

The Accountant

The city of Paradise has a position in its finance department called "accountant," whose FLSA classification has recently been called into question. The primary job duties of the position are several. They are to

- post and balance the general and subsidiary ledger;
- prepare a variety of financial records, reports, and analyses;
- provide technical guidance to technical accounting staff;
- update the fixed-asset system for additions and deletions, assign asset numbers, and reconcile fixed-asset detail to fixed-asset account group;
- interpret and enforce fiscal policies and practices;
- assist and respond to requests by external auditors;
- supervise the processing and accounting for payroll and related reports, such as state and federal withholding reports, balancing and calculating payments by fund category; calculate health insurance payments;
- issue quarterly and annual tax reports and W-2 yearly withholding for employees;
- prepare quarterly fuel tax reports and prepare oil and gas analyses;
- review and distribute end-of-the-month reports to department heads;
- participate in budget preparation and administration as requested by the finance director; and
- serve as acting finance director in the absence of the finance director.

This position clearly satisfies the first prong of the administrative duties test—the work is nonmanual office work that is directly related to management and, perhaps even more so, to general business operations. The Paradise human resources director and attorney must now move on to the second prong of the administrative duties test and consider whether the position entails work requiring the exercise of discretion and independent judgment on matters of significance to the city. The accountant position includes duties that both do and do not require the exercise of discretion and independent judgment.

The duties that seem likely to involve the exercise of discretion and independent judgment include

- preparing a variety of financial records, reports, and analyses;
- interpreting and enforcing fiscal policies and practices;
- assisting and responding to requests by external auditors;
- preparing oil and gas analyses;

- participating in budget preparation and administration as requested by the finance director; and
- serving as acting finance director in the absence of the finance director.

The duties that do *not* appear likely to include the exercise of discretion and independent judgment (although they may require training and skill) are

- posting and balancing the general and subsidiary ledgers;
- providing technical guidance to technical accounting staff;
- updating fixed-asset system for additions and deletions, assigning asset numbers, and reconciling fixed-asset detail to fixed-asset account group;
- supervising the processing and accounting for payroll and related reports, such as state and federal withholding reports; balancing and calculating payments by fund category; calculating health insurance payments;
- issuing quarterly and annual tax reports and W-2 yearly withholding for employees;
- preparing quarterly fuel-tax reports; and
- reviewing and distributing end-of-the-month reports to department heads.

While we can, for purposes of this hypothetical, assume that the duties mentioned above as requiring the exercise of discretion and independent judgment do so, a real-life human resources director cannot make that assumption. The list of the accountant position's job duties illustrates well the limited utility of job descriptions in accurately classifying positions as exempt or nonexempt for FLSA purposes. The job description says that the person in this position will prepare "a variety" of financial records, reports, and analyses. What this means is anyone's guess. What it means in the City of Paradise may be different from what it means in Paradise County government. Some records and reports may require the employee to discern important differences, exercise judgment about whether or not an asset or a practice fits into a given category, and draw conclusions from data. Other reports will require only that the employee plug data into an already-existing framework or formula. In the job duty described as "interpreting and enforcing fiscal policies and practices," the word "interpret" suggests that the person in the position will be exercising discretion and independent judgment. That might not be the case, however. Not all policies are written in such a way as to allow for interpretation. The human resources director and attorney must ask whether the particular policies with which the accountant will work are likely to need interpretation in different sets of circumstances. Furthermore, does "enforce" mean that the person in this position has the authority to override a decision made by a subordinate or to choose among different practices? To accurately classify this position as exempt or nonexempt in a particular city or county, the human resources director will have to interview the person(s) currently holding this position, his or her supervisor and department head, and, possibly, people who previously held this position.

The human resources director will have to ask similar kinds of questions about the next two sets of duties, as well: assisting and responding to requests by external auditors and preparing oil and gas analyses. The human resources director must understand what these duties entail on a day-to-day basis.

The last two items on the list of the accountant's primary duties—participating in budget preparation and administration as requested by the finance director and serving as acting finance director in the absence of the finance director—strongly imply use of discretion or independent judgment in matters of significance to the city. Does that mean that their inclusion in the job description automatically makes this position exempt? No, it does not. Whether or not these duties make the position exempt turns on how frequently they are performed and how important it is that they be performed and be performed by the person in this position.

The human resources director must also consider whether the position makes decisions on matters of significance *to the employer.* Although we might say that "finance" is a matter of significance to the city, that answer is not good enough. The question of whether the *particular* judgments this employee makes are on matters of significance cannot be determined on the basis of this general list of duties. Once again, the human resources director will have to dig deeper into the meaning of this duty to make the correct call on classification.

Once the human resources director determines that a job duty requires the exercise of discretion and independent judgment on matters of significance to the city, he or she must evaluate whether this duty or a set of duties requiring discretion and independent judgment are important enough in the overall scheme of the job to make that position exempt. When the U.S. Department of Labor revised the regulations setting forth the duties tests for FLSA exemptions in 2004, it eliminated from the analysis any measure of percentage of time spent on a duty or group of duties. Instead, the rules now advise employers to consider only the job's *primary* duty or duties in classifying it as an executive, administrative, or professional position. The FLSA regulations define the phrase "primary duty" as meaning the "principal, main, major or most important duty that the employee performs."[50] The regulation goes on to say that while employees who spend more than 50 percent of their time on exempt work are *likely* to be exempt, there is no minimum time *requirement.* Employees who spend less than 50 percent of their time on exempt work may still qualify for an exemption. The time spent on exempt duties may be a factor in determining the primary duty, the rule says, but the emphasis should be on "the character of the employee's job as a whole."[51] As explained earlier in the discussion of the executive exemption, in determining whether a duty is a primary duty, important factors to consider are

- the relative importance of the duty or group of duties being examined compared with the employee's other duties;
- the amount of time spent performing this duty or group of duties;
- the employee's relative freedom from direct supervision in performing this duty/these duties; and

---

50. 29 C.F.R. § 541.700(a).
51. 29 C.F.R. §§ 541.700(a), (b).

- the relationship between the employee's salary and the wages paid to other employees for the kind of nonexempt work, if any, performed by the employee.[52]

Applying this framework to the accountant position, the Paradise human resources director will want to know how important the position's budget responsibilities are—in other words, does this position play an integral role in budget development? How does this position's contributions to budget development compare to those of others in the department? How frequently are this person's budget recommendations adopted? The human resources director will also want to know how frequently the person in this position is called upon to serve as acting finance director and whether the person is actually called upon to exercise the finance director's duties and make decisions when acting in that role. The Paradise human resources director and the city's attorney agree that more work needs to be done. The accountant position cannot be correctly classified as exempt or nonexempt under the FLSA based on the job description alone.

The Management Analyst

The last position that the city is reevaluating is that of "management analyst," a title that suggests exempt status. "Don't let the position title fool you into prejudging its exempt status," the human resources director warns the human resources trainee who is working on this project with him. "Whether or not a position is exempt under the FLSA is solely a function of whether the duties as performed by the incumbent satisfy one of the executive, administrative, or professional duties tests." The job duties of the Paradise management analyst position are to

- find and research grant opportunities and work with departments with the relevant substantive expertise to prepare grant applications;
- gather information for the city's annual report;
- assist with budget analysis;
- recommend outside vendors for the city's recycling program and options for single-stream recycling, prepare contracts for single-stream recycling, and maintain Big Company's corporate sponsorship of the recycling program;
- draft reports about various city initiatives for legislators in order to garner support and funding;
- engage in marketing work, such as drafting the content of flyers distributed to citizens with their utility bills;
- coordinate community outreach projects, such as chamber of commerce events and events to encourage citizens to participate in government programs; and
- perform preparatory and clean-up work for meetings, such as cleaning coffee mugs, making coffee, serving food at meetings, and cleaning up after meetings.

---

52. *See* 29 C.F.R. § 541.700(a).

The human resources director quickly and correctly concludes that the management analyst position qualifies for an exemption under the administrative duties test. Why does this position, which seems to have far fewer responsibilities than the accounting position discussed above, clearly qualify for the administrative exemption while there were so many open questions about the accounting position? First, as was the case with both the accountant and the city planner, the management analyst position involves nonmanual office work. Second, all the position's duties, with the exception of coffee preparation, are clearly related to management and general business operations, as all of them are related either to generating revenue for the city (grant writing, budget analysis, supporting Chamber of Commerce community development, maintaining corporate sponsorships, legislative outreach) or spending it (budget analysis, recommending vendors, and preparing contracts). The FLSA regulations expressly recognize the development of marketing projects and materials, such as those done for community outreach events and for flyers, as a type of work directly related to management or general business operations of the employer.[53]

Third, all but two of the duties appear by their very nature to involve the exercise of discretion and independent judgment in matters of significance to the city. Finding grant opportunities appropriate for a range of departments requires the employee to make judgments about which funding opportunities are most appropriate and most likely to be successful for a variety of different departments, as does determining the substantive content of marketing projects (in contrast, doing the graphic design of marketing material does not involve discretion and independent judgment within the meaning of the FLSA). Even if the person in the management analyst position is not the final decision maker, sifting through possible vendors, identifying the most promising candidates, and explaining why they are the best choices are classic examples of the exercise of discretion and independent judgment. So, too, is the drafting of contract terms. Furthermore, the decision about whom the city should contract with for recycling is a matter of significance. Similarly, where the purpose of a report is to gain the support of legislators for a city program, the author of the report will necessarily have to exercise good judgment about what to highlight and what to minimize; doing so is a necessary part of the job. Persuading legislators of the value of the city's programs is not only generally significant, but sometimes of paramount importance.

"What about the job duty identified as assisting with budget analysis?" asks the human resources trainee. "Excellent question!" says the human resources director. "In general, the use of the term 'assist' or 'assisting' in a job description should raise a red flag because it means that the position does not have the responsibility for the task or project in question but is merely working in a subordinate capacity with someone who does. The person 'assisting' is therefore unlikely to be exercising discretion and independent judgment on matters of importance to the employer," the human resources director explains. Nevertheless, depending on the circumstances, the position may have significant responsibility for a part of the project. The use of the word "assist," therefore, is a sign that the human resources director should

---

53. *See* 29 C.F.R. § 541.201.

be asking questions of the employee in that position and his or her supervisors to understand that particular job duty correctly. Here, in the case of the management analyst, there appear to be enough other job duties that clearly satisfy the discretion and independent judgment requirement that the classification of the position as exempt is not in doubt. If, however, the primary job duty was assisting in budget analysis and the other duties were but a small part of the position's responsibilities, the answer might be different.

The trainee pipes up again, noting that making coffee is not an exempt job duty. The trainee is, of course, correct. "Thankfully," says the attorney, "the inclusion of some nonexempt duties, such as those involving the preparation and cleaning up of coffee, does not turn what would otherwise be an exempt position into a nonexempt position." The touchstone of FLSA classification is the concept of the primary duty. If the primary duty of the management analyst position were to be serving as a barista and the other revenue-generating and business-related duties were secondary, the position would be nonexempt. But that's not the way the position is structured in Paradise (and probably not in many other jurisdictions either).

The administrative duties test is, by far, the most challenging and difficult of the three tests for exempt status. More than either the executive exemption or the professional exemption, the administrative duties test frequently requires a local government's human resources staff to investigate the details of the way in which a job is actually performed in order to understand whether it qualifies for exempt status. That is not to say that the professional duties test, which evaluates whether the position is one that requires an advanced academic degree or other high-level training, does not also have its challenges.

The Professional Exemptions from Overtime Pay

The professional duties exemption involves not one kind of exemption but is actually several exemptions gathered together in one name. As with the executive exemption and the administrative exemption, the professional exemption applies only if, in addition to satisfying the professional duties test, the employee is paid on a salary basis and is paid at least $684 per week.

The general requirements for satisfying the professional duties test are set out in the U.S. Department of Labor's (DOL) regulations at Title 29, Section 541.300 of the Code of Federal Regulations (C.F.R.). These requirements apply to all the subcategories of the professional exemption: the learned professional, the creative professional, the teaching professional, and the computer professional. To qualify as an exempt professional, an employee must have a primary duty of performing work that requires

- knowledge of an advanced type in a field of science or learning that is customarily acquired by a prolonged course of specialized intellectual instruction *or*
- invention, imagination, originality, or talent in a recognized field of artistic or creative endeavor.[54]

---

54. *See* 29 C.F.R. § 541.300(a)(2).

In subsequent sections, the regulations set out more specific requirements for each category of exempt professional. Because schoolteachers and creative professionals such as actors, musicians, painters, and novelists are not positions generally found in local government employment, they will not be discussed here. Readers may find the regulations governing the exemptions for teachers and creative professionals at C.F.R. Title 29, Sections 541.303 and 541.302, respectively.

The Learned Professional Exemption

The test for the learned professional exemption is set out in DOL's FLSA regulations at C.F.R. Title 29, Section 541.301. To qualify for this exemption, an employee's primary duty must be the performance of work requiring advanced knowledge in a field of science or learning customarily acquired by a prolonged course of specialized intellectual instruction. This primary duty test requires that three elements be satisfied.

- The employee must perform work requiring advanced knowledge.
- The advanced knowledge must be in a field of science or learning.
- The advanced knowledge must be customarily acquired by a prolonged course of specialized intellectual instruction.[55]

In most cases, this means that an employee must have a graduate degree to be able to perform the position's duties. A bachelor's degree will not usually suffice, except with respect to an engineering degree or a nursing degree that leads to an RN license.

Advanced Knowledge

"Work requiring advanced knowledge" means work that is predominantly intellectual in character. It is further defined as work that "includes work requiring the consistent exercise of discretion and judgment" and is contrasted with performance of routine mental, manual, mechanical, or physical work. To quote the rule directly, "an employee who performs work requiring advanced knowledge generally uses the advanced knowledge to analyze, interpret or make deductions from varying facts or circumstances."[56]

A Field of Science or Learning

The regulations define "field of science or learning" as including the study of law; medicine; teaching; accounting; actuarial science; engineering; architecture; pharmacy; and the physical, chemical, and biological sciences.[57]

---

55. *See* 29 C.F.R. § 541.301(a).

56. 29 C.F.R. § 541.301(b).

57. *See* 29 C.F.R. § 541.301(c).

A Prolonged Course of Specialized Intellectual Instruction

Again, this generally means a graduate degree of some kind. In most cases, a bachelor's degree does not suffice to meet this requirement, as the regulations instruct that the exemption "is not available for occupations that customarily may be performed with only the general knowledge acquired by an academic degree in any field."[58]

The learned professional exemption does not apply to occupations in which most employees have acquired their skill by experience rather than by advanced specialized intellectual instruction. Nevertheless, employees who work in fields where specialized academic training is a standard requirement but who do not have the requisite degree may qualify for the exemption if they have obtained similar knowledge through a *combination* of work experience *and* intellectual instruction.[59] For example, a certified public accountant would qualify for the professional exemption. Accountants who are not CPAs but whose job duties require knowledge that is the same as that acquired by a CPA would probably qualify for the professional exemption.[60]

It is important to note that a position may qualify for the professional exemption only if it *requires* the person to have advanced knowledge in a field of science or learning acquired by a prolonged course of specialized instruction. If the person in the position possesses an advanced degree but the position does not require the person to have such a degree, neither the position nor the person in it will qualify for the professional exemption. Two local government positions where this issue frequently arises are those of planner and social services caseworker. A planning department position that requires a job applicant to have a master's degree in planning before being considered for the position will qualify for the professional exemption. A planning position in which a master's degree is a preferred qualification but where applicants with bachelor's degrees will nonetheless be considered will not qualify for the professional exemption. Similarly, a social services position that requires a master's degree in social work will satisfy the professional duties test. A position that requires either a bachelor's degree or a master's degree in social work will not qualify for the exemption.

Some Examples of Local Government Positions Likely to Satisfy the Learned Professional Duties Test

Certain local government positions will automatically satisfy the learned professional test: city and county attorneys, physicians and licensed pharmacists on the staff of county health departments, and city and county engineers. In the regulations, DOL sets out some examples of occupations whose typical primary duties make them likely to satisfy the learned professional test. For local governments,

---

58. 29 C.F.R. § 541.301(d).

59. *Id.*

60. *See* 29 C.F.R. § 541.301(e)(5).

these occupations are most likely found in the health sciences field and include registered nurses, medical technologists, dental hygienists, and physician assistants.[61]

Registered Nurses but Not Licensed Practical Nurses

The regulations recognize registered nurses (RNs) as learned professionals on the basis that registration by the appropriate state examining board (here, the North Carolina Board of Nursing) attests to their having completed the requisite advanced study. The rule makes the position of licensed practical nurses (LPNs) clear: LPNs generally do not qualify as exempt learned professionals "because possession of a specialized advanced academic degree is not a standard prerequisite for entry into such occupations."[62] Although LPNs must also be licensed by the state, typical LPN training is a one-year post–high school course of study, usually in a community or technical college. Registered nurses, by contrast, must have completed a minimum two-to-three-year academic course of study; some will have completed a four-to-five-year program.

Medical Technologists, Dental Hygienists, and Physician Assistants

The DOL regulations explicitly recognize dental hygienists and physician assistants, like registered or certified medical technologists, as likely to meet the requirement for the professional exemption if their training satisfies specific criteria.

- Registered or certified medical technologists must have successfully completed three academic years of pre-professional study in an accredited college or university plus a fourth year of professional course work in a school of medical technology approved by the Council of Medical Education of the American Medical Association.[63]
- Dental hygienists must have successfully completed four academic years of pre-professional and professional study in an accredited college or university approved by the Commission on Accreditation of Dental and Dental Auxiliary Educational Programs of the American Dental Association.[64]
- Physician assistants must have successfully completed four academic years of pre-professional and professional study, including graduation from a physician assistant program accredited by the Accreditation Review Commission on Education for the Physician Assistant, and be certified by the National Commission on Certification of Physician Assistants.[65]

Paralegals Unlikely to Satisfy the Professional Duties Test

DOL has also provided examples of occupations whose primary duties make them unlikely to satisfy the learned professional test. For public employers, the most relevant example is that of the paralegal supporting the work of in-house or staff attor-

---

61. *See* 29 C.F.R. § 541.301(e).
62. 29 C.F.R. § 541.301(e)(2).
63. *See* 29 C.F.R. § 541.301(e)(1).
64. *See* 29 C.F.R. § 541.301(e)(3).
65. *See* 29 C.F.R. § 541.301(e)(4).

neys. Paralegals and legal assistants do not qualify because they are generally not required to have an advanced, specialized academic degree to work in the field.[66] This is true notwithstanding the fact that many will have attended certification programs through a college or community college, sometimes after completing a four-year bachelor's degree.

The Computer Professional Exemption

The exemption for the computer professional is different from all the other exemptions in that it does **not** require that the employee be paid on a salary basis. Instead, a position may be paid on either a salary basis or an hourly basis, provided that the hourly rate is a minimum of $27.63 per hour. That hourly figure was set by Congress when it added the computer professional exemption to the FLSA.[67] Like all other exempt employees, however, a computer professional paid on a salary basis will have to earn a minimum of $684 per week.

The primary duties test for the computer professional requires that an employee's work focus on

- the application of systems analysis techniques and procedures, including consulting with users, to determine hardware, software, or system functional specifications; or
- the design, development, documentation, analysis, creation, testing, or modification of computer systems or programs, including prototypes, based on and related to user or system design specifications; or
- the design, documentation, testing, creation, or modification of computer programs related to machine operating systems; or
- a combination of these duties, requiring the same level of skills.[68]

As discussed above, "primary duty" means "the principal, main, major or most important duty that the employee performs."[69]

Educational Requirements

Unlike the learned professional exemption, the computer professional exemption does not require the employee to have any particular degree—or to have a degree at all. Employees frequently do have a bachelor's or more advanced degree because the level of expertise and skill required to do the work covered by this exemption is generally gained through education. But this expertise may be acquired through a combination of education and experience or through experience alone.

---

66. *See* 29 C.F.R. § 541.301(e)(5).
67. *See* 29 U.S.C. § 213(a)(17).
68. *See* 29 C.F.R. § 541.400(b).
69. 29 C.F.R. § 541.700(a).

Positions That Typically Satisfy the Computer Professional Exemption

The computer professional exemption is available for information technology directors, provided that their actual job duties satisfy the primary duties test, and for systems analysts, programmers, and software developers. The regulations note that many systems analysts and computer programmers will have additional responsibilities that qualify them for the general administrative exemption, and some of the lead people in those areas will likely have management and supervisory responsibilities that qualify them for the executive exemption as well.[70]

Positions That Do Not Qualify for the Computer Professional Exemption

The regulations expressly exclude employees involved in the operation, manufacture, repair, or maintenance of computer hardware and related equipment from qualifying for the computer professional exemption, just as they do those whose work is dependent upon the use of computers and computer software, such as draftsmen and those working with computer-assisted design (CAD) software.[71]

Exempt or Nonexempt?

Local government employers trying to determine whether a particular position is exempt under the computer professional test should keep in mind a pair of distinctions. The first is between highly-specialized knowledge in computer systems analysis, computer programming, and software engineering on the one hand, and highly-specialized knowledge about computers and software on the other. The second distinction is between designing, creating, and modifying computer systems and programs, and identifying the computer needs and solutions of a department or unit of government. In both instances, the former set of tasks requires knowledge and skills needed to perform work qualifying for the computer professional exemption, while the latter does not.

A 2004 case from the federal Sixth Circuit Court of Appeals helps illuminate this distinction. The employer in *Martin v. Indiana Michigan Power Co.*[72] classified the plaintiff's position—Information Technology (IT) Support Specialist—as exempt under the computer professional test. The power plant employer described plaintiff Anthony Martin's job as belonging to a team that functioned as "a maintenance organization that takes care of computer systems" and defined "computer systems" as work stations at individual desks connected to a local area network (in contrast to the computer system that ran the plant's nuclear reactors).[73] The company described Martin's individual job duties as follows:

- maintaining computer workstation software, including responding to helpdesk tickets and installing software and software patches on individual workstations;

---

70. *See* 29 C.F.R. § 541.402.
71. *See* 29 C.F.R. § 541.401.
72. 381 F.3d 574 (2004).
73. *Id.* at 576–77.

- troubleshooting and repairing workstation problems,
- installing hardware and cable for the local network, including hubs, switches, and routers, and verifying their connections by phoning the system administrator to confirm that the hubs were on the network; and
- documenting the network to reflect what was physically present in wiring closets.[74]

When responding to helpdesk requests, Martin reported those problems he could not solve to his supervisor, who then determined whether to request service from a particular manufacturer or order a replacement part or unit. Martin did not design the configuration of the local network but only installed its cables and hardware. He did not install programs onto the network. Although the computer professional exemption does not require an employee to have any specific education or training, courts look to an employee's educational background as an indicator of the level of technical expertise the position requires. Martin had a high school degree but no college-level classes and no computer certifications. He had a few computer-training classes.[75]

The federal district court decision from which Martin appealed found that he was a computer professional, finding that his work required "highly specialized knowledge of computers and software" and that he customarily and regularly exercised discretion and independent judgment.[76] The appeals court disagreed, finding that

> . . . the district court made an understandable mistake, one that arises from the common perception that all jobs involving computers are necessarily highly complex and require exceptional expertise. However, the regulations provide that an employee's primary duty must require theoretical and practical application of highly-specialized knowledge *in computer systems analysis, programming, and software engineering*" not mere "highly-specialized knowledge *of computers and software*." This is an important difference. The former is a narrower class of jobs that requires a different level of knowledge and training than the latter.[77]

The Sixth Circuit found that Martin's job duties were all nonexempt: he did not do computer programming, software engineering, or perform systems analysis, which would have required him to make actual, analytical decisions about how the computer network should function. Instead, his work required him to install, upgrade, configure, replace, and troubleshoot in accordance with specifications in a system design that had been determined by others. "Maintaining the computer system within the predetermined parameters," the court said, "does not require 'theoretical and

---

74. *Id.*
75. *Id.* at 577–78.
76. *Id.* at 580.
77. *Id.*

practical application of highly-specialized knowledge in computer systems, analysis, programming, and software engineering.' "[78]

Comparison of the *Martin* case with a 2014 case from North Carolina involving the exempt status of a local area network (LAN) engineer shows how difficult correctly classifying a computer professional can be. Jeffrey Campbell, the plaintiff in *Campbell v. Kannapolis City Schools Board of Education*,[79] had many of the same job responsibilities as did Anthony Martin: he installed local area networks, including installing servers, hubs, routers, and workstations; he operated and maintained those same networks, tracking significant problems, monitoring performance, and performing upgrades to network hardware and software as needed; he also maintained the documentation about network configurations, operating procedures, and service records. Campbell testified that he was often called upon to solve problems involving desktop computers that helpdesk support team members could not resolve. By his own admission, troubleshooting individual desktops was not among his assigned job duties; he said that he was called upon to do just that because his knowledge base was greater than that of other computer employees.[80]

While Campbell emphasized his role in maintaining network systems, the federal district court judge focused on his broader responsibilities and determined that Campbell's position satisfied the requirements of the computer professional exemption. The job advertisement for Campbell's position, for example, described the LAN engineer role as being "responsible for *designing* and implementing local area networks in a school environment. Employee *supervises* the installation, maintenance, and operation of local area networks and associated computer hardware and software . . . ."[81] In finding that (1) Campbell's job duties involved the higher-level analysis required for the exemption and (2) he exercised discretion and independent judgment, the judge found persuasive Campbell's own testimony that it was his responsibility to make sure that individual schools and school system facilities had access to the network because he was the only person who could solve connectivity issues and the school system relied on him to do whatever he needed to do to make sure users had network access.[82]

Like the court in the *Martin* case, the judge in *Campbell* looked to the educational requirements for the position for further evidence of the nature of the job duties.

---

78. *Id.* at 580–81. *See also* Longlois v. Stratasys, Inc., 88 F. Supp. 3d 1058, 1069–71 (D. Minn. 2015) (court found that core duties of employee's job—servicing of computer and related equipment—did not fall within scope of computer professional exemption).

79. *See* 55 F. Supp. 3d 821, 824 (M.D.N.C. 2014).

80. *See id.* at 828.

81. *See id.* at 824 (emphasis added).

82. *See id.* at 825–26, 830. *See also* Bagwell v. Fla. Broadband, LLC, 385 F. Supp. 2d 1316, 1327–28 (S.D. Fla. 2005) (network engineer, whose primary duty was developing, improving, and making employer's computer network system function reliably, was exempt as computer professional); Bombadilla v. MDRC, No. Civ. 9217, 2005 WL 2044938 (S.D.N.Y. Aug. 24, 2005) (network administrator who made decisions about network modification and design was exempt computer professional despite being called upon for assistance by helpdesk staff).

The position description called for a B.S. degree in computer science; five years of increasingly responsible experience in networks; as well as a preference for certification as a Novell Administrator, Novell Engineer, or Microsoft Engineer. Campbell met those requirements.[83] The contrast between the education and training that Campbell needed to perform his job and the education and training that Martin needed is significant. This comparison of the two cases shows that what separates an exempt from a nonexempt network computer position is the formulation of a design or program that involves the application of higher-level abstract thinking, even where the same person is responsible for overseeing or performing the manual tasks associated with the installation of such a design or program.

Computer Employees as Exempt Employees under the Administrative Duties Test

The administrative duties test requires that an employee's primary duty be office or nonmanual work to qualify for exemption from the FLSA's overtime provisions. Many tasks performed by members of an information technology staff involve manual labor. For example, building a server involves organizing and running cable into rooms, manually placing components into a computer box, and placing the computer box in an office or room. Other positions may involve technical support duties, such as installing software on individual machines; physically repairing printers, scanners, and fax machines; or transferring computer files from one computer to another. A position that primarily performs duties such as these without also having responsibilities for planning and designing systems and writing specifications and protocols is likely to be nonexempt.

In a limited number of instances, however, computer and information technology personnel who do not qualify for the computer professional exemption may satisfy the administrative duties test. In *Koppinger v. American Interiors, Inc.*,[84] for example, a federal district court found that the job duties of the defendant's one-man information technology department employee, Lee Koppinger, satisfied the administrative duties test.[85] Koppinger performed some duties that might be considered manual, such as loading software and fixing computers and other equipment; these duties, he argued, made him a nonexempt employee. But the court found that his problem-solving, planning, and purchasing duties were the most important of his responsibilities: he made recommendations about what software and hardware his employer should purchase and was instrumental in his employer's decision to upgrade its server and software and to purchase laptops. Koppinger was responsible for managing the company's computer systems from end to end, and the court found that in doing so he exercised discretion and independent judgment on a regular basis.

---

83. *See Campbell*, 55 F. Supp. 3d at 824–25.

84. 295 F. Supp. 2d 797 (N.D. Ohio 2003).

85. *Id.* at 806. This case was decided under the pre-2004 version of the FLSA regulations (29 C.F.R. pt. 541), which were substantially similar to those in effect today.

This responsibility was integral to his employer's general business operations. As such, the court said, Koppinger was in an exempt administrative position.[86]

Similarly, in *Lee v. Megamart, Inc.*,[87] a federal district court found that the defendant grocery market's information technology manager, Jung Chan Lee, could satisfy the administrative duties test if his primary duties were to install, implement, and manage the defendant's databases and server; identify and remediate problems with the databases and servers; consult, recommend, and hire outside vendors to purchase and/or upgrade databases and inventory systems; troubleshoot inventory database problems; train new employees to use the database; implement a new data-order system that the company's Korean stores were using; and create and implement coding that would strengthen the company's computer systems. These are job duties that the employer claimed Lee performed. Lee, on the other hand, claimed that he did nothing more than basic troubleshooting. Accordingly, the court denied a motion for summary judgment, finding that there were questions of material fact about what Lee's job duties were.[88]

More often, however, information technology positions will be nonexempt. As noted above, courts easily find that the maintenance of an employer's computer systems is not only directly related—but is essential—to an employer's business operations. The stumbling block is the requirement that the employee exercise discretion and independent judgment on matters of significance to the employer. An oft-cited opinion letter from DOL makes clear that although computer-troubleshooting work can be unusually complex or require specialized technical knowledge, and despite the fact that there can be significant consequences or losses if employees do not perform their duties properly, this does not mean that the work relates to significant matters in the management or general business operations of the employer.[89] The position at issue in this opinion letter was that of IT Support Specialist. The primary duties identified by the employer were installing, configuring, testing, and troubleshooting computer applications, networks, and hardware. DOL applied the discretion and independent judgment requirement to the position and found as follows

> Maintaining a computer system and testing by various systematic routines to see that a particular piece of computer equipment or computer

---

86. *Id.* at 799–806.

87. 223 F. Supp. 3d 1291 (N.D. Ga. 2016).

88. *See id.* at 1300–01 (N.D. Ga. 2016). *See also* Cruz v. Lawson Software, Inc., 764 F. Supp. 2d 1050, 1065–68 (D. Minn. 2011) (implementing and configuring software to run business in a more efficient way is directly related to general business operations and requires exercise of independent judgment on matters of significance); Bagwell v. Fla. Broadband, LLC, 385 F. Supp. 2d 1316, 1322–26 (S.D. Fla. 2005) (employee with primary duty of developing, improving, and making employer's computer network function reliably was exempt under the administrative duties test).

89. See U.S. Dep't of Labor, Emp't Standards Admin., Wage & Hour Div., Wage & Hour Opinion Letter, FLSA 2006-42 (Oct. 26, 2006), https://www.dol.gov/whd/opinion/FLSA/2006/2006_10_26_42_FLSA.pdf (citing 29 C.F.R. §§ 541.202(c), (e), and (f), as well as *Clark v. J.M. Benson Co.*, 789 F.2d 282. 2887 (4th Cir. 1986)).

application is working properly according to the specifications designed by others are examples of work that lacks the requisite exercise of discretion and independent judgment within the meaning of the administrative exemption. Employees performing such activities are using skills and procedures or techniques acquired by special training or experience. Their duties do not involve, with respect to matters of significance, the comparison and the evaluation of possible courses of conduct, and action or making a decision after the various possibilities have been considered . . . . Such work does not involve formulating management policies or operating practices, committing the employer in matters that have significant financial impact, negotiating and binding the company on significant matters, planning business objectives . . . .[90]

Human resources professionals drafting or updating job descriptions for computer or information technology positions should beware of using overly broad characterizations of a position's essential duties. The description of an individual job duty should capture a reasonably finite or definite set of tasks. Broad, generalized descriptions of tasks may encompass some actual job duties that are exempt and some that are nonexempt. For example, an employee who "troubleshoots problems" with an email program is likely to be nonexempt, while one who "troubleshoots problems" and has the discretion to implement system-wide solutions to problems is more likely to be exempt.

Highly-Compensated Employees

The FLSA provides for an exemption from overtime for employees who make at least $107,432 per year but who do not satisfy any of the duties tests for exemption. An employee may be exempt from overtime as a "highly compensated employee" if he or she makes a minimum of $107,432 per year, performs office or nonmanual work (as in the requirement for the administrative exemption), and customarily and *regularly* performs at least one of the exempt duties set forth in the executive, administrative, or professional duties tests.[91] The rationale for not requiring a highly-compensated

---

90. *Id.* at 5. *See also* Martin v. Ind. Mich. Power Co., 381 F.3d 574, 581–84 (6th Cir. 2004); Turner v. Genome Scis., Inc., 292 F. Supp. 2d 738, 745, 747 (D. Md. 2003) (employee whose primary duties were to troubleshoot and correct problems with employer's computer and phone systems did not exercise requisite discretion and independent judgment so as to satisfy administrative duties test).

91. *See* 29 C.F.R. § 541.601. *See also* Zannikos v. Oil Inspections (U.S.A.), Inc., 605 F. App'x 349, 359–60 (5th Cir. 2015) (employee who earned slightly more than $100,000 annually who primarily performed non-manual work directly related to the management or general business operations of the employer's customers fell within the "highly compensated employee" exemption to the FLSA's overtime requirements); Boyd v. Bank of Am. Corp., 109 F. Supp. 3d 1273, 1303–04 (C.D. Cal. 2015) (appraisers' duties must be viewed as separate, whole tasks for the purposes of the highly-compensated exemption; appraisers have only one duty (appraising real property), which does not meet any prong of any exemption; therefore, appraisers cannot satisfy the highly-compensated employee exemption from overtime).

employee to satisfy one of the duties tests in full is that, in the words of the U.S. Department of Labor (DOL), a "high level of compensation is a strong indicator of an employee's exempt status, thus eliminating the need for a detailed analysis of the employee's job duties."[92] No matter how highly paid they may be, working supervisors and others who perform duties that require physical skill and energy or use of their hands cannot be exempt from overtime as a highly-compensated employee.[93]

The $107,432 minimum must include a salary of at least $684 per week (like all other exempt employees) but may also include any non-discretionary bonuses or other non-discretionary compensation, such as commissions, earned during the year. It cannot include the value of health insurance premium payments or other benefits.[94] The year may be measured by any fifty-two-week period, but unless a period other than the calendar year is identified in advance in the employer's records, DOL will assume that the measurement period is the calendar year.[95]

Combination Exemptions

DOL also allows for an exemption from overtime for employees who meet both the salary-basis and the salary-threshold tests and who perform a combination of exempt duties as set forth in the executive, administrative, professional, and computer employee tests.[96] This is different from the highly-compensated employee exemption, which only requires that the employee perform one exempt task to qualify. To qualify for the combination exemption, the employee must perform more than one exempt task, and the tasks must be from different duties tests.

The combination exemption is designed for situations where an employee performs a basket of duties that fall under different exemption tests, but no single one of these duties can be considered the employee's primary duty. Instead, these duties combined constitute the employee's primary duty.[97] The federal regulation covering "combination exemptions" is Section 541.808 of Title 29 of the Code of Federal Regulations. Courts have generally looked askance at use of the combination exemption where there is no clear set of mixed exempt duties that can be seen as a primary duty.[98] Employers should therefore exercise care in classifying a position as exempt using Section 541.708.

---

92. 29 C.F.R. § 541.600(c).

93. *See* 29 C.F.R. § 541.600(d).

94. *See* 29 C.F.R. § 541.600(b).

95. *See* 29 C.F.R. § 541.601(b)(4).

96. *See* 29 C.F.R. § 541.708; IntraComm, Inc. v. Bajaj, 492 F.3d 285, 294 (4th Cir. 2007) (deferring to Secretary of Labor's interpretation of 29 C.F.R. § 541.708, court held that because employee did not meet the salary requirement, he could not qualify for combination exemption).

97. *See IntraComm, Inc.*, 492 F.3d at 294; Dalheim v. KDFW-TV, 918 F.2d 1220, 1232 (5th Cir. 1990) (news producers did not do any executive or administrative work and thus could not qualify for combination exemption).

98. *See Dalheim*, 910 F.2d at 1232; Clark v. Centene Co. of Tex., L.P., 44 F. Supp. 3d 674, 685 (W.D. Tex. 2014), *aff'd*, 656 F. App'x 688 (5th Cir. 2016); Longlois v. Stratasys, Inc., 88 F. Supp. 3d 1058, 1069–71 (D. Minn. 2015); Kadden v. VisuaLex, LLC, 910 F. Supp. 2d 523, 542 (S.D.N.Y. 2012).

Chapter 2

Deductions from Wages: Allowable and Prohibited Deductions from the Wages of Exempt and Nonexempt Employees

As a general rule, the Fair Labor Standards Act (FLSA) requires employers to pay their employees their wages in full, subject only to federal and state income tax, Social Security, Medicare, and unemployment tax withholding, on the next regular payday. This chapter considers what happens when an employer does not pay an employee's wages in full. Some deductions from wages are permissible, while others are not, and making them can have serious consequences. For example, if an employee is exempt from overtime under the FLSA, the failure to pay his or her full salary could result in the loss of that exempt status and make that position and others like it nonexempt. Other deductions from pay—whether from exempt or nonexempt employees—constitute violations of the FLSA for which an employer may be required to pay back employees and pay the Department of Labor a penalty. The first part of this chapter looks at those deductions that will take away an employee's exempt status—that is, deductions that will turn an exempt employee into a nonexempt one. The second part of this chapter will discuss when deductions that simply have the effect of reducing an employee's pay—whether that employee is exempt or nonexempt—are consistent with the FLSA.

Permissible Deductions from the Salaries of Exempt Employees

What happens if an employer makes deductions from the salary of an exempt employee? Remember that to be exempt, an employee must be paid on a salary basis, and that requires that the employee be paid the same predetermined amount each week regardless of the amount and quality of that employee's work.[1] A deduction should, therefore, destroy a position's exemption, making the employee eligible for overtime. In most cases, that is precisely what happens. There are, however, four circumstances in which the FLSA allows public employers to make deductions from the salary of an exempt employee *without* destroying the exemption.

Deductions for Absences in Excess of Accrued Sick or Vacation Leave

This is probably the most frequently used of the permissible exceptions to the rule prohibiting deductions from the pay of an exempt employee. Under this exception, an employer may make deductions from the salary of an exempt employee in full-day increments or on a pro rata basis for less than a full day when an employee has already used all of his or her accrued paid leave. This exception also applies when an employee does not bother to ask for permission to take time off or when the employee asks for permission to take leave, it is denied, and the employee takes time off anyway. The exception also applies when an employee has accrued paid leave but asks to be put on unpaid leave and the employer agrees. This exception to the salary-basis test may only be used if the employer has adopted a policy (1) granting employees paid

---

1. *See* 29 C.F.R. § 541.602(a). See chapter 1 of this book for a discussion of this test and other tests used to determine exemption from the overtime requirements of the FLSA.

sick, vacation, or personal leave and (2) requiring that an employee's pay be docked when he or she is absent for personal reasons or because of sickness or injury and has no accrued paid leave available.[2] This exception is sometimes referred to as the "public accountability" exception, reflecting the fact that paid time-off is a benefit funded by taxpayer dollars, and may be used only by public employers. Private employers may also make deductions from the salaries of exempt employees when they are absent for personal reasons or because they are ill, but private employers may only make deductions in full-day increments.[3]

Note that the regulation addressing these issues, Section 541.710 of Title 29 of the Code of Federal Regulations (C.F.R.), also authorizes public employers to furlough exempt employees by temporarily categorizing them as nonexempt (thus requiring employers to pay these employees for any overtime worked) in workweeks during which the jurisdiction wishes to furlough its employees for budgetary reasons.[4]

Deductions for Full-Day Disciplinary Suspensions for Exempt Employees

Under this second exception, an exempt employee who violates a generally applicable rule of workplace conduct may be placed on an unpaid disciplinary suspension without affecting his or her exempt status, but only in increments of a full day. In other words, the employer may dock the employee's salary in increments of one day, two days, three days, etc. It may not dock the employee's salary for the equivalent of two-and-one-half days of work, for example. The workplace misconduct must be a violation of a rule that is written and that applies to all employees. As was the case with the excess leave exception discussed above, an employer must have a written policy in place before it can use the unpaid disciplinary suspension exception.[5] The relevant federal regulation is Section 541.602 of C.F.R. Title 29.

The regulation does not define the term "workplace conduct." It does give two examples, however. The first is of a violation of an employer's sexual harassment policy, and the second is of a violation of a policy prohibiting workplace violence.[6] Both examples involve serious misconduct by the employee, with the potential for employer liability for damages suffered by other employees. In the Preamble Discussion that accompanied the publication of the rule in the Federal Register, the U.S. Department of Labor gave two additional examples—a violation of an employer's written drug or alcohol policy and a violation of an employer's written

---

2. *See* 29 C.F.R. § 541.710.

3. *See* 29 C.F.R. §§ 541.602(b)(1), (2).

4. *Id.*

5. *See* 29 C.F.R. § 541.602(b)(5). *See also* Martinez v. Hilton Hotels Corp., 930 F. Supp. 2d 508, 522 (S.D.N.Y. 2013) (an employer may make deductions for full-day unpaid disciplinary suspensions, imposed pursuant to formal written policy, without jeopardizing an employee's exempt status); Wetzel v. Town of Orangetown, No. 06 Civ. 15190 (LAP), 2013 WL 1120026, at *6 (S.D.N.Y. Mar. 18, 2013), *aff'd*, 556 F. App'x 46 (2d Cir. 2014) (all that the FLSA requires as to suspending employees for disciplinary matters is a "written policy").

6. *See* 29 C.F.R. § 541.602(b)(5).

policy concerning off-duty conduct or violations of law.[7] Cases provide some further examples: a nurse anesthetist who admittedly reported to work under the influence of alcohol violated the employer's conduct rules;[8] a registered nurse who failed to update a patient's care plan and neglected to initiate a care plan for another patient also engaged in workplace misconduct within the meaning of Section 541.602(b)(5);[9] and a pharmacy manager who violated both state law and her employer's policy by not immediately conducting an investigation and contacting a patient upon learning of a technician's error in filling a prescription engaged in misconduct that justified a full-day suspension without pay.[10]

Given these examples, discretion would say that employers should not place exempt employees on unpaid disciplinary suspensions for more minor offenses such as insubordination, excessive tardiness, or for the vague offense of "conduct unbecoming a government employee." The result could be the destruction of the exempt status of the disciplined employee.

Docking an Exempt Employee's Pay for Major Safety Violations

The FLSA regulations for this third exception have long included a provision allowing employers to dock an exempt employee's pay as a penalty for violating a safety rule of major significance. This exception is poorly understood, and North Carolina public employers have not made much use of it. It is found at Section 541.602(b)(4) of C.F.R. Title 29. The rule explains that "[s]afety rules of major significance include those relating to the prevention of serious danger in the workplace or to other employees, such as rules prohibiting smoking in explosive plants, oil refineries and coal mines."

The relatively few cases involving this regulation demonstrate that this is a rule intended to prevent serious danger *to the workplace or other employees. The exemption does not appear to cover violation of safety rules designed to prevent danger to the general public.* For example, a law enforcement officer's failure to remain at his assigned post, sleeping while on duty, or failing to report the loss of her service weapon have been found to put fellow officers at risk and thus to be violations of safety rules of major significance.[11] A police officer's failure to respond to a traffic accident has been found to jeopardize EMTs working at the scene and to be a violation of a major safety rule.[12] A fire truck driver's failure to respond to the correct

7. *See* 69 Fed. Reg. 22,122, 22,177 (Apr. 23, 2004).

8. *See* Cavanaugh v. S. Cal. Permanente Med. Grp., Inc., 583 F. Supp. 2d 1109, 1137 (C.D. Cal. 2008).

9. *See* Richardson v. Regeis Care Ctr., LLC, No. 16 Civ. 3538(LGS), 2017 WL 432806, at *3 (S.D.N.Y. Jan. 30, 2017).

10. *See* Parmar v. Safeway Inc., No. C10-421 MJP, 2011 WL 888238, at *5 (W.D. Wash. Mar. 14, 2011).

11. *See* Kelly v. City of New York, Nos. 91CIV.2567(JFK), 91CIV.9343(JFK), 91CIV.7755(JFK), 2000 WL 1154062, at *14, *15 and *17 (S.D.N.Y. Aug. 15, 2000), *aff'd sub nom.* Abramo v. City of New York, 54 F. App'x 708 (2d Cir. Jan. 6, 2003).

12. *See* Childers v. City of Eugene, 922 F. Supp. 403 (D. Or. 1996) *aff'd*, 120 F.3d 944 (9th Cir. 1997).

address was found to be a violation of a safety rule of major significance because the delay in its arrival at the scene endangered fellow firefighters already at the scene.[13]

In contrast, law enforcement officers did not violate a safety rule when they accepted free sausage sandwiches from a merchant,[14] nor did an employee who failed to report absences from work.[15] A fire captain's failure to prevent subordinates from downloading pictures of nude women from the Internet was also not a violation of a safety rule of major significance.[16]

The FLSA regulation provides that a deduction for a violation of a safety rule of major significance may be made in any amount and need not be tied to the employee's salary rate.[17] Thus, this rule may be used to fine exempt employees as well as to suspend them.

Deductions for Partial First or Last Week of Work or for Partial Week of FMLA Leave

The fourth exception recognizes that an exempt employee's first or last week of work may not be a full workweek. The FLSA allows an employer to pay a proportionate part of an exempt employee's full salary for the time actually worked in the first and last week. This exception is found in subsection (b)(6) of C.F.R. Title 29, Section 541.602. Similarly, an employee may begin or end a block of unpaid Family and Medical Leave Act (FMLA) leave midweek or may take intermittent FMLA leave—in blocks of time amounting to less than a full workweek, perhaps for the flare-up of chronic conditions or for scheduled medical treatments. Subsection (b)(7) of the regulation allows employers to pay a proportionate part of an exempt employee's full salary for the time actually worked in a week in which FMLA leave has been used.

Deductions from Pay Affecting *Both* Exempt and Nonexempt Employees

There are a number of situations in which an employer is owed money by an employee. Perhaps an employee has accidentally been overpaid or has been advanced paid vacation or sick leave. Perhaps an employer rightly feels that it should be reimbursed by an employee who has lost or damaged employer property or has failed to return equipment at the end of employment. Perhaps the employer has paid for expensive training for the employee but has not received the benefit of that expense because the employee quits soon afterward. Perhaps an employee who resides in the

---

13. *See* Watkins v. City of Montgomery, 930 F. Supp. 2d 1302, 1310 (M.D. Ala. 2013), *aff'd*, 775 F.3d 1280 (11th Cir. 2014).

14. *See* Pautlitz v. City of Naperville, 781 F. Supp. 1368, 1371 (N.D. Ill. 1992).

15. *See* Shockley v. City of Newport News, 997 F.2d 18, 25 (4th Cir. 1993).

16. *See* Prickett v. DeKalb Cty., 92 F. Supp. 2d 1357, 1371 (N.D. Ga. 2000), *aff'd in part, rev'd in part*, 254 F.3d 74 (11th Cir. 2001).

17. 29 C.F.R. § 541.602(c).

jurisdiction has unpaid property taxes or utility bills that the employer wishes to deduct from the employee's paycheck. Perhaps outside creditors of an employee ask an employer to deduct what they are owed from the employee's wages and to pay the amount directly to the creditor. The Fair Labor Standards Act (FLSA) has detailed rules governing each of these situations. In some cases, the rules are the same for exempt and nonexempt employees. In other cases, they are different. As applied to nonexempt employees, the rules may be different in overtime and nonovertime weeks. Employers must pay close attention to the requirements governing deductions from pay for each kind of situation.

Deductions for the Overpayment of Wages

When an employer has accidentally paid an employee more than it owes the employee in wages, it may deduct the amount of overpayment from the employee's future wages either in a lump sum or over time. This will *not* destroy the exemption status of an exempt employee. With respect to nonexempt employees, "the principal may be deducted from the employee's earnings even if such deduction cuts into the minimum wage or overtime pay due the employee under the FLSA." This is in contrast to deductions for loss or damage to employer property (discussed below).[18]

Deductions for Advances of Vacation and Sick Leave

No FLSA regulations and no cases the author can find from the federal Fourth Circuit Court of Appeals, a North Carolina federal district court, or courts in other jurisdictions address deductions from employee pay to repay advanced paid vacation or sick leave. Nevertheless, certain principles may be inferred from existing rules and from opinion letter guidance from the U.S. Department of Labor (DOL).

First, nothing prohibits an employer from deducting from current wages an earlier advance of wages. Vacation and sick leave are an alternate form of compensation that have a cash value, so an advance of leave is equivalent to an advance of wages. DOL's *Field Operations Handbook* says that an advance of accrued paid leave may be considered an advance of salary. As with an advance of salary, the deduction for repayment of an advance of vacation or sick leave *may* reduce below minimum wage the amount of money the employee receives after the deduction is made. Deductions must be made based on the hourly rate the employee was earning at the time that leave was advanced, **not** at the rate the employee was earning at the time of the deductions (because if the deduction is made at the end of employment, that rate may be significantly higher). The practice of deducting any advance of vacation or sick leave from final wages must be incorporated into an employer's personnel policy before it may make such deductions.[19]

18. *See* U.S. Dep't of Labor, Emp't Standards Admin., Wage & Hour Div., Wage & Hour Opinion Letter, FLSA 2004-19NA (Oct. 8, 2004), https://www.dol.gov/whd/opinion/FLSANA/2004/2004_10_08_19FLSA_NA_recoup.pdf.

19. *See* U.S. Dep't of Labor, Emp't Standards Admin., Wage & Hour Div. (DOL), Field Operations Handbook § 30c10(c), https://www.dol.gov/whd/FOH/FOH_Ch30.pdf;

Deductions for the Destruction or Loss of Employer Property or Money

An employer's desire to deduct the cost of lost or damaged property or of missing funds is one place where the FLSA treats exempt and nonexempt employees differently.

Exempt Employees

Employers may not deduct the cost of lost or damaged property or of missing funds from the wages of an exempt employee. To do so will destroy the exemption and turn the exempt employee into a nonexempt employee. The rationale behind this prohibition is that when an employer seeks from an employee reimbursement for the destruction or loss of employer property or for missing money, it is holding the employee responsible for the loss. It is, in effect, counting the loss as a failure by the employee in the performance of his or her duties. To deduct from the wages of an exempt employee for deficiencies in the quality of the employee's work is inconsistent with payment on a salary basis, which requires that the salary be guaranteed irrespective of the quality or quantity of work.[20] The deduction would also violate the FLSA's requirement that wages be paid unconditionally and "free and clear," with no deductions being made for the benefit of the employer.

The "Free and Clear" Rule

The FLSA requires that wages be paid unconditionally and "free and clear." According to DOL's FLSA regulations, "[t]he wage requirements of the Act will not be met where the employee 'kicks-back' directly or indirectly to the employer or to another person for the employer's benefit the whole or part of the wage delivered to the employee."[21] Thus, as a general matter, deductions from an employee's paycheck that benefit the employer are unlawful.[22]

Nonexempt Employees

Deductions from employee pay to pay back an employer for lost or damaged uniforms, property, or equipment are arguably for the employer's benefit and will run afoul of the free and clear rule, discussed immediately above, which makes deductions from pay that benefit the employer unlawful. That being said, an employee may voluntarily allow his or her employer to make deductions for lost or damaged property if certain requirements, discussed in the sections below, are met. There are different requirements for workweeks without overtime and those in which overtime is owed.

DOL, Wage & Hour Opinion Letter, FLSA 2004-17NA (Oct. 6, 2004), https://www.dol.gov/whd/opinion/FLSANA/2004/2004_10_06_17FLSA_NA_unearned_vacation.pdf.

20. *See* U.S. Dep't of Labor, Emp't Standards Admin., Wage & Hour Div., Wage & Hour Opinion Letter, FLSA 2006-7 (Mar. 10, 2006), https://www.dol.gov/whd/opinion/FLSA/2006/2006_03_10_07_FLSA.pdf.

21. 29 C.F.R. § 531.35.

22. *Id.*

Workweeks without Overtime

In a workweek in which a nonexempt employee has not earned overtime pay, a deduction made for lost or damaged property or missing funds cannot reduce below the rate of the minimum wage the amount of money the employee is paid that week.[23] If an employee admits to or is convicted of stealing or other misappropriation of funds, the amount may be deducted in full from the employee's wages even if it reduces the employee's wages below minimum wage.[24]

Overtime Workweeks

Deductions for lost or damaged property or missing funds may only be made in an overtime workweek if there is an agreement between the employer and the employee that deductions will be made for specific items.[25] The reason for the requirement that there be an agreement is that under Section 778.315 of Title 29 of the Code of Federal Regulations (C.F.R.), employers must pay employees all of their straight-time compensation due under an express or implied employment contract (which all employees have) for the non-overtime hours worked before it can be said that the employer has paid proper time-and-one-half overtime compensation for the overtime hours worked.

To be valid and for deductions to be permissible in an overtime workweek, the agreement must meet all of the following conditions.

1. The agreement must be reached before the employee performs the work that becomes subject to the deductions.

2. The agreement must be specific concerning the particular items for which the deductions will be made, and the employee must know how the amount of the deductions that are covered by the agreement will be determined.

3. The employee must affirmatively agree or assent to the employer's deduction policy, and while the employee's assent to the policy may be written or unwritten, the burden of proof that an employee has agreed to the deduction policy rests on the employer.[26]

---

23. *See* 29 U.S.C. § 206; 29 C.F.R. §§ 531.35, .36. *See also* Brock v. Phillips, No. 84-92-Civ-T-15, 1986 WL 6849, at *2 (M.D. Fla. Jan. 30, 1986) (employer willfully violated FLSA's minimum wage provisions by deducting shortages resulting from mathematical errors or other unaccountable circumstances from wages of their employees); Hodgson v. Frisch's Dixie, Inc., No. 6641, 1971 WL 837, at *5 (W.D. Ky. Aug. 16, 1971) (same).

24. *See* Mayhue's Super Liquor Stores, Inc. v. Hodgson, 464 F.2d 1196, 1198 (5th Cir. 1972) ("If the agreement required only repayment of money that the employee himself took or misappropriated it obviously would not collide with the Act. As a matter of law, the employee would owe such amounts to the employer, and as a matter of fact, the repayment of moneys taken in excess of the money paid to the employee in wages would not reduce the amount of his wages.").

25. *See* 29 C.F.R. § 531.37(a).

26. *See* U.S. Dep't of Labor, Emp't Standards Admin., Wage & Hour Div., Wage & Hour Opinion Letter, FLSA 2001-7 (Feb. 16, 2001), https://www.dol.gov/whd/opinion/FLSA/2001/2001_02_16_7_FLSA.pdf.

The total amount that an employer may deduct from an employee subject to overtime pay in an overtime workweek may not exceed the amount that could be deducted if the employee had only worked a forty-hour week. In other words, the deduction cannot reduce below the minimum wage the amount of money the employee receives in compensation for straight-time hours. In addition, the employee's regular rate for calculating time-and-one-half overtime pay cannot be affected by the deduction and remains the regular hourly rate or regular salary before the deductions are made.[27] In other words, the deduction cannot reduce the amount of overtime pay that the employee receives. The bottom line is that where there is no express or implied agreement as to deductions for particular items, or if the employer reduces an employee's wages for a reason not addressed in the contractual arrangement or for no legitimate reason, the deductions are considered illegal and are not allowed during overtime workweeks.

Deductions for the Cost of Training

Few things are as aggravating to local government employers as paying for the cost of an expensive training program only to have the employee who received the training leave immediately to go to work for another local government employer. The new employer gets the benefit of the training for which the old employer paid. Small and rural cities and counties commonly suffer this loss among their entry-level law enforcement and firefighter ranks. In response, numerous local governments have adopted policies requiring police officers or firefighters to repay a portion of their training costs if they voluntarily leave the local government's employment before completing a specified number of years of service. This practice appears to be permissible so long as employees are advised of the policy at the outset of employment and the deduction does not bring the employee's regular rate of pay below minimum wage, as with deductions from pay for damage to or loss of the employer's equipment.

Viewing Payment of the Cost of Training as a Loan

There is no regulatory guidance and there are relatively few judicial decisions that address the lawfulness of deducting the cost of training from employee pay. Neither the FLSA regulations nor any federal Fourth Circuit Court of Appeals cases address deductions for the cost of training. Two cases from other circuits, however, and a few trial court cases, provide a rationale for allowing the deductions.

In a 2010 decision from California, *Gordon v. City of Oakland*,[28] the federal Ninth Circuit Court of Appeals held that a city's deduction of the cost of training from an employee's final paycheck was lawful. The court noted that the city could choose to require applicants to obtain their police training independently prior to beginning employment, which the city could do by hiring only individuals already possessing law enforcement certification. Instead, the city elected to make available to police

---

27. *See* 29 C.F.R. § 531.37(b).
28. 627 F.3d 1092 (9th Cir. 2010).

officer trainees what was essentially a loan of the cost of their police academy training. In this case, the conditional offer of employment the plaintiff signed explained that the city would forgive her repayment obligation at a specified rate and that she would owe nothing after five years of service. Because the plaintiff chose not to serve the five years necessary to secure complete loan forgiveness, the city became the plaintiff's creditor. The city made a deduction from her final paycheck to partially repay the loan. Because it satisfied the FLSA's requirements by paying her at least minimum wage for her final week of work, the city did not violate the law.[29]

In the 2002 federal Seventh Circuit Court of Appeals case *Heder v. City of Two Rivers*,[30] the city funded its firefighters' mandatory paramedic training but required a firefighter to reimburse the city for the costs of training if he or she left the city's employ before completing three years of service. The Seventh Circuit upheld the reimbursement agreement, comparing it to a loan; the cost of the training was a loan the city made to its firefighters, repayment of which was forgiven after three years. If, however, a firefighter left before three years of service, the loan became due. The court held that as long as the city paid departing firefighters at least the statutory minimum wage, it could deduct the training costs from wages.

Two federal district court cases featured similar reasoning. In one, financial advisors at a financial services company alleged that an agreement providing that they would have to repay the company for the costs of training if they left employment within three years and continued to work in the field violated the Fair Labor Standards Act (FLSA). The court disagreed, saying that the tuition-cost reimbursement provision did not violate the FLSA because it was not a kickback that violated the free and clear rule but was instead a loan.[31] In the second case, an informational technology consulting company required its trainees to pay a termination fee of $30,000 if they left within the first year of employment, and $20,000 if they left in the second year. The plaintiff left her position shortly before the start of her second year. She paid the termination fee of $20,000, but she also sued. The court rejected her claim that the tuition and training reimbursement was a kickback that violated the FLSA, noting that

> [t]he Termination Fee is characterized in the Employment Agreement as liquidated damages approximating the damages FDM [the employer] suffered by reason of breach of the Employment Agreement prior to the completion of the two-year contracted period. The Employment Agreement includes the consultant's acknowledgment that the Company incurred significant costs in training the employees and that the two-year term was contracted in consideration of such costs. . . . It is not a deduction for tools used or costs incurred in the course of Plaintiff's performance of her job as a consultant. Indeed, if Plaintiff had performed the full two

---

29. *See id.* at 1096.
30. 295 F.3d 777 (7th Cir. 2002).
31. *See* Bland v. Edward D. Jones & Co., L.P., 375 F. Supp. 3d 962 (N.D. Ill. 2019).

years of her contract, she would not have had to pay anything back at all. Such liquidated damages provisions in employment agreements are not unusual, and even those that are explicitly tied to repayment of the costs of a training program have been upheld as akin to loan repayment provisions.[32]

Conclusion
Based on the cases discussed above,[33] it appears that the deduction of the cost of an employee's training from his or her paychecks is permissible so long as

- the arrangement is structured as a loan that will be forgiven if the employee remains with the employer for a specified period of time,
- employees sign individual agreements that specify the terms of repayment, and
- no paycheck brings the employee's regular rate of pay below minimum wage for that pay period.

Deductions for Unpaid Utility Bills Owed to the Employing Jurisdiction
Unlike the cost of training or the replacement cost of damaged or lost property, unpaid utility bills are not debts related to a person's employment. There is no authority for a local government employer to deduct payment for those bills from the wages of an employee who owns property within the jurisdiction. Applying the general principles governing exempt status and deductions from the wages of nonexempt employees necessarily leads to the conclusion that an agreement by the employee allowing such a deduction would violate the FLSA's free and clear rule and would constitute an impermissible waiver of the employee's rights under the FLSA. Don't do it.

Deductions in Response to Garnishments and Court Orders
Public employers may garnish wages pursuant to orders of the North Carolina Superior Court or the U.S. Bankruptcy Court. In three circumstances, public employers may garnish wages without a court order.

Garnishment Pursuant to a Court Order
Public employers must, of course, obey a court order related to garnishment. Courts are restricted by the federal Consumer Credit Protection Act (CCPA), located at Sections 1671–1677 of Title 15 of the U.S. Code, in the amounts that they may order

---

32. *See* Park v. FDM Grp. (Holdings) PLC, No. 16-CV-520-LTS, 2017 WL 946298, at *4 (S.D.N.Y. Mar. 9, 2017), *order vacated in part on reconsideration sub nom.* Park v. FDM Grp., Inc., No. 16-CV-520-LTS, 2018 WL 4100524 (S.D.N.Y. Aug. 28, 2018).

33. There is one additional case from a North Carolina federal district court involving deductions for the cost of training, *Ketner v. Branch Banking & Trust Co.*, 143 F. Supp. 3d 370 (M.D.N.C. 2015), that contains a lengthy but ultimately inconclusive discussion of the issue.

to be deducted from an employee's wages as a garnishment. Any court order imposing a garnishment will take the CCPA's restrictions on garnishment into account in
calculating the amount of the garnishment. In general, the CCPA limits the amount
of earnings that may be garnished in any workweek or pay period to the lesser of

- 25 percent of disposable earnings or
- the amount by which disposable earnings are greater than thirty times the
  federal minimum hourly wage.[34]

Note that the reason complying with a garnishment does not violate the FLSA is
because the employer is still in effect paying the employee—the law is simply directing that the employee's wages be directed to someone or some entity with a greater
legal claim to them.

Garnishments That Do Not Require a Court Order

There are three kinds of garnishments that do **not** require a court order: federal and
state tax garnishments, non-tax federal administrative garnishments, and garnishments for child support and alimony.

Tax Garnishments or Levies

The first type of garnishment that does not mandate a court order prior to being
issued is a garnishment for unpaid federal or state taxes.[35] Not only do garnishments for unpaid federal or state taxes not require a court order, they are also not
subject to the CCPA's limitations on the amounts that may be garnished. For federal
tax garnishments, the Internal Revenue Service simply issues a "Notice of Levy on
Wages" (IRS Form 668-W) to an employer. The employer is then required to begin the
garnishment of the employee's wages. An IRS garnishment (technically, a "levy") is
continuous, meaning that it remains in place until the employer receives a release of
levy from the IRS. The method for calculating the amount that is to be garnished is
beyond the scope of this book, but Form 668-W is usually accompanied by IRS Publication 1494, which provides detailed instructions on how to comply with an IRS levy.

Similarly, a garnishment for delinquent *state* taxes is initiated when the North Carolina Department of Revenue issues a notice of garnishment to an employer.[36] A North
Carolina state tax garnishment is subject to a limitation of 10 percent of disposable
income.[37] For delinquent *local* taxes, local tax collectors are also authorized to garnish
employee wages. They do so by sending to the employer a notice that complies with
G.S. 105-368(b). A local tax garnishment is also subject to a limitation of 10 percent
of disposable income.[38]

---

34. *See* 15 U.S.C. § 1673(a).

35. *See* 15 U.S.C. § 1673(b)(1)(C).

36. *See* Chapter 105, Section 242.1 of the North Carolina General Statutes (hereinafter G.S.).

37. *See* G.S. 105-242(b).

38. *See* G.S. § 105-368(a).

Federal Administrative Garnishments Unrelated to Tax Liability

Non-tax federal administrative garnishments may also be issued without a court order and are also exempt from the CCPA's restrictions. The most common types of garnishments in this category spring from debts owed to federal student loan guaranty agencies pursuant to the federal Higher Education Act (under which garnishment is limited to 10 percent of disposable income)[39] and debts covered by the federal Debt Collection Improvement Act (under which garnishment is limited to 15 percent of disposable income).[40] There are other sources of federal administrative garnishments as well.

Garnishments for Child Support and Alimony

In North Carolina, garnishments for child support and alimony will be issued either by the superior court or by a child support enforcement agency (without a court order but impliedly under the authority of a court order). They are not subject to the limitations imposed by the CCPA on general creditors. Under the CCPA, garnishments for child support and alimony are limited to 50 percent of disposable income if the employee is supporting a spouse or child not covered by the alimony or child support order and 60 percent of disposable income if the employee is not supporting another spouse or child. The amount may be increased by an additional 5 percent if the employee is more than twelve months in arrears.[41]

Bottom Line on Garnishments

The court or agency issuing the garnishment will reference the applicable limitations on the amount to be garnished. If an employer complies with the instructions in a garnishment order or notice, it will not violate the FLSA if it makes deductions from an employee's wages.

Across-the-Board Pay Cuts

The FLSA sets the minimum wage and governs the payment of overtime and use of comp time but, beyond that, it has nothing to say about wage increases or decreases—they remain within the discretion of the employer. Thus, except where there is an employment agreement for a specific term (like those that cities and counties frequently enter into with their managers), public employers are generally free to either increase or decrease employees' future compensation as they see fit.

Pay cuts imposed on all employees across the board are lawful, as are any pay cuts that do not bring an employee below the minimum wage, even if they apply only to employees of some departments but not others, or to employees with more seniority but not to newer hires, or the other way around. Public employees have on occasion challenged reductions to their compensation, but the courts have routinely

---

39. *See* 20 U.S.C. § 1095a.
40. *See* 31 U.S.C. § 3720D.
41. *See* 15 U.S.C. § 1673(b)(2).

rejected the notion that a public employee has a vested right in any rate or method of compensation.[42]

Wages may not, however, be reduced in retrospect. Employees must know the amount the employer is willing to pay for a day's work before they begin work. But there is no statutory minimum amount of notice that must be given before an employer institutes an across-the-board cut. It need only be prospective.

Furloughs

The decision to institute a furlough is one that units of government never take lightly. A primary concern is the effect that a temporary reduction in hours and pay will have on employees and their abilities to support their families and honor their financial commitments. A second concern arises from the FLSA. The government employer may worry that furloughing an exempt employee will trigger a violation of the salary-basis test and destroy exempt status. When a public employer institutes a furlough, nonexempt employees continue to be paid as they always are: at a set rate of pay for those hours actually worked in a given workweek. The FLSA permits a government employer to furlough exempt employees by *treating them as nonexempt* during a furlough week and paying them at a pro-rata rate for those hours actually worked. If a public employer does this, it will not lose the exemption for that position in non-furlough weeks:

> Deductions from the pay of an employee of a public agency for absences due to a budget-required furlough shall not disqualify the employee from being paid on a salary basis except in the workweek in which the furlough occurs and for which the employee's pay is accordingly reduced.[43]

In other words, the employer must require exempt employees to track their time during the furlough week, if they do not already do so, and must ensure that they limit the number of hours worked. For a furlough to serve the purpose for which it

---

42. *See, e.g.,* Adams v. State, 790 S.E.2d 339 (N.C. Ct. App. 2016) (unless specifically prohibited by the North Carolina Constitution, as a general rule, the legislature may reduce or increase the salaries of public officers during their terms of office but cannot deprive them of the whole); Abeyounis v. Town of Wrightsville Beach, 102 N.C. App. 341, 344 (1991); Keeling v. Grand Junction, 689 P.2d 679, 680 (Colo. App. 1984) (firefighters and police do not have vested contract rights and could have reasonably relied on continuance of a particular rate or method of compensation); Chicago Patrolmen's Benevolent Ass'n v. City of Chicago, 309 N.E.2d 3, 6 (Ill. 1974) (public employees have no property rights in the continuance of any specific rate or method of compensation). *But cf.* Baltimore Teachers Union v. Mayor & City Council of Baltimore, 6 F.3d 1012 (4th Cir. 1993) (holding that inclusion of wage rate negotiated by teachers' and police officers' unions with city in city budget ordinance created a contractual right to that rate of compensation for the life of the budget).

43. 29 C.F.R. § 541.710(b). This exception has generated very little reported litigation. In *Bozzo v. City of Gilroy*, 982 F. Supp. 2d 1057 (N.D. Cal. 2013), the court found that DOL's regulation was reasonable and that the city's furlough of fire department chiefs did not destroy their exempt status.

is undertaken—to save money in difficult financial times—the employer must make sure that it specifies the number of hours exempt employees may work and enforce that limit. If an exempt employee regularly works in excess of forty hours a week in order to get his or her work done and works a similar number of hours during the furlough week, he or she must be paid overtime at time-and-one-half. This will likely undo the purpose of having a furlough week in the first place. But the employee cannot simply work his or her usual number of hours and accept the temporary pay cut without jeopardizing the employer's FLSA compliance and exposing the employer to liability.

Chapter 3

Compensable Time

If you don't work, you don't get paid. This is a straightforward idea, easily understood by employees and employers alike. But what about times when employees work but don't get paid? Under the Fair Labor Standards Act (FLSA), time worked by a non-exempt employee is either "compensable" or "noncompensable"—time that must be paid or time that does not have to be paid even though the employee has provided some benefit to the employer. By far, most time is compensable. There are, however, exceptions to this principle. They are the subject of this chapter.

What Does It Mean to "Work"?

The FLSA does not define the term "work." It does, however, define the term "employ" as "to suffer or permit to work."[1] Accordingly, the U.S. Supreme Court has attempted to answer in practical terms the question, "What is work time for which an employee must be compensated?" In a series of decisions in the 1940s, the Court held that "work" is time spent primarily for the benefit of the employer in physical or mental exertion, remaining in a state of readiness to serve, or lying in wait for threats to the safety of the employer's property.[2] It held that work is all of the time during which an employee is required to be on the employer's premises, on duty or at a prescribed work site.[3] Critically, work time is also all time during which an employee is allowed to work (or is not prohibited from working), even where the work has not been requested. Work time generally includes all time that an employee is required to be on the employer's property, but work time may also include time spent off the employer's premises or time spent performing work for the employer at the employee's home.[4] If an employer knows or has reason to believe that the work is being performed, it must count the time as hours worked.[5]

The Continuous Workday Principle

An understanding of compensable work time must begin with an understanding of the continuous workday rule. The relevant FLSA regulation, Section 790.6 of Title 29 of the Code of Federal Regulations (C.F.R.), defines the compensable workday as all the time between the time when an employee begins to perform his or her principal activities and the time when the employee stops performing the principal activities:

> "Workday" . . . means, in general, the period between the commencement and completion on the same workday of an employee's principal activity or activities. It includes all time within that period whether or not the employee engages in work throughout all of that period . . . . If an employee is required to report at the actual place of performance of his principal activity at a certain specific time, his "workday" commences at the time he reports there for work in accordance with the employer's requirement, even though through a cause beyond the employee's control,

---

1. *See* 29 U.S.C. § 203(g).
2. *See* Tenn. Coal, Iron & R.R. Co. v. Muscoda Local No. 123, 321 U.S. 590, 601–03 (1944) (FLSA required employer to pay miners for all hours worked mining ore rather than by the quantity of ore produced); Armour & Co. v. Wantock, 323 U.S. 126, 133–34 (1944) (daytime employees required to remain on employer's premises at night to respond to fire calls were engaged in work); Skidmore v. Swift, 323 U.S. 134, 137–40 (1944) (same). *See also* 29 C.F.R. § 785.7.
3. *See* Anderson v. Mt. Clemens Pottery Co., 328 U.S. 680, 689–91 (1946). *See also* 29 C.F.R. § 785.7.
4. *See* 29 C.F.R. § 785.12.
5. *See id.*

he is not able to commence performance of his productive activities until a later time. In such a situation the time spent waiting for work would be part of the workday.[6]

The regulation goes on to say that even rest periods and lunch periods are part of the compensable continuous workday unless an exception found in the text of the FLSA itself or in the regulations applies.[7] Two of the most important of these exceptions, those for meal time and sleep time, will be discussed later in this chapter.

The Continuous Workday Principle and Work Performed Before or After the Scheduled Workday

A typical work schedule for FLSA nonexempt employees scheduled to work a forty-hour work week might look like this: Monday through Friday, 8 a.m. to 5 p.m. with a mandatory unpaid lunch break of one hour. Sometimes, however, nonexempt employees may come to work before 8 a.m. or stay later than 5 p.m. without being asked to do so by their supervisors. They may begin to perform their regular job duties during those early morning hours or continue to perform their regular duties into the early evening. Sometimes nonexempt employees come to work before 8 a.m. to prepare equipment or dress themselves in special gear so that they can begin to perform their actual job duties at 8 a.m. Similarly, employees must sometimes remain on the employer's premises after they stop performing their job duties at 5 p.m. to put away equipment or change into civilian clothing from protective gear. While these are all situations of "work" performed before or after the scheduled workday, the FLSA treats very differently performance of an employee's primary job duties before the scheduled starting time and after the scheduled stopping time on one hand, and, on the other, tasks undertaken before starting and stopping time that enable the employee to perform his or her primary job duties. The former kind of work is referred to as "off-the-clock" work. The U.S. Department of Labor (DOL) has named the latter "preliminary and postliminary" work. This chapter will refer to preliminary and postliminary work by the less cumbersome terms *pre-work* and *post-work* activities.

"Off-the-Clock" Work

Imagine the following situation.

Andrew is a nonexempt city employee who is scheduled to work a thirty-seven-and-one-half-hour workweek: from 8:30 a.m. until 4:30 p.m., with a half-hour unpaid lunch period, from 12:30 to 1 p.m., during which he is to leave his work station and perform no work. Recently, the volume of work in Andrew's department has increased. He has come in early and begun working at 8:00 a.m. this week. As a result, Andrew has worked an

6. 29 C.F.R. § 790.6(b).
7. See id.

additional two and one-half hours for a total of forty hours. He duly records this on his timesheet. Should Andrew be paid for the additional two and one-half hours he has worked beyond his scheduled hours?

Andrew has performed work that has benefitted his employer. His supervisor knows that Andrew has worked those extra two and one-half hours because she has seen his recorded time. The city must pay Andrew for the extra two and one-half hours—even though it did not ask him to work additional hours—because he began his principal work activity and started his continuous workday at 8 a.m. each day that week. If the city does not want Andrew to work more than thirty-seven and one-half hours—even if it means falling behind in his work—his supervisor or department head must tell him so.

Suppose Andrew's supervisor does instruct him not to start work early but he continues to do so, working an additional two and one-half hours the next week. He reports it on his timesheet. Must the city pay him for the additional time worked during the second week? Once again, the answer is "yes." The city must pay Andrew for the additional hours worked, as he has done the work for the city's benefit.[8] To keep Andrew from continuing to work additional hours, the city will have to find a way to physically prevent him from doing so—by taking away his access to the building before and after hours, perhaps, or by programming the city's computer system to lock him out except between the hours of 8:30 a.m. and 4:30 p.m. Alternatively, the city could discipline Andrew, perhaps by suspending him without pay for a period of time. Or the city could dismiss Andrew from employment. The bottom line is that the city knows that Andrew is working a greater number of hours than he is scheduled to work, and it must take steps to prevent him from doing so. As the FLSA regulations instruct:

> In all such cases it is the duty of the management to exercise its control and see that the work is not performed if it does not want it to be performed. It cannot sit back and accept the benefits without compensating for them. The mere promulgation of a rule against such work is not enough. Management has the power to enforce the rule and must make every effort to do so.[9]

The same would hold true if Andrew came in on time at 8:30 but worked until 5 p.m., half an hour later than scheduled, or if he began work at 8:30, left at 4:30, and worked through his half-hour lunch period.

---

8. *See* 29 C.F.R. § 785.11. *See also* Chao v. Gotham Registry, Inc., 514 F.3d 280, 288 (2d Cir. 2008); Forrester v. Roth's IGA Foodliner, Inc., 646 F.2d 413, 414 (9th Cir. 1981); Reich v. Stewart, 121 F.3d 400, 407 (8th Cir. 1997).

9. *See* 29 C.F.R. § 785.13.

Unauthorized Overtime Due to "Working Off the Clock"

Although Andrew in the hypothetical presented above worked more than his scheduled weekly hours, he did not work more than forty hours. So, his additional hours would be compensated at his regular hourly rate. But what if he had worked overtime? The same principles apply when nonexempt employees work unscheduled hours that take them above the forty-hour overtime threshold. The compensable continuous workday ends only when an employee stops working. When employees work unscheduled or unauthorized extra hours and report the hours on their timesheets, they must be paid straight time for all hours up to and including forty hours, and time-and-one-half their regular rate for all hours above forty. It is up to the employer to put a stop to unauthorized hours of work when supervisors, department heads, human resources staff, or payroll personnel become aware of it. This is true even if the employer has adopted a policy that prohibits employees from working overtime without prior authorization. Merely stating a policy is not enough. Consider the following example.

> Betsy is a nonexempt employee in the county social services department. Committed to her clients, Betsy frequently ends up working more than her scheduled forty hours. The county's and the department's personnel policies state clearly that no employee is to work overtime hours without the express permission of his or her immediate supervisor. Betsy knows this but works the extra overtime hours anyway, believing that the needs of her clients, many of them minors, should come first.
>
> Betsy does not record the overtime hours on her timesheets, thinking that the county will not pay her for them since the overtime was not authorized by her supervisor. She is more concerned with getting her clients the assistance they need than with the extra pay. But she keeps a record of her overtime hours for herself—"just in case."
>
> Recently, Betsy has soured on her job. She feels that her new supervisor plays favorites. On the advice of a friend, she brings a record of her overtime hours to the human resources department and tells the director that she needs to be compensated for all of those additional hours she has worked over the years.

How does Betsy's situation differ from that of Andrew, who also worked additional hours without prior permission?

The difference lies in what Andrew's employer knew compared to what Betsy's employer knew. Andrew had recorded his additional hours. The city knew about them and was obligated to pay him for them and to take some action to prohibit him from working additional hours in the future. The county, on the other hand, may not know that Betsy has been working overtime, as she never formally recorded or submitted that time for payment. If the county does not know about Betsy's extra hours, it does not have to pay her for what was unauthorized overtime—unless Betsy can show that the county had *constructive* knowledge that she was working overtime.

Constructive Knowledge

An employer is liable for unpaid overtime if it had actual knowledge of the overtime work.[10] If the time was reported on the employee's time sheet, for example, or if the employee can show that his or her supervisor directed the employee not to record all of the hours worked, then actual knowledge on the part of the employer is clear. On the other hand, it is entirely possible that an employee has worked extra hours and the employer really does not know about it. For example, where employees admit that they worked overtime hours upon their own initiative and fail to submit timesheets reflecting the extra hours, it may be possible to conclude that the employer did not have direct knowledge of the overtime hours and thus is not liable for them. The general rule is that where an employee prevents an employer from learning about uncompensated overtime, there is no FLSA violation.[11]

But the employer can be liable in situations in which it might be said that while the employer did not have *actual knowledge* of overtime hours, it had mere *constructive knowledge* of the extra hours worked, meaning that the circumstances show that the employer surely should have known of the extra hours worked. The burden is on the employees claiming that they are due compensation for extra hours worked to prove that the employer had this constructive knowledge. It is not an easy matter for employees to prove. Courts have routinely found that employees failed to meet this burden when they argued that managers had seen them on the employer's premises after hours, that managers should have noticed that the employees sent them emails after hours, or that they had mentioned to their managers on isolated occasions that they had worked overtime without receiving permission but had not recorded the time.[12]

Employers should note, however, that DOL investigators may not employ the same high standard of proof as the courts. DOL has introduced a mobile app for the iPhone that employees can use to record overtime hours.[13] On its website, the agency

---

10. *See* Bailey v. Cty. of Georgetown, 94 F.3d 152, 157 (4th Cir. 1996) (employees failed to show that county employer had actual or constructive knowledge of overtime work where only evidence presented was isolated and general comments over three-year period in question); Davis v. Food Lion, 792 F.2d 1274, 1276 (4th Cir. 1986) (supermarket manager failed to show that employer knew or should have known that he was working secret overtime hours to meet employer's scheduling system).

11. *See* Allen v. Bd. of Pub. Educ., 495 F.3d 1306, 1319 (11th Cir. 2007) (question of material fact existed as to whether employees told supervisors that they worked overtime, precluding summary judgment).

12. *See, e.g.*, Darrikhuma v. Southland Corp., 975 F. Supp. 778 (D. Md.), *aff'd*, 129 F.3d 1258 (4th Cir. 1997) (seen on employer premises on weekend); Faery v. Weigand-Omega Mgmt., Inc., No. H-11-2519, 2012 WL 3063899, at *5 (S.D. Tex. July 26, 2012) (after-hours email); *Bailey*, 94 F.3d at 157 (isolated comments about overtime worked).

13. The app is available on DOL's website: https://www.dol.gov/general/apps/timesheet.

describes the tool as "a timesheet to record the hours that you work and calculate the amount you may be owed by your employer. It also includes overtime pay calculations at a rate of one and one-half times (1.5) the regular rate of pay for all hours you work over 40 in a workweek."[14] Whether DOL investigators would then shift the burden of proof onto employers to show that an employee did not work the hours recorded on the app is unclear.

Courts generally allow lawsuits alleging constructive knowledge to proceed to trial. Employer attempts to have these cases dismissed frequently fail, as courts often find the mere allegation that an employee has worked uncompensated hours sufficient to state a claim for a violation of the FLSA, even where the employee has not alleged a specific list of hours and dates on which uncompensated hours were worked.[15] The parties frequently offer conflicting evidence as to whether the employer had actual or constructive knowledge, which makes the claim one not appropriate for decision without a trial.[16] The employer may ultimately prevail, but at the cost of litigating the claim through a full trial.

The most effective strategy to prevent employees from bringing claims alleging uncompensated work over a period of years involves three steps. First, employers should adopt and publicize a policy that clearly prohibits work outside a nonexempt employee's scheduled hours without permission. This should be part of new employee orientation and should be re-published or addressed at department meetings at least once a year.

Second, supervisors should (1) immediately send home any employee discovered to be working when not scheduled to do so and (2) consider taking disciplinary action.[17] If an employee turns in a current timesheet recording unauthorized hours, supervisors should take disciplinary action. That action should take any form the supervisor believes will be most effective: a written warning in jurisdictions that require warnings prior to more serious discipline, a suspension without pay (perhaps for the number of hours that are needed to recoup the payment the employer must

---

14. *Id.*

15. *See, e.g.,* Alston v. Becton, Dickinson & Co., No. 1:12CV452, 2013 WL 4539634, at *4 (M.D.N.C. Aug. 27, 2013); Butler v. DirectSat USA, LLC, 800 F. Supp. 2d 662, 668 (D. Md. 2011).

16. *See, e.g.,* Mahshie v. Infinity Ins. Co., No. 12-20148-CIV, 2012 WL 5818150, at *6 (S.D. Fla. Nov. 15, 2012) (summary judgment denied, as jury could conclude, notwithstanding employer's denial that it had knowledge of overtime, that based on the record of the employee's emails to supervisors, employer should have known employee was working overtime).

17. *See, e.g.,* Davis v. Food Lion, 792 F.2d 1274, 1277–78 (4th Cir. 1986) (where evidence showed that (1) employee was aware of employer's established policy prohibiting employees from working unrecorded overtime hours and providing for discipline for violations of the policy and (2) managers gave employee warnings and reprimands on occasions where he was discovered working off-the-clock, employer was not liable for overtime hours). *See also Faery,* 2012 WL 3063899, at *5 (employer did not have constructive knowledge of unauthorized overtime where employee was aware of employer's written policy against unauthorized overtime, supervisor reminded employee of policy and encouraged employee to request permission for overtime if there was legitimate need, and employee neither advised supervisor of any specific overtime hours she had worked nor provided her with a legitimate reason for overtime).

make for the unauthorized work), or demotion or even discharge for repeat offenders. It is possible that this could drive employees working unauthorized overtime "underground," leading to situations where they work and record overtime surreptitiously. Even if that is the case, the case law is clear that employees who deliberately try to conceal their overtime work from their employers cannot prove actual or constructive knowledge and will be unable to recover the unpaid wages.[18]

Third, supervisors should investigate any suspicions they may have that an employee is working overtime without recording it on his or her timesheets. Depending on the circumstances, supervisors might interview department employees individually to see if others have observed anyone working off-the-clock or heard co-workers talking about doing so. It is virtually impossible to show that an employer who polices unauthorized work hours and who takes disciplinary action against those employees who violate a rule against unauthorized overtime hours "knew or should have known" that an employee was working overtime. The only way in which an employer who is serious about stopping off-the-clock work can be ignorant of it is if employees seek to hide it.

Pre-Work and Post-Work Activities

Section 254 of the FLSA (sometimes known as the "Portal-to-Portal Act") exempts from compensation "activities which are preliminary to or postliminary to" the performance of an employee's principal activities.[19] Another way of putting this is to say that an employee does not generally have to be paid for activities he or she undertakes before the start of the continuous workday. Sometimes, however, it is unclear whether an activity that an employee performs at either the start or the conclusion of a workday is part of the employee's principal activities or is more in the nature of a preliminary or subsequent activity.

Integral and Indispensable Part of the Principal Activity

In an attempt to add some clarity to the distinction between a compensable principal activity and a noncompensable preliminary or concluding activity, the U.S. Supreme Court has defined the term "principal activities" to include all activities that are an "integral and indispensable part of the principal activities."[20] Integral and indispensable activities are those activities that are intrinsic elements of the employee's principal activities and that the employee must perform in order to perform the principal activities of his or her job.[21] In its FLSA regulations, DOL gives several examples of activities that would be considered integral and indispensable to a principal activity:

> (1) In connection with the operation of a lathe an employee will frequently at the commencement of his workday oil, grease or clean his machine,

---

18. *See, e.g.*, Allen v. Bd. of Pub. Educ., 495 F.3d 1306, 1319 (11th Cir. 2007); Holland v. Distribution Servs. Int'l, Inc., No. 4:14-cv-60, 2014 WL 6473677, at *4 (S.D. Ga. Nov. 18, 2014).

19. *See* 29 U.S.C. § 254(a)(2).

20. *See* Steiner v. Mitchell, 350 U.S. 247, 252–53 (1956). *See also* 29 C.F.R. § 790.8(b).

21. *See Steiner*, 350 U.S. at 249, 251. *See also* 29 C.F.R. § 790.8(c).

or install a new cutting tool. Such activities are an integral part of the principal activity, and are included within such term.

(2) In the case of a garment worker in a textile mill, who is required to report 30 minutes before other employees report to commence their principal activities, and who during such 30 minutes distributes clothing or parts of clothing at the work-benches of other employees and gets machines in readiness for operation by other employees, such activities are among the principal activities of such employee.[22]

Similarly,

[i]f an employee in a chemical plant . . . cannot perform his principal activities without putting on certain clothes, changing clothes on the employer's premises at the beginning and end of the workday would be an integral part of the employee's principal activity. On the other hand, if changing clothes is merely a convenience to the employee and not directly related to his principal activities, it would be considered as a "preliminary" or "postliminary" activity rather than a principal part of the activity.[23]

FLSA Section 254 lists three preliminary and post-work activities that are not compensable, namely, "walking, riding, or traveling to and from the actual place of performance of the principal activity or activities which [the] employee is employed to perform."[24] The FLSA regulations elaborate and make clear that the kind of "walking, riding, or traveling" that is not compensable is that which occurs on the trip between home and the workplace. Walking, riding, or otherwise traveling between the entrance to the employer's premises and the actual place at which the employee performs his or her work is also not considered integral and indispensable to the employee's principal activities and thus is not compensable.[25] Any walking, riding, or traveling that occurs during an employee's work day, such as trips between the location of one principal activity and another, or traveling to an out-of-town location that occurs during working hours, is, by contrast, compensable under the FLSA's continuous workday rules.[26] The regulations also say that changing clothes, as well as washing up or showering, do not generally constitute compensable activities.[27]

Below are some pre-work and post-work activities about which questions of compensability arise most frequently in public sector employment.

- changing into uniforms and required safety gear,

22. 29 C.F.R. §§ 790.8(b)(1), (2). *See also id.* § 785.24.
23. 29 C.F.R. § 790.8(c). *See also id.* § 785.24.
24. 29 U.S.C. § 254(a).
25. *See* 29 C.F.R. §§ 790.8(c), (f).
26. *See* 29 C.F.R. § 790.7(c).
27. *See* 29 C.F.R. § 790.7(g).

- cleaning machines and vehicles used in the performance of the principal activity,
- driving a government vehicle between home and work,
- caring for and transporting police dogs, and
- reporting to work ten or fifteen minutes early or staying ten or fifteen minutes late so that an incoming shift may be briefed.

For most of these activities, the case law is relatively consistent.

Changing into Uniforms and Required Safety Equipment

The U.S. Supreme Court first addressed the question of whether changing in and out of a uniform ("donning and doffing," as the regulations and cases call it) is compensable in 1956 in the case *Steiner v. Mitchell*.[28] *Steiner* involved workers in a battery plant who were regularly exposed to toxic materials and therefore needed to change clothes and shower on-site after they finished work. The time involved was substantial: ten minutes before beginning work and twenty minutes after a shift ended, for a total of thirty minutes each day. The Court found that changing clothing and showering after this type of work was "a recognized part of industrial hygiene programs in the industry" and noted that state law required employers to install showering facilities in these circumstances.[29] Given how quickly regular clothing deteriorated when exposed to battery acid and associated chemicals, the employer actually provided clothing for its employees to wear on the job.[30] The Court found that showering and changing were "integral" and "indispensable" to the workers' principal activity and that their employer therefore had to compensate them for the time spent showering and changing, as well as for the time spent performing their principal activities within the plant.[31]

In the public sector, claims regarding time spent changing into uniform and putting on safety gear are brought most frequently by law enforcement officers—although they are not the only positions in which government employees wear uniforms. Officers have generally argued that the wearing of a uniform is vital to the performance of the officers' jobs, that donning a uniform and safety gear minimizes the potential for injury to officers, which in turn benefits the employing agency by facilitating a ready and healthy police force, and that donning the uniform and equipment helps police officers do their jobs more efficiently. Courts, on the other hand, have regularly rejected such claims, although their rationale for doing so may differ from case to case. Sometimes courts have found for the government employer because the plaintiff officers failed to establish that the donning and doffing of uniforms and equipment was integral and indispensable to their principal work,[32] sometimes

---

28. 350 U.S. 247 (1956).

29. *Id.* at 250.

30. *Id.* at 250–51.

31. *See id.* at 253, 256.

32. *See* Huff v. City of L.A., 468 F. App'x 773 (9th Cir. 2012); Reed v. Cty. of Orange, 716 F. Supp. 2d 876 (C.D. Cal. 2010); Martin v. City of Richmond, 504 F. Supp. 2d 766 (N.D. Cal. 2007).

because the officers had the option of changing at home before leaving for work.[33] But other times courts have found that changing in and out of uniform is integral and indispensable to an employee's duties, and thus compensable under the FLSA, where either the law or employer policy *requires* that donning and doffing activities take place at the workplace. This finding is particularly common in cases where the workplace dangers that accompany the employee's principal activities go above and beyond ordinary risks and require specialized protective gear.[34]

DOL considers a requirement that employees change into uniforms or safety equipment at the workplace as making the donning and doffing a part of the continuous workday:

> . . . donning and doffing of required gear is within the continuous workday only when the employer or the nature of the job mandates that it take place on the employer's premises. It is our longstanding position that if employees have the option and the ability to change into the required gear at home, changing into that gear is not a principal activity, even when it takes place at the [place of employment].[35]

Donning and doffing the protective gear that a law enforcement officer wears in addition to a uniform, such as a "duty belt," a radio case, pepper mace, a baton strap, a magazine pouch, handcuffs, a holster, a first-responders pouch, a flashlight, and/ or a ballistics vest—is more likely to be compensable as "integral and indispensable" to the officer's performance of his or her duties, as such equipment directly helps the officer apprehend and deal with suspects, protect physical locations, and protect himself or herself.[36]

Time That Is De Minimis

Sometimes pre-work or post-work activities may be an integral and indispensable part of an employee's primary activity but take so little time as to be impractical to record or compensate. This situation arises most frequently in the area of donning and doffing required clothing or protective gear. The FLSA regulations address this issue at Section 785.47 of C.F.R. Title 29:

---

33. *See* Dager v. City of Phoenix, 380 F. App'x 688 (9th Cir. 2010); Bamonte v. City of Mesa, 598 F.3d 1217 (9th Cir. 2010); Musticchi v. City of Little Rock, 734 F. Supp. 2d 621, 626 (E.D. Ark. 2010). *Contra* Lemmon v. City of San Leandro, 538 F. Supp. 2d 1200 (N.D. Cal. 2007).

34. *See* Perez v. City of New York, 832 F.3d 120 (2d Cir. 2016) (denying summary judgment where genuine issues of material fact existed as to whether or not the donning and doffing of uniforms by assistant urban park rangers was integral and indispensable to their principal activities when such uniforms included utility belts holding a baton, pepper spray, and handcuffs and bulletproof vests).

35. U.S. Dep't of Labor, Wage & Hour Div., Advisory Memorandum No. 2006-2 (May 31, 2006), https://www.dol.gov/whd/FieldBulletins/AdvisoryMemo2006_2.htm (memorandum for DOL regional administrators and district directors on *IBP v. Alvarez*, 546 U.S. 21 (2005)).

36. *See* Lesane v. Winter, 866 F. Supp. 2d 1, 7 (D.D.C. 2011).

... insubstantial or insignificant periods of time beyond the scheduled working hours, which cannot as a practical administrative matter be precisely recorded for payroll purposes, may be disregarded. The courts have held that such trifles are de minimis. (Anderson v. Mt. Clemens Pottery Co., 328 U.S. 680 (1946)) This rule applies only where there are uncertain and indefinite periods of time involved of a few seconds or minutes duration, and where the failure to count such time is due to considerations justified by industrial realities. ...

De minimis is a Latin term meaning "about insignificant things" and, as a legal term, it has come to be used to denote things too insignificant to count or measure. Just how much time is necessary for a period to be considered *de minimis* can be determined only on a case-by-case basis. The federal Fourth Circuit Court of Appeals has held that the aggregate amount of time that employees spend in pre-work or post-work activities is the standard against which to measure compensability. The court rejected an employer's argument that each task or group of tasks should be evaluated separately to determine if the time period is *de minimis*.[37] The court held that three factors must be considered when conducting a *de minimis* analysis: (1) the practical difficulty the employer would encounter in recording the additional time, (2) the total amount of the employee's compensable time (each day and over time), and (3) the regularity of the additional work.[38]

Cleaning Machines and Vehicles Used in the Performance of the Principal Activity

Courts have generally found time spent on the care and cleaning of clothing, equipment, and vehicles necessary for the performance of an employee's principal duty to be compensable. For example, where police officers spent time after the scheduled workday cleaning and caring for police equipment such as uniforms and weapons, a court found the time to be compensable under the FLSA because the city employer derived significant benefit from such activities.[39] Similarly, where canine officers spent time outside the scheduled workday cleaning, fueling, and maintaining their vehicles, the same court found that the activity was not preliminary or subsequent

---

37. *See* Perez v. Mountaire Farms, Inc., 650 F.3d 350, 373 (4th Cir. 2011) (holding that poultry-processing plant employees were entitled to compensation for 10.204 minutes per work shift for the time that they spend donning and doffing their protective gear at the beginning and the end of their shifts).

38. See *Mountaire Farms*, 650 F.3d at 373, *citing* Lindow v. United States, 738 F.2d 1057, 1062–63 (9th Cir. 1984), and cases from other circuits. *See also* Reich v. Monfort, Inc., 144 F.3d 1329, 1334 (10th Cir. 1998) (ten minutes each day spent donning and doffing, cleaning, and sanitizing safety gear was not *de minimis* and was compensable); Rutti v. Lojack Corp., Inc., 596 F.3d 1046, 1059 (9th Cir. 2010) (summary judgment denied on question of whether fifteen-minute post-work transmissions on portable data terminal were *de minimis*); *Lesane*, 866 F. Supp. 2d at 10 (summary judgment denied on question of whether six- or eight-minute period spent donning and doffing of protective gear was *de minimis*).

39. *See* Treece v. City of Little Rock, 923 F. Supp. 1122 (E.D. Ark. 1996).

to their principal activity of driving vehicles and transporting dogs but was, instead an integral and indispensable part of that work.[40]

In a non–law enforcement context, the federal Fifth Circuit Court of Appeals found that pre-shift activities performed by electricians and their helpers, including the filling out of time sheets, material sheets, supply sheets, and cash requisition sheets, and the fueling, loading, and cleaning of trucks were within the broad range of "principal activities" performed at the employer's behest and for benefit of its business and were, therefore, compensable activities.[41]

Driving a Government Vehicle between Home and Work

Driving an employer-issued car between the employee's home and workplace is never compensable time unless the employee is performing some other activity at the direction of the employer during the trip. The general rule governing travel from home to work is found in the FLSA itself, and it omits from compensation any time spent "walking, riding, or traveling to and from the actual place of performance of the principal activity or activities which such employee is employed to perform . . . ,"[42] as does DOL's corresponding interpretive regulation at C.F.R. Title 29, Section 785.35:

> An employee who travels from home before his regular workday and returns to his home at the end of the workday is engaged in ordinary home to work travel which is a normal incident of employment. This is true whether he works at a fixed location or at different job sites. Normal travel from home to work is not worktime.

The FLSA is clear that the fact that an employee may use an employer-issued vehicle is irrelevant:

> For purposes of this subsection, the use of an employer's vehicle for travel by an employee and activities performed by an employee which are incidental to the use of such vehicle for commuting shall not be considered part of the employee's principal activities if the use of such vehicle for travel is within the normal commuting area for the employer's business or establishment and the use of the employer's vehicle is subject to an agreement on the part of the employer and the employee or representative of such employee.[43]

Nevertheless, public employees sometimes argue that commuting from home to work in a government-issued vehicle *is* a different situation: the vehicles are not issued as perks but are instead generally issued to employees who may have to respond to emergencies outside of scheduled work hours. Law enforcement officers, fire officials, utility repair workers, public works employees, and on-call social services workers are among the positions most frequently issued government-owned vehicles. The

---

40. *See id.*

41. *See* Dunlop v. City Elec., Inc., 527 F.2d 394 (5th Cir. 1976).

42. 29 U.S.C. § 254(a) (Section 254 is the codified version of the 1947 Portal-to-Portal Act amendment to the FLSA).

43. *Id.*

courts, however, have rejected this argument, holding that the time a government employee spends commuting in a government-issued vehicle is not an integral and indispensable part of an employee's principal activities—even where employees must monitor radio calls or stop or re-route for emergencies while en route from home to the workplace.[44] Of course, time actually spent dealing with an emergency that arises during the commute is compensable.

The 2006 case *Adams v. United States* provides a good example of the application of this principle. The case was brought by a group of federal law enforcement officials from various agencies, all of whom were required to commute from home to work in government vehicles. All of the officers were subject to rules applicable to their commutes: they were each required to have their weapons and other law enforcement–related equipment in their vehicles and to monitor the vehicles' communications equipment. They were not allowed to run any personal errands in their government vehicles and thus had to proceed directly from home to work and back again without unauthorized detours or stops. There was no question that these requirements facilitated their employers' law enforcement missions, since they made the cars available to the officers for rapid response to emergency calls at any time, whether the officers were at home after hours or on their way to work.[45]

The court held that for the commuting time to be compensable, the requirements and restrictions placed on the officers' commutes had to be significant and to turn the commute into an activity performed for the employer's benefit. It found that the commutes were not compensable. In reaching its conclusion, the court cited with approval the reasoning of the federal Second Circuit Court of Appeals in an earlier case:

> The more the preliminary (or postliminary) activity is undertaken for the employer's benefit, the more indispensable it is to the primary goal of the employee's work, and the less choice the employee has in the matter, the more likely such work will be found to be compensable. . . . The ability of the employer to maintain records of such time expended is a factor. And, where the compensable preliminary work is truly minimal, it is the policy of the law to disregard it.[46]

In a 2008 case from the same Second Circuit, *Singh v. City of New York*, the details differ but the result is the same. In *Singh*, the city's fire-alarm inspectors did not report back to their offices four of the five days of the workweek. They went directly home from inspection sites. But they were required to carry home briefcases that held necessary documents and weighed 15 to 20 pounds; they then had to carry the cases back out to inspections each day. The inspectors argued first, that the required carrying of the briefcases, which was done solely to benefit their employer, turned

---

44. *See* Aiken v. City of Memphis, 190 F.3d 753, 759 (6th Cir. 1999) (mere monitoring of police radio did not turn commute into compensable time).

45. *See* Adams v. United States, 471 F.3d 1321, 1323 (Fed. Cir. 2006).

46. *See id.* at 1327, *citing* Reich v. N.Y. City Transit Auth., 45 F.3d 646, 650 (2d Cir. 1995) (commute of law enforcement dog-handlers not compensable); *see also* Bobo v. United States, 136 F.3d 1465, 1467 (Fed. Cir. 1998) (same).

their commutes into compensable time, and second, that the added weight of the briefcases made them slower and thus increased the amount of time it took them to travel home and back. The court found that the mere carrying of briefcases did not turn noncompensable travel time into work time since it did not impinge on the commute in any other way. It further found that any lengthening of the time it took to make the trip from home to work was so minimal as to not be compensable.[47]

Maybe an employee completes some work tasks from home before beginning his or her trip to the workplace. This does not transform commuting time into compensable time. The time spent performing duties for the employer before starting the commute may be compensable, but the commute is a noncompensable break in the continuous workday.[48]

Briefing an Incoming Shift

Public safety employees are often required to come into work ten to fifteen minutes early or to stay ten to fifteen minutes beyond the end of their shift so that the employees from the outgoing shift can brief those on the incoming shift. The regulations address this practice directly at C.F.R. Title 29, Section 553.225:

> It is a common practice among employees engaged in fire protection activities to relieve employees on the previous shift prior to the scheduled starting time. Such early relief time may occur pursuant to employee agreement, either expressed or implied. This practice will not have the effect of increasing the number of compensable hours of work for employees employed under section 7(k) where it is voluntary on the part of the employees and does not result, over a period of time, in their failure to receive proper compensation for all hours actually worked. On the other hand, if the practice is required by the employer, the time involved must be added to the employee's tour of duty and treated as compensable hours of work.

Several things about this section are worth noting. First, although the text of Section 553.225 speaks of "employees engaged in fire protection activities," the courts regularly apply it to law enforcement personnel as well.[49] Second, if the employer

---

47. *See* Singh v. City of New York, 524 F.3d 361, 367–72 (2d Cir. 2008) (applying a predominant benefit test to determine whether the carrying of the briefcases was an integral and indispensable part of the employee's principal activities).

48. *See* Kuebel v. Black & Decker Inc., 643 F.3d 352, 360 (2d Cir. 2011) (fact that employee performed some tasks at home, on his own schedule, did not make his commute time compensable any more than it made his sleep time or his dinner time compensable).

49. In fact, most of the reported cases involve law enforcement, rather than fire protection, employees. *See, e.g.*, Brubach v. City of Albuquerque, 893 F. Supp. 2d 1216 (D.N.M. 2012) (plaintiffs who worked a fifteen-minute mandatory pre-shift briefing period may be entitled to overtime compensation); Lindow v. United States, 738 F.2d 1057 (9th Cir. 1984) (same); Adair v. City of Kirkland, 16 F. App'x 644 (9th Cir. 2001) (collective-bargaining agreement provision including pre-shift briefing time as part of officers' normally scheduled work day did not violate the FLSA); Robertson v. Bd. of Cty. Commr's, 78 F. Supp. 2d 1142 (D. Colo. 1999) (plaintiffs who worked a fifteen-minute mandatory pre-shift briefing period may be entitled to overtime compensation).

requires employees to report to work for pre-shift briefings or to stay at work for post-shift briefings, the time is compensable unless it is *de minimis.* In one New Mexico case, the issue was whether a five-minute pre-shift briefing was compensable. The employer argued that attendance at the briefing was voluntary, and therefore not compensable, pointing to its written policy that provided that officers "should" arrive for duty five minutes prior to their assigned shifts. The court, however, noted that even if the language of a policy is in the form of a recommendation, any pressure or encouragement to report early would be evidence of an FLSA violation.[50] The court found that a reasonable juror could find that attendance at the pre-shift briefing was required: eight of the plaintiffs claimed that they were told by at least seven different sergeants, two lieutenants, and one supervisor that they were required to arrive to work five minutes prior to the start of their shift times for briefing, and one said that a sergeant informed her that he would "write her up" if she did not arrive five minutes early.[51]

This does not mean that public employers must always compensate employees who perform or attend shift-change briefings. A written agreement to the effect that attendance at a pre-shift or post-shift briefing is part of a *salaried*, nonexempt employee's workday will make clear that the briefing time is not separately compensated unless an employee works in excess of the overtime threshold. This is especially useful for employers scheduling law enforcement officers and firefighters in accordance with the FLSA's Section 207(k) exemption[52] for fewer hours than 171, 212, or whatever the applicable overtime threshold may be.

Sometimes employers do not think it necessary for employees to come in early to be briefed and do not want them to do so. In a federal Ninth Circuit Court of Appeals case involving the Army Corps of Engineers, the court found that a written statement or policy to the effect that employees were not required to arrive early to review the previous shift's activities rendered any early arrivals voluntary and noncompensable.[53] That case, *Lindow v. United States*, had a complicated fact pattern and, consequently, a complicated holding, but it illustrates well the nuances

---

50. *See Brubach*, 893 F. Supp. 2d at 1225. *See also Lindow*, 738 F.2d at 1061.

51. *See Brubach*, 893 F. Supp. 2d at 1225.

52. "The 207(k) exemption allows employers to compute overtime for law enforcement and firefighters on the basis of extended work schedule—usually 28 days. Under 207(k), nonexempt law enforcement officers must work 171 hours in 28 days before the employer becomes liable for overtime. In other words, for law enforcement, hours up to and including 171 are paid at the employee's regular straight time rate. Hours in excess of 171 are paid as overtime at the time-and-one-half rate. If the employer has adopted a policy that provides for use of compensatory time off ("comp time") in lieu of cash overtime, then an officer would earn one-and-one-half hours paid time-off for every hour worked over 171 in that 28-day period.... Firefighters must work 212 hours on a 28-day schedule." Diane M. Juffras, *How Does the FLSA's 207(k) Exemption for Law Enforcement and Firefighters Work?* (UNC School of Government), https://www.sog.unc.edu/resources/faqs/how-does-flsa%E2%80%99s-207k-exemption-law-enforcement-and-firefighters-work.

53. *See Lindow*, 738 F.2d at 1060.

of pre-shift briefing compensability. The plaintiffs were power-plant operators, control-room operators, and general foremen of some of the Corps' hydroelectric dams. They alleged that the Corps required each of them to report to work fifteen minutes before their scheduled starting time to familiarize themselves with the previous shift's activities and plant conditions, exchange information, clarify log entries with employees clocking out of the previous shift, and relieve outgoing employees operating navigational locks. The plaintiffs sought three years of back overtime pay they claimed they were owed because of working an additional fifteen minutes each day.

At trial, the federal district court found that employees had not routinely used the entire fifteen minutes to brief themselves in preparation for their shifts. Instead, employees sometimes used seven or eight minutes per day before their shifts for that purpose, while other times they spent the fifteen minutes socializing, getting coffee, and performing non-work-related activities. Sometimes employees got the necessary information after their shifts had begun. The trial court also found that the Army Corps did not require the employees to report to work early, though it was customary for them to do so. The Corps did not reprimand employees for arriving early, but at one point it did issue a policy letter saying that employees were not required to report to work early to review information. Interestingly, the court noted that there was evidence that employees felt pressure from their coworkers on the outgoing shifts to arrive early so that they could be relieved early.

In its decision, the Ninth Circuit held that any of the seven or eight minutes that employees actually spent performing pre-shift work prior to the Corps' issuance of the policy letter was compensable (but that, as we shall see, it was *de minimis*) because it was an integral and indispensable part of their principal activities and the Corps had suffered or permitted the work to be done. The pre-work socializing, coffee-drinking, and availability to relieve outgoing shifts early, however, was not for the employer's benefit and was not compensable.[54]

But, the court said, once the policy letter was issued, the Corps was not liable—even for the seven or eight minutes of pre-shift work that was sometimes performed.[55] That outcome is somewhat surprising, since the Corps did not discipline any employee for engaging in information exchanges before the start of shifts, and those exchanges were for the Corps' benefit. The court based its distinction on the fact that the employees could have performed the work during their scheduled hours.[56]

Pre-shift or post-shift briefings outside the scheduled workday are also not compensable if they are *de minimis*. In a case involving detention-officer employees of a for-profit prison management company, the detention officers brought a lawsuit alleging that they were not paid for pre-shift briefings. The evidence showed, however, that the briefings consisted of each officer receiving his or her post assignment for the day, which sometimes included getting information about what had been happening

---

54. *See id.* at 1061.
55. *See id.* at 1061–62.
56. *See id.*

at that post before the officer's arrival; a briefing on operational and security issues at the facility; and the distribution of paperwork for the assigned post. The briefings took an additional one to two minutes of the officers' time, which the court found to be too small and administratively difficult an amount to be compensable.[57] In the *Lindow* case discussed above, the court found that even the seven or eight minutes of pre-work that would otherwise be compensable was *de minimis*—and therefore not compensable—primarily because, with respect to each employee, the compensable work occurred so irregularly as to make accounting for it difficult.[58]

On-Call Time

Most local governments require that at least some employees be available to return to work in the event of an emergency. Departments with on-call requirements may include water, sewer, and other utilities; public works; law enforcement; fire; emergency medical services (EMS); emergency management; social services; and information technology. Whether such employees must be paid for the time they are on call can be a vexing question.

The DOL's On-Call Regulation

The FLSA regulations devote only one section to on-call time, Section 785.17 of Title 29 of the Code of Federal Regulations (C.F.R.), which reads as follows:

> An employee who is required to remain on call on the employer's premises or so close thereto that he cannot use the time effectively for his own purposes is working while "on call". An employee who is not required to remain on the employer's premises but is merely required to leave word at his home or with company officials where he may be reached is not working while on call.

In interpreting this section, both the wage and hour administrators at the U.S. Department of Labor (DOL) and the federal courts have said that the most important question is whether the time is being spent primarily for the benefit of the employer or the employee. In other words, as a practical matter, can the employee use the time for his or her own benefit even though he or she is waiting for the possibility of a call? Time can be considered spent for an employee's own benefit even where an employer imposes some restrictions on employees who are on call—such as requiring them to abstain from alcohol consumption. Modest restrictions do not make on-call time compensable.

---

57. *See* Aguilar v. Mgmt. & Training Corp., No. 16-00050 WJ/GJF, 2017 WL 4804361, at *1 (D.N.M. Oct. 24, 2017).

58. *See Lindow*, 738 F.2d at 1063–64.

Factors in Determining the Compensability of On-Call Time

The mere fact that employees may not use on-call time precisely as they might wish or that they may have to be home when they might want to be somewhere else does not turn on-call time into compensable time. Neither does the simple frequency of the calls received. Whether on-call time must be paid turns on a number of factors in light of all of the circumstances. The factors include

- any agreement between the employer and employee;
- whether the employee may carry a phone or beeper and travel freely or whether the employee must remain in one place;
- how quickly the employee must take action in response to a call and whether that action involves driving back to the workplace or taking some action electronically—the shorter the response time, the more likely it is that the on-call time is compensable;
- whether employees can easily trade on-call shifts;
- how restricted the employee is geographically;
- the extent to which the employee is able to engage in personal activities; and
- the number and frequency of calls during an on-call period in relation to the time spent without having to respond to calls.[59]

Reported cases reflect a far greater number of examples in which on-call time has been found **not** to be compensable than examples of such time being ruled compensable.

Examples of Compensable On-Call Time: Engaged to Wait

The text below discusses three cases in which appellate courts found on-call time to be compensable.

In a 2000 case involving a utility company employer, the federal Tenth Circuit Court of Appeals found that electronics technicians employed by a gas and electric company were entitled to compensation for on-call time. The technicians were on call to monitor building alarms weekdays from 4:30 p.m. to 7:30 a.m. On weekends they were on call twenty-four hours a day. In other words, the technicians were on-call whenever they were not on duty. Each technician typically fielded three to five calls per on-call period. The technicians did not always have to return to the workplace after making service calls, but even when they did not have to do so, they still had to take action by computer within fifteen minutes of receiving an alarm call.[60]

In an earlier Tenth Circuit case involving municipal firefighters, the court found on-call time to be compensable where the firefighters were called back into work an average of three to five times per twenty-four-hour on-call period and were required to report to the station house within twenty minutes of receiving a call. The firefighters

---

59. *See* Whitten v. City of Easley, 62 F. App'x 477, 479 (4th Cir. 2003); U.S. Dep't of Labor, Emp't Standards Admin., Wage & Hour Div., Wage & Hour Opinion Letter, FLSA 2008-14NA (Dec. 18, 2008), https://www.dol.gov/whd/opinion/FLSANA/2008/2008_12_18_14NA_FLSA.pdf.

60. *See* Pabst v. Okla. Gas & Elec. Co., 228 F.3d 1128 (10th Cir. 2000).

could trade on-call shifts only with great difficulty and were effectively precluded by their schedules from obtaining a second job. The court found that, effectively, they could not use their on-call time for personal pursuits at all.[61]

Similarly, in a federal appeals court case from Arkansas, the court found on-call time to be compensable for state forestry service firefighters who were required to remain within fifty miles of their work sites while on-call and to respond to an emergency call within thirty minutes. The firefighters were on-call twenty-four hours per day and could not, therefore, trade shifts. They were unable to take part in any activities that prevented them from simultaneously monitoring radio transmissions.[62]

In each of these three cases, the employer scheduled employees for long stretches of on-call time with little opportunity for relief. In addition, the employees regularly received at least a handful of calls that required some action on their part during every on-call shift. Two of the three cases feature mandatory response times on the order of fifteen to twenty minutes, and in two of the cases the court expressly found that the number of calls and relatively short response times rendered the employees effectively unable to use the on-call time for their own purposes.

Examples of On-Call Time That Is Not Compensable: Waiting to Be Engaged
Law enforcement officers and firefighters figure predominantly in on-call cases. The variety of employer practices in these cases allows us to gain an idea of why, in most instances, on-call time is not compensable. Key factors that have led courts to find that on-call time was **not** compensable appear to be

- the ability of employees to trade on-call shifts,
- the ability of employees to freely move about geographically when a cellphone or pager is used as the method of contact,
- the relative infrequency of calls that necessitate a response from the on-call employee, and
- whether the employee was, in actual fact, able to engage in personal activities.

In *Whitten v. City of Easley*,[63] an unpublished 2003 case from the federal Fourth Circuit Court of Appeals, the court found that municipal firefighters spent their on-call time predominantly for their own benefit and were not entitled to compensation. The court reached this conclusion (1) because the firefighters (a) were on-call only to respond to relatively rare second-alarm calls, (b) were allowed to trade on-call shifts, (c) carried pagers, and (d) responded to an average of only six second-alarm calls per month and (2) because the fire department did not require the firefighters to respond to every second-alarm call or even to a set percentage of calls.[64] Similarly,

---

61. *See* Renfro v. City of Emporia, 948 F.2d 1529, 1539 (10th Cir. 1991).
62. *See* Cross v. Ark. Forestry Comm'n, 938 F.2d 912, 917 (8th Cir. 1991).
63. 62 F. App'x 477 (4th Cir. 2003).
64. *See id.*

in *Ingram v. County of Bucks*,[65] the federal Third Circuit Court of Appeals held that where county deputy sheriffs were not required to remain at the sheriff's office or wear their uniforms, and where they carried beepers, could trade on-call shifts, and experienced call frequency that was not so great as to keep them from engaging in personal activities, on-call time was not compensable.[66]

Even a requirement that employees must report to work within five minutes of receiving an emergency call does not render on-call time compensable where other factors give employees the freedom to pursue their own interests. In one small Iowa town, two emergency medical technicians (EMTs) could choose the shifts during which they would be on call. In the majority of on-call shifts, the two EMTs worked two or fewer hours during their twelve-hour on-call shifts. One EMT did not have to respond to a single call during 55 percent of his shifts, and the other did not respond to a single call during 39 percent of his shifts. Because this was a small town, both EMTs lived less than a five-minute drive away from the EMS station where they worked, so that even when they were not at home while on call, the town's small size meant that they could freely move around town and engage in a number of personal activities quickly and efficiently.[67]

Two other cases in which the court emphasized the infrequency with which employees were actually called back to work are *Reimer v. Champion Healthcare Corp.*[68] and *Dinges v. Sacred Heart St. Mary's Hospitals, Inc.*[69] The *Reimer* case involved on-call nurses, who were required to be reachable by telephone or beeper during on-call shifts and had to be able to report to the hospital within twenty minutes of receiving a call. Other than a requirement that they abstain from alcohol or recreational drug use, the nurses could do what they pleased while on call. The court noted that over a three-year span, only about one-quarter of nurses were called in more than once during their scheduled on-call times.[70] In *Dinges*, on-call rural EMTs worked under a system where their hospital employer paid them a relatively low on-call rate plus time-and-a-half for any time they spent taking care of medical emergencies. The EMTs brought suit, alleging that the entirety of the on-call periods (which each lasted fourteen to sixteen hours) amounted to working time, thus entitling them to higher wage totals than they had received. The EMTs were required to report to the hospital within seven minutes of receiving a page. The court found the on-call time not to be compensable, primarily because the EMTs had less than a 50 percent chance of being called into work during any fourteen-to-sixteen-hour period.[71]

---

65. 144 F.3d 265 (3d Cir. 1998).
66. *See id.* at 268–70.
67. *See* Dickhaut v. Madison Cty., 707 F. Supp. 2d 883 (S.D. Iowa 2009).
68. 258 F.3d 720 (8th Cir. 2001).
69. 164 F.3d 1056 (7th Cir. 1999).
70. *See Reimer*, 258 F.3d at 725–26.
71. *See Dinges*, 164 F.3d at 1057–59.

Evaluating whether on-call time is compensable should be an ongoing project, not a once-and-done determination, as the relevant circumstances may change over time. Employers should periodically investigate how frequently on-call employees are being called to take action or to return to work. Employers should also know whether employees do, in fact, engage in personal pursuits while on-call. Those in charge of determining compensable time should know not only whether there is a standard reporting time, but also whether the employing department penalizes employees who do not meet the reporting standard, as this may be a factor in making the time compensable. Even if supervisors prefer having regular, assigned on-call shifts, human resources should encourage all departments to allow employees to trade on-call shifts.

Breaks from Work: Rest Periods, Meal Periods, and Sleep Time

To an employer, it can surely seem (1) that when employees take a break with a cup of coffee, sit down to eat a meal, or catch a few hours of sleep on an overnight shift, the employees are no longer engaging in their principal activities and (2) that these break periods are for the employee's benefit, rather than that of the employer. These times don't seem like they should be compensable work time, do they? The Fair Labor Standards Act (FLSA) addresses the issue raised by breaks from work in five separate regulations: the rest-time regulation found at Section 785.18 of Title 29 of the Code of Federal Regulations (C.F.R.), the meal-time regulation found at Section 785.19 of this same title, and three sleep-time regulations found at Sections 785.20 through .22 of C.F.R. Title 29.

Rest Periods

Brief rest periods are generally compensable time. The regulation setting out the rest-time rule provides as follows:

> Rest periods of short duration, running from 5 minutes to about 20 minutes, are common in industry. They promote the efficiency of the employee and are customarily paid for as working time. *They must be counted as hours worked.* Compensable time of rest periods may not be offset against other working time such as compensable waiting time or on-call time.[72]

The regulation suggests that rest periods are as much for the employer's benefit (increased efficiency and production) as for the employee's.

There are, of course, other periods during the workday when employees stop working for a brief time, most obviously to use the restroom. In the normal course of events, the time an employee spends away from the principal activity while using the

---

72. 29 C.F.R. § 785.18 (emphasis added).

restroom is too insignificant to constitute an interruption of the continuous workday; this time is *de minimis*.[73] The time is compensable.

Meal Periods

The rules governing the compensability of meal breaks follow from the continuous workday rule. Under that rule, all time between the start of an employee's principal activity and the conclusion of that activity is compensable. What about breaks for meals, whether for lunch, dinner, or snacks, that take place during the course of the continuous workday? Without a regulation that said otherwise, time spent on such meal breaks would be compensable.

But the FLSA does have regulations that say otherwise: a general meal-period regulation found at Section 785.19 of C.F.R. Title 29, a meal-period regulation for employees whose shifts last longer than twenty-four hours found at Section 785.22 of the same title, and a meal-period regulation for law enforcement officers and firefighters who are scheduled using the 207(k) overtime exemption[74] found at Section 553.253 of C.F.R. Title 29.

The General Bona Fide Meal-Period Rule (29 C.F.R. § 785.19)

The general-meal period rule allows for a noncompensable meal break during a continuous workday. The rule requires that employees be given thirty minutes of relatively uninterrupted time to eat a meal before that time may be deducted from hours worked and considered noncompensable:

a). Bona fide meal periods. Bona fide meal periods are not worktime. Bona fide meal periods do not include coffee breaks or time for snacks. These are rest periods. The employee must be completely relieved from duty for the purposes of eating regular meals. Ordinarily 30 minutes or more is long enough for a bona fide meal period. A shorter period may be long enough under special conditions. The employee is not relieved if he is required to perform any duties, whether active or inactive, while eating. For example, an office employee who is required to eat at his desk or a factory worker who is required to be at his machine is working while eating.

b). Where no permission to leave premises. It is not necessary that an employee be permitted to leave the premises if he is otherwise completely freed from duties during the meal period.[75]

The rule is clear: for meal time to be noncompensable, it must last for a period of no less than thirty minutes and the employee must not be substantially interrupted

---

73. For more on *de minimis* time, see also 29 C.F.R. § 785.47.

74. *See* note 52, *supra*, for more on this exemption.

75. *See* 29 C.F.R. § 785.19. *See also* Perez v. Mountaire Farms, Inc., 650 F.3d 350, 363 (4th Cir. 2011) ("This Court has determined, however, that the continuous workday does not include time spent during a 'bona fide meal period.'").

by co-workers, citizens, customers, or anyone else on matters associated with the employee's work during that time.

Reality is rarely so simple, however. Consider the lunch time situation of Christy, clerk for the city of Paradise.

> *The city's policy requires all full-time nonexempt employees to take a thirty-minute unpaid lunch break. Christy has no deputy or assistant clerks to help her out. Because her job is one that interfaces with the public, finding thirty minutes in which to take lunch is a challenge, especially since her job duties include answering calls to the city's main telephone number. More often than not, Christy records herself as out for half an hour on her timesheet, begins to eat her lunch at her desk, and is interrupted by a citizen with a question or by a phone call. While Christy always manages to finish her lunch at some point, she never has the half-hour of uninterrupted time to which she is entitled. But because she is required to take a half-hour unpaid lunch, she records the time as taken. It isn't a matter of being untruthful or deceptive. Each time Christy signs out for lunch, she wants and intends to take the half-hour off. Circumstances do not let her.*

Is this okay? Or has the city—or Christy—violated the FLSA?

Let's take Christy first. Christy certainly has not violated the FLSA—only an employer can violate the Act. Christy may have violated the city's lunch policy by not actually taking a half-hour uninterrupted break and may have violated the city's policy about accurately recording time. But she has not violated the FLSA.

The city, on the other hand, is potentially in violation of the FLSA. There are two crucial issues here. The first is a threshold issue. Notwithstanding the fact that the meal-time regulation, C.F.R. Title 29, Section 785.19, says that employees must be "completely relieved" of duties during meal-time breaks, the courts have interpreted that phrase to mean something less than it appears. In the words of one of the most-cited decisions on compensable meal time, "[a]s long as the employee can pursue his or her mealtime adequately and comfortably, is not engaged in the performance of any substantial duties, and does not spend time predominantly for the employer's benefit, the employee is relieved of duty and is not entitled to compensation under the FLSA."[76]

The question is whether, on balance, Christy has been able to use the lunch break as her own time or whether she has had to spend it on matters that are primarily for the city's benefit. In practice, the answer to that question may vary from day to day. On some days, the interruptions may be minimal: Christy may transfer a call to the manager's office and direct a visitor to the restroom but have the rest of the meal time

---

76. *See* Hill v. United States, 751 F.2d 810, 814 (6th Cir. 1985) (a requirement that the plaintiff postal worker exercise reasonable care for items in his care and for mail secured in postal vehicles and relay boxes did not interfere with the free use of his lunch period and, thus, did not make the lunch period compensable), *cited by* Roy v. Cty. of Lexington, 141 F.3d 533, 545 (4th Cir. 1998).

to herself. On days like this, Christy's lunch break is not compensable. But on days where the phone rings incessantly and there is a constant stream of citizens, board members, and fellow employees in and out of the clerk's office during Christy's half-hour "break," her meal time is probably compensable. The frequency and duration of the interruptions are such that the time is spent predominantly for the city's benefit.

The second crucial issue in determining the compensability of meal-time breaks is whether the city knew or should have known that Christy was working during her lunch break. It doesn't matter whether Christy is supervised on a day-to-day basis by the manager, whether she reports to the council, or whether she turns her timesheet into the city's human resources or finance department. If the manager, the council, the human resources director, the finance director, or the payroll administrator is aware that Christy is working while taking her lunch break (or should be aware because they routinely see her scarfing down bites of a chicken sandwich between answering telephone calls or other interruptions), then the time is compensable. But if no one with management or payroll responsibility ever comes into Christy's workspace and becomes aware that she is working through her break, and if Christy herself never mentions it, a court might not find the time compensable. Maybe the reason no one sees Christy eat lunch is that she takes her lunch somewhere other than her desk—somewhere where she is less likely to be interrupted.

The same principles apply here as apply when nonexempt employees work unscheduled straight-time or unauthorized overtime.[77]

> ... [I]t is the duty of the management to exercise its control and see that the work is not performed if it does not want it to be performed. It cannot sit back and accept the benefits without compensating for them. The mere promulgation of a rule against such work is not enough. Management has the power to enforce the rule and must make every effort to do so.[78]

This means that if the city does not want Christy's meal period to be compensable, it must take steps to ensure that her time is uninterrupted as soon as it becomes aware that she is primarily engaging in work activities during this period.

Law enforcement officers frequently find themselves interrupted during meal breaks—so much so that there is an entire body of case law devoted to the question of whether their meal times are compensable or not. The rules applicable to law enforcement officers and other public safety personnel are not, however, different than those that apply to employees like Christy, the city clerk. Consider the following hypothetical.

> *Delia is a patrol officer for the City of Paradise. The city's policy that all nonexempt employees take a half-hour unpaid meal break applies to police officers and others whose work is performed out in the community, as well*

---

77. See the discussion on pages 62 through 67 of this chapter.
78. *See* 29 C.F.R. § 785.13. *See also* Chao v. Gotham Registry, Inc., 514 F.3d 280, 288 (2d Cir. 2008); Reich v. Stewart, 121 F.3d 400, 407 (8th Cir. 1997).

as to employees like Christy who work in an office environment. In good weather, Delia likes to take her break in Paradise Park and eat at one of the picnic tables there or on a bench. In bad weather, Delia usually runs into Luke's Diner for a quick bite. Whether she is in the park or at Luke's, Delia cannot count on having an uninterrupted half-hour. First, she's required to carry her radio with her to monitor dispatcher communications. When she is directed to respond to a call, she must do so immediately. Second, citizens regularly approach Delia when they see her sitting out in the park or at Luke's. Sometimes, it is to give her a pleasurable "Hi! We appreciate all that you do" greeting. Other times, it is to report behavior that a citizen deems suspicious or to seek her advice.

Is Delia working if she must monitor the radio during her meal break? Is she working if her break is interrupted by a citizen?

Absent other interruptions, the mere requirement that Delia must monitor the radio during her half-hour break does not make the time compensable. A meal break that requires passive monitoring or readiness to respond is not compensable if the employee is not otherwise called upon to begin performing his or her regular duties.[79] However, if Delia is called to respond to a situation before her half-hour break is complete, then she is working for some part of that break and will not have had an uninterrupted half-hour. The entire "break" period will revert to being compensable time.

---

79. *See* Ruffin v. MotorCity Casino, 775 F.3d 807, 812 (6th Cir. 2015) (monitoring a radio is generally a peripheral activity that security employees can perform while spending their meal-break times however they like); Jones-Turner v. Yellow Enter. Sys., LLC, 597 F. App'x 293, 297 (6th Cir. 2015) (where EMTs had to eat within one mile of an assigned stand-by location, maintain radio contact, and were subject to any call, their meal breaks were not compensable). *See also* U.S. Dep't of Labor, Emp't Standards Admin., Wage & Hour Div., Wage & Hour Opinion Letter, FLSA 2004-7NA (Aug. 6, 2004) (meal breaks of transit employees who were responsible for counting and safeguarding fare revenue and who were not allowed to leave the lunchroom, change clothes, make phone calls, smoke, or leave the building were not compensable where the employees were completely relieved from their duties during break times, allowed to take meals uninterrupted by their employer, and had sufficient time to eat); Myracle v. Gen. Elec. Co., 33 F.3d 55, at *5 (6th Cir. 1994) (per curiam) (unpublished) (lunch breaks were compensable when maintenance mechanics were required to maintain responsibility for their machines and to remain on call during their lunch breaks in case the machine malfunctioned but were free to leave the plant and were only rarely interrupted for emergencies or power outages); Henson v. Pulaski Cty. Sheriff Dep't, 6 F.3d 531, 536 (8th Cir. 1993) (where the only potential restrictions on the plaintiff officers' and deputies' use of their meal periods for their own purposes were the monitoring of radios for emergency calls and the possibility that citizens might ask them questions, the meal times were for the officers'/deputies' benefit and were not compensable). *Cf.* Lamon v. City of Shawnee, 972 F.2d 1145, 1156 (10th Cir. 1992) (where, during meal periods, police officers were restricted to locations in close proximity to the station, required either to leave a telephone number or to monitor a portable radio, had to respond to emergency calls, were mandated to answer to personnel shortages if needed, had to respond to citizen inquiries, were required to confront crimes committed in the officers' presence, and were prohibited from conducting personal errands, their meal breaks were compensable).

Determining whether being approached by a citizen will turn Delia's meal break into compensable time is more complicated. This determination must be made on a day-by-day basis, as different circumstances will lead to different conclusions. For example, if someone screams for help in the park or jumps up in the diner and yells, "Stop! Thief! He's got my wallet!", Delia might spring into action, putting an end to her meal break and turning it into compensable time. But what about the following two situations?

> *On Monday, Delia eats in the park. As she takes the first bite of her sandwich, an older couple approach her. They tell Delia that they live two blocks down and that there has been a lot of late-night activity recently, with people coming and going in the house across the street. Delia listens to them carefully and asks them the street address of the house in question. She promises to take a look after her break and to mention it to her supervisor to pass on to the night shift. She also gives the couple a number to call at night whenever they observe the suspicious activity. The couple thanks her, and Delia resumes eating her lunch.*
>
> *On Tuesday, Delia goes to Luke's Diner for lunch. Before she even orders, she is approached by Luke, the owner, who tells her that someone keeps emptying out the tip jar that sits by the register. Delia and Luke discuss some options for about five minutes or so, after which she finally places her order. While she is waiting for her meal, a woman approaches and confides to Delia that she is worried that her teenage son is hanging out with the "wrong crowd" and that they might get him into trouble. Delia asks whether the woman has spoken with the school resource officer and gives her the officer's contact information. She also gives her suggestions for afterschool activities at the local community center and the Y. Delia's order arrives and she starts to eat, hoping that folks will refrain from asking her advice when they see her actually eating rather than waiting. Suddenly, there is a crash. At the back of the diner, one patron has punched another, sending him sprawling, knocking over and breaking several glasses. Delia stops the fight. After speaking with the victim and with Luke, both of whom decline to press charges, what is left of Delia's lunch is cold. She pushes it aside, pays, and returns to her patrol car.*

Is Delia's meal break on Monday compensable? What about on Tuesday?

As noted earlier, notwithstanding the clear statement set forth in C.F.R. Title 29, Section 785.19(a) that an "employee is not relieved if he is required to perform any duties, whether active or inactive, while eating," courts have moved away from interpreting this requirement strictly. Instead, most courts apply the "predominant benefit test," assessing whether the employee's meal time is spent primarily for the employer's benefit.[80] Law enforcement cases frequently phrase the inquiry by asking whether employees are "primarily engaged in work-related duties" during their meal breaks. In *Lamon v. City of Shawnee*,[81] the federal Tenth Circuit Court of Appeals explained:

> [A] police officer must primarily be engaged in work-related duties during meal periods to warrant compensation therefor. That a police officer is on-call and has some limited responsibilities during meal periods does not perforce mean the officer is working. . . . If during meal periods a police officer's time and attention are primarily occupied by a private pursuit, presumably the procurement and consumption of food, then the officer is completely relieved from duty and is not entitled to compensation under FLSA. Conversely a police officer is entitled to compensation for meal periods if the officer's time or attention is taken up principally by official responsibilities that prevent the officer from comfortably and adequately passing the mealtime.[82]

Another court observed that "there is a universe of possibilities about when a meal is "interrupted" so as to require compensation."[83] What is important is the *frequency* and *extent* of the interruptions on any given day (or every day) rather than the mere possibility of interruption.[84]

To return to Delia, on Monday, the day she eats in the park and is approached by the couple worried about the goings-on across the street, it seems reasonable to conclude that her attention and time are primarily occupied by taking a break and eating her lunch. Her interaction with the couple is brief and is the only interruption that

---

80. *See* Kohlheim v. Glynn Co., 915 F.2d 1473, 1477 (11th Cir. 1990) (firefighters' meal periods compensable because they were subject to "significant" duties during these periods); Burgess v. Catawba, Co., 805 F. Supp. 341, 346–47 (W.D.N.C. 1992) (EMS workers' mealtimes were compensable where employees were subject to call, needed to be prepared to respond, and recorded timesheets showing frequent interruptions); Wahl v. City of Wichita, 725 F. Supp. 1133, 1144 (D. Kan. 1989) ("What matters in meal period cases is whether the employee is subject to real limitations on his personal freedom which inure to the benefit of his employer.").

81. 972 F.2d 1145 (10th Cir. 1992), *cert. denied*, 507 U.S. 972 (1993).

82. *Id.* at 1157–58. *See also* Alexander v. City of Chicago, 994 F.2d 333, 337 (7th Cir. 1993) (adopting *Lamon* standard); Lee v. Coahoma Cty., 937 F.2d 220, 225 (1991) (affirming noncompensability of deputy sheriffs' meal periods where being on call in event of emergency did not constitute being on duty), *modified on other grounds*, 986 F.2d 100 (5th Cir. 1993); Bagrowski v. Md. Port Auth., 845 F. Supp. 1116, 1118–20 (D. Md. 1994) (being on call in case of an emergency, doing occasional mail runs, and responding to minor citizen inquiries did not make meal breaks of port administration police officers compensable).

83. *Alexander,* 994 F.2d at 339–40.

84. *See id.* at 339–41; Avery v. City of Talladega, 24 F.3d 1337, 1347 (11th Cir. 1994) (meal times not compensable where plaintiff police officer had to listen to citizen complaints during meal breaks but, according to his own testimony, had a break from duties during these periods 95–98 percent of the time); Albee v. Vill. of Bartlett, 861 F. Supp. 680, 685 (N.D. Ill. 1994) (meal times not compensable when officers are only called out for emergencies a few times each month).

occurs during her lunch break. The time is not compensable. By contrast, it seems reasonable to conclude that Delia's lunch break on Tuesday has primarily been spent working as a police officer: she has given advice on theft to Luke, advised a citizen worried about the possibility that her teenage son might get into trouble, and interceded in an assault. The interruptions were frequent and time-consuming, and Delia was not able to eat her meal. The time is compensable.

So, what is an employer to do? How can an employer ensure that (1) employees actually have uninterrupted breaks and (2) employees who do not always get the benefit of uninterrupted breaks are appropriately compensated? How can an employer avoid a claim that two years of meal breaks should have been compensated when the matter was called to its attention a long time after the fact?

The Bottom Line

Public employers that do not wish to compensate their employees for their meal breaks should first adopt policies that require employees to take daily thirty-minute lunch breaks during which they are to perform no work. The policy should also instruct employees who do spend a significant amount of time on work duties during lunch either to record that time as time worked or, where meal breaks are automatically deducted from hours worked automatically, have some other process for reporting uncompensated work time. *Under the FLSA, if an employer establishes a reasonable process for an employee to report uncompensated work time, the employer is not liable for non-payment if the employee fails to follow the established process.* That is because when an employee fails to follow reasonable time-reporting procedures, he or she prevents the employer from knowing its obligation to compensate the employee and thwarts the employer's ability to comply with the FLSA.[85]

Meal Periods for Employees Whose Shifts Last Longer than Twenty-Four Hours (29 C.F.R. § 785.22)

In contrast to the general rule about the compensability of meal periods, the FLSA regulations provide that when an employee's shift is *longer* than twenty-four hours, an employer may deduct a bona fide meal period of thirty uninterrupted minutes from the employee's compensable time only if the employer and employee mutually agree to the deduction.[86] No such "agreement" is required for employees working conventional shifts of eight to twelve hours. What constitutes agreement in these circumstances? This question has been litigated in cases involving sleep time, but oddly, not meal time. But from the sleep-time cases it is possible to say that where a government employer has in place a policy of deducting thirty-minute meal periods from the hours worked by employees on shifts longer than twenty-four hours, a new hire is considered to have impliedly agreed to this policy upon accepting the job.

---

85. *See* White v. Baptist Mem'l Health Care Corp., 699 F.3d 869, 876 (6th Cir. 2012). *See also* Hertz v. Woodbury Cty., 566 F.3d 775, 781–82 (11th Cir. 2009); Newton v. City of Henderson, 47 F.3d 746, 749–50 (5th Cir. 1995); *Maus v. City of Towanda, Kansas*, 165 F. Supp. 2d 1223, 1230 (D. Kan. 2001).

86. *See* 29 C.F.R. § 785.22(a).

Where an employer adopts a new policy, those employees who do not object, continue to report to work, and accept the employer's compensation will be considered to agree to the new policy. Those employees who object at the time of the adoption of the policy and who continue to object might not be said to have agreed to the practice and their meal times may be compensable. Whether or not a court finds agreement in this last circumstance will depend upon all of the relevant circumstances.

Bona Fide Meal Periods for Law Enforcement Officers Scheduled under the Section 207(k) Exemption (29 C.F.R. § 553.223)

There are separate rules covering meal breaks for law enforcement officers and firefighters, who work on cycles of between seven and twenty-eight days under the special overtime exemption provided by FLSA Section 207(k).[87] The rules vary depending on whether an employee is engaged in law enforcement or fire suppression and on whether the 207(k) shifts are less than or greater than twenty-four hours. The rules are set forth in Section 553.223 of C.F.R. Title 29.

The underlying rule for the exclusion of meal times from compensable time for employees scheduled under the 207(k) exemption is the same as the rule set forth in C.F.R. Title 29, Section 785.19 for all other employees: the break must be at least thirty minutes long (although shorter periods may be excluded under special circumstances) and the law enforcement officer or firefighter must be able to eat without interruption.[88] These requirements are set forth in subsection (a) of Section 553.223. Subsection (b) of this regulation adds a distinction with respect to law enforcement officers whose shifts are exactly twenty-four or fewer than twenty-four hours long:

> . . . [T]he public agency may, in the case of law enforcement personnel, exclude meal time from hours worked on tours of duty of 24 hours or less, provided that the employee is completely relieved from duty during the meal period, and all the other tests in § 785.19 of this title are met. On the other hand, where law enforcement personnel are required to remain on call in barracks or similar quarters, or are engaged in extended surveillance activities (e.g., "stakeouts"), they are not considered to be completely relieved from duty, and any such meal periods would be compensable.[89]

The provision stating that officers who remain on call at an employer-provided facility or those who are required to remain in a fixed location in a stakeout are to be considered working—and that because of this any meal times they take are compensable—is consistent with the general rules for the compensability of on-call time discussed in the preceding section of this chapter.

Subsection (c) of Section 553.223, meanwhile, provides for a different rule for firefighters whose shifts are exactly twenty-four or fewer than twenty-four hours long:

---

87. *See* note 52, *supra*, for more on the 207(k) exemption.
88. *See* 29 C.F.R. § 553.223(a).
89. 29 C.F.R. § 553.223(b).

meal breaks may not be excluded from compensable time. This is true even where the meal break is thirty minutes long and there is no interruption.[90]

When law enforcement officers and firefighters are scheduled for shifts that exceed twenty-four hours by any amount (this includes shifts of twenty-four and one-quarter hours, where the additional fifteen minutes is used for shift-change briefings), employers may exclude meal periods of thirty minutes, provided that the employee is substantially relieved of duty and there is an agreement between the employer and the employee to exclude meal periods. In the absence of such an agreement, the time is compensable.[91] For a detailed discussion of what constitutes agreement, see the provisions on sleep time exclusion for 207(k) personnel below.

Sleep Time

In the interpretative rules accompanying the FLSA regulations, the U.S. Department of Labor (DOL) notes that "[u]nder certain conditions an employee is considered to be working even though some of his time is spent in sleeping or in certain other activities."[92] That interpretation flows from the continuous workday rule and is consistent with the rules governing on-call time: the employee is present at the workplace at the direction of the employer, is not free to leave the workplace, and cannot be said to be spending time for his or her own benefit. Nevertheless, DOL recognizes that sometimes the nature of a given job requires that employees work day-long shifts during which there will be sufficient down time such that an employee may be able to sleep and not perform any useful work for the employer. It has, therefore, developed rules allowing employers to deduct sleep time from the number of hours worked if certain requirements are met. For public employers, these rules are set forth in Part 553 of C.F.R. Title 29, which contains the substantive regulations that address government employment, as supplemented by the interpretive regulations found in Part 785 of this same title. The rules for sleep time are slightly different for law enforcement and fire service personnel scheduled under the 207(k) exemption, and the rules are slightly different depending on the length of the shift.

General Sleep-Time Rule

Shifts of Fewer Than Twenty-Four Hours

The rule here is simple. An employer cannot deduct sleep time from the hours of any employee whose shift is fewer than twenty-four hours long.[93] This is true regardless of the position an employee holds or the department in which he or she works. For law enforcement and fire service employees, this rule applies whether they are scheduled to work a forty-hour workweek or are scheduled under the 207(k) exemption.

---

90. *See* 29 C.F.R. § 553.223(c).

91. *See* 29 C.F.R. § 553.223(d).

92. 29 C.F.R. § 785.20.

93. *See* 29 C.F.R. §§ 553.222(b)(1). 785.21. *See also* U.S. Dep't of Labor, Emp't Standards Admin., Wage & Hour Div., Field Operations Handbook ch. 31, at 3, § 31b00 (revision effective Aug. 10, 2016) (hereinafter FOH), https://www.dol.gov/whd/FOH/FOH_Ch31.pdf.

Shifts That Are Exactly Twenty-Four Hours Long and Shifts That Are More Than Twenty-Four Hours Long

An employer may exclude an employee's sleep time from compensable time if shifts are exactly twenty-four hours or greater than twenty-four hours long, provided *all* of the following requirements are met:

- the employer excludes *no more than* eight hours of sleep time, even if the employee has slept more than eight hours,
- the employer has either the express or implied agreement of the employee to exclude sleep time,
- the employer provides adequate sleeping facilities, and
- the employee is able to get at least five hours of uninterrupted sleep.[94]

This general rule applies to law enforcement officers and firefighters who are not scheduled under the 207(k) exemption from overtime, as well as to all other local government employees who may work longer than usual shifts.

Sleep-Time Rules for Section 207(k) Personnel

For a 207(k) employee, the only difference in the rules governing sleep time is that a shift must be *more than* twenty-four hours long before sleep time can be excluded. If a shift is exactly twenty-four hours long, a public employer may not exclude sleep time from compensation.[95] For shifts of more than twenty-four hours, the same four requirements must be met before sleep time can be excluded: (1) no more than eight hours of sleep time may be excluded, (2) there must be express or implied agreement with the employer's sleep-time exclusion, (3) the employer must provide adequate sleeping facilities, and (4) the employee must be able to get at least five hours of uninterrupted sleep.[96]

Express or Implied Agreement to Sleep-Time Deduction by the Employee

Before an employer may deduct sleep time for shifts of exactly twenty-four or more than twenty-four hours, the FLSA regulations require that the employer have the express or implied agreement of any affected employee. Does this mean that an employer must negotiate a sleep-time exclusion with each individual employee? Or can mere notice of the employer's practice of deducting eight hours of sleep time constitute agreement when an employee reports to work knowing that the sleep-time deduction is one of the terms and conditions of employment? Both Section 785.22 (the general sleep-time rule) and 553.222(c) (the sleep-time rule applicable to 207(k) employees) of C.F.R. Title 29 say clearly that absent agreement, the sleep time must be paid. But they do not define what "agreement" means in these circumstances.

---

94. *See* 29 C.F.R. §§ 785.21, .22; U.S. DEP'T OF LABOR, EMP'T STANDARDS ADMIN., WAGE & HOUR DIV., WAGE & HOUR OPINION LETTER, FLSA 2002-6 (Aug. 13, 2002), https://www.dol.gov/whd/opinion/FLSA/2002/2002_08_13_6_FLSA.pdf.

95. *See* 29 C.F.R. § 553.222(b)(2).

96. *See* 29 C.F.R. § 553.222(c).

An express agreement is one in which the terms and obligations of the parties are set out clearly and unambiguously, as is their mutual intent to abide by them. Express agreements are usually—but do not have to be—written agreements. Where the employer has a written policy and the employee has signed an acknowledgment of that policy, there is an express agreement. A written employer policy, assent to which is indicated by the employee's signature, would likely constitute an express agreement. More difficult are circumstances where the agreement may be merely implied—where it is inferred by the parties' conduct. In either case, the employer bears the burden of showing that an actual agreement existed.[97]

Long-standing Fourth Circuit precedent holds that where an employee acquiesces without complaint in a schedule that includes the exclusion of sleep time, the employee has impliedly agreed to the exclusion of sleep time from compensable time. In *Bodie v. City of Columbia*,[98] firefighter Alvin Bodie sued his municipal employer *after his retirement* for unpaid overtime, claiming that the city had unlawfully deducted eight hours of sleep time from his wages over a period of several years. At the time the city adopted the schedule that excluded sleep time, thirty-six firefighters, but not Bodie, sent letters to the city manager asserting that they did not consent to the exclusion. Bodie claimed that he had not sent a letter when the other firefighters did because he was out of town at the time, but in fact he did not indicate his lack of consent either orally or in writing upon his return or at any time during his active employment. Citing a number of cases from other circuits that had reached the same conclusion under similar factual circumstances, the Fourth Circuit held that Bodie had impliedly agreed to the exclusion of sleep time and that those hours were not compensable.[99] The court expressly distinguished the case from the earlier federal district court decision in *Local 2962 v. City of Jacksonville* (North Carolina), which found that firefighters had not impliedly agreed to the exclusion of sleep time from compensable work time by continuing to work, where those firefighters filed a petition with the city manager protesting the policy.[100]

Another case was decided by the Fourth Circuit around the same time as *Bodie* and arose out of the very same circumstances with the same city defendant. This second case considered the question of whether an agreement to a sleep-time exclusion could be valid where the employer threatened the employee with termination if he did not sign an express agreement to that effect. In *Johnson v. City of Columbia*,[101] firefighter Randolph Johnson, Jr. (along with thirty-six other firefighters) sent

---

97. *See* Johnson v. City of Columbia, 949 F.2d 127, 130 (4th Cir. 1991).

98. 934 F.2d 561 (4th Cir. 1991).

99. *See id.* at 563–66, *citing* Rousseau v. Teledyne Movible Offshore, Inc., 805 F.2d 1245 (5th Cir. 1986), *cert. denied*, 484 U.S. 827 (1987); Shepler v. Crucible Fuel Co., 140 F.2d 371 (3d Cir. 1944); Ariens v. Olin Mathieson Chem. Corp., 382 F.2d 192 (6th Cir. 1967); Gen. Elec. Co. v. Porter, 208 F.2d 205, 811–12 (9th Cir. 1953), *cert. denied*, 347 U.S. 951 (1954).

100. *See Bodie*, 934 F.2d at 567. *See also* Jacksonville Prof'l Fire Fighters Ass'n Local 2961 v. City of Jacksonville, 685 F. Supp. 513, 519–20 (E.D.N.C. 1987).

101. 949 F.2d 127.

a letter to the city manager advising the manager that he did not consent to the new sleep-time policy (this occurred during the time that Alvin Bodie said he did not object to that policy because he was out of town). In response to the letters from the firefighters, the Columbia city manager (1) gave each objecting firefighter a written agreement setting forth consent to the sleep-time exclusion policy and (2) told each firefighter that anyone who did not sign the agreement would be terminated. Johnson signed the agreement and continued to work for the city. He filed his lawsuit alleging uncompensated sleep time against the city four years later while continuing to work for the city as a firefighter. In response to the lawsuit, the manager again gave Johnson the choice of signing a new agreement consenting to the sleep-time exclusion or losing his job. Johnson signed the agreement but continued his lawsuit.

The Fourth Circuit contrasted the facts of *Johnson* with those of *Bodie*, noting that although it had found that there was an implied agreement to the sleep-time deduction in *Bodie*, the issue in *Johnson* was whether there was a valid express agreement. The court found that under South Carolina contract law, which governed the validity of the agreement, the actions by the city constituted duress and that Johnson would not have signed the agreement were it not for the "improper" threat of termination.

> In our view, the City could not force Johnson to sign an "express agreement" by threatening discharge in order to circumvent his already stated views. As noted above, the City had the burden of showing that Johnson expressly agreed to the exclusions. We find that the City failed to carry its burden when the evidence shows that there was no meeting of the minds between Johnson and the City.[102]

Were the facts of the *Johnson* case to arise in North Carolina, North Carolina contract law would apply. While the rules governing duress in contracting are not expressed in precisely the same language in North Carolina cases as they are in the South Carolina cases cited by the *Johnson* court, they are similar in broad outline.[103] A North Carolina employer who threatened employees with termination if they did not agree to a sleep-time exclusion would therefore also be likely to be found to have violated the FLSA by coercing employees into agreeing to the exclusion. North Carolina law would likely find such an agreement invalid and not to be a meeting of the minds.

In an unpublished opinion issued two years after the *Bodie* decision, the Fourth Circuit reaffirmed and expanded its reasoning with respect to implied agreements. In *Holb v. City of Beaufort* (South Carolina),[104] the court consolidated several cases

---

102. *Id.* at 132. *See also* Burgess v. Catawba Cty., 805 F. Supp. 341, 346 (W.D.N.C. 1992) (citing *Johnson* and finding that county did not meet its burden of showing existence of implied agreement to exclude sleep time where EMS employees expressed concerns and objections contemporaneously with employer's adoption of sleep-time policy).

103. *See, e.g.*, Link v. Link, 278 N.C. 181, 194 (1971); Smithwick v. Whitley, 152 N.C. 369, 371 (1910); Radford v. Keith, 160 N.C. App. 41, 43–44 (2003), *aff'd*, 358 N.C. 136 (2004).

104. 996 F.2d 1211 (1993) (unpublished disposition).

arising out of a similar set of circumstances to those set forth in *Bodie*. In the *Holb* case, the court found that

- employees who, like Bodie, were already hired when the sleep-time policy went into effect but did not complain about it until the end of their employment impliedly agreed to the sleep-time exclusion;[105]
- firefighters already employed when the new policy went into effect who complained about it orally up the chain of command but did not file a formal grievance with the city impliedly agreed to the policy by continuing to work;[106] and
- firefighters hired after the sleep-time policy was already in effect who complained about it but neither filed a formal complaint nor refused a paycheck impliedly agreed to the sleep-time exclusion.[107]

The Fourth Circuit used different reasoning to reach its respective conclusions about firefighters who were employed with the city at the time the sleep-time policy was adopted and those who were hired after it was already in place. The court looked at the case in traditional contract terms. For those who were already employed, the city was unilaterally introducing new terms into the firefighters' ongoing employment contract with the city. The *Holb* court noted that unlike in the *Johnson* case discussed above, there were no threats of termination and no economic duress. Hence, it was appropriate in such circumstances to consider whether, by their actions, the firefighters impliedly agreed to the sleep-time terms.[108] For those hired after the sleep policy was in place, the policy was part of the terms of employment offered to new firefighters. In accepting their job offers, the firefighters were accepting terms that included the sleep policy. If they later complained, it was because they overlooked that term in accepting their offers of employment.[109]

From the *Bodie*, *Holb*, and *Johnson* cases, we can conclude the following about the existence of an agreement to deduct sleep time from compensable hours of work.

- First, where a government employer has a sleep-time exclusion policy in place, new hires will be considered to have agreed to the policy as part of the terms and conditions of employment. If a new hire complains about the policy but continues to work and accept wages from the employer, he or she will nonetheless be considered to agree to the policy. Although the Fourth Circuit did not say so, it appears that the only option for a new hire who is dissatisfied with such a policy is to quit and seek employment elsewhere.

---

105. *See id.* at *3.
106. *See id.* at *5–*7.
107. *See id.* at *4–*5.
108. *See id.* at *5–*7.
109. *See id.* at *4.

- Second, where a government employer newly adopts a sleep-time exclusion policy, current employees who do not voice any objection to the policy will be considered to impliedly agree to the policy.
- Third, where a government employer newly adopts a sleep-time exclusion policy, reasonably contemporaneous and continuing oral objections or protests to the employer's actions may indicate lack of agreement to the sleep-time exclusion and employers may be liable for employees' time spent sleeping (both for straight time and any resulting overtime hours) if the sleep time is judged to be compensable. Determination of whether objecting employees impliedly agreed by continuing to work can only be made on a case-by-case basis in light of all the circumstances.
- Finally, where a government employer newly adopts a sleep-time exclusion policy, it cannot compel employees to sign or otherwise indicate agreement with the policy by threatening termination. The courts have never expressly considered whether the termination of an employee who objects to the deduction of sleep time is unlawful because it has the effect of coercing other employees to agree. But the reasoning in the cases discussed above suggests that such a motive would violate the FLSA.

Training Time

Section 785.27 of the FLSA regulations provide that employees do not have to be compensated for time spent training if all of the following conditions apply:

1. attendance is outside the employee's regular working hours,
2. attendance is voluntary,
3. the course is not directly related to the employee's job, and
4. the employee does not perform any productive work during time in attendance at the course.[110]

While employee time spent on training and similar activities must satisfy all four requirements to be treated as not compensable, an employer may choose to pay non-exempt employees for their training time—even if these four conditions are not satisfied. These rules apply regardless of whether the training or class is offered in-house by the employer or by an outside organization.

Outside Regular Working Hours

The requirement that attendance at training activities be outside of an employee's regular working hours for training time to be noncompensable is fairly straightforward. Imagine that Amanda, a nonexempt employee working in the human resources department of Paradise County, is attending the week-long Introduction to Public

110. *See* 29 C.F.R. § 785.27.

Employment Law course at the University of Paradise. The class meets Monday through Friday from 8:30 to 5:30, with an hour free for lunch. Those are Amanda's normal working hours, so her participation in the course will be compensable. If class time spills over into Amanda's nonworking hours, the other three factors would have to be considered to determine whether those hours are compensable.

Voluntary Attendance

The FLSA regulations expressly state that attendance at training activities is not voluntary if the employer requires the employee to take the class, workshop, etc. It is also not voluntary if employees are led to believe that their present working conditions or their continued employment would be adversely affected by not attending the training activity.[111]

What if employees undertake training activities outside of regular working hours in order to pass a test that is required by the employer? Is this voluntary or is this required training time that is compensable? This question frequently arises in the context of public safety, where law enforcement officers, firefighters, and sometimes paramedics and EMTs may be required to pass a physical abilities test on a regular basis. In cases such as these, the training time would be compensable if the employer *required* its employees to take a particular fitness class outside of work or to follow a specific training regimen in preparation for the test. But where employees are not required to spend a specific amount of time training for the test or do specific exercises or activities, the training time is not compensable. This is true even where it would be quite difficult to pass the test without training or preparation.

The Eleventh Circuit Court of Appeal's decision in *Dade County v. Alvarez*[112] is an excellent example of the how the training-time regulation applies to situations where an employer requires public safety employees to pass a physical fitness exam. The conclusion in the case is consistent with other FLSA principles. The plaintiffs in *Alvarez* were members of the (Miami) Metro-Dade Police Department's Special Response Team, or SRT. SRT officers were highly trained in the use of special weapons, equipment, and techniques designed to minimize the risk of harm to officers and civilians in situations involving barricaded subjects, snipers, hostages, riots, and high-risk search and arrest warrants. Accordingly, excellent physical fitness was a continuing requirement for assignment to the SRT. SRT officers worked two weeks on primary duty, during which they trained in SRT tactics and responded to calls for SRT assistance, and two weeks on warrant duty, in which they served felony arrest warrants on high-risk individuals. When on primary duty, SRT officers were allotted two hours of on-duty physical fitness training each day, which they used to conduct long-distance runs, weight training, and calisthenics. At one time, SRT members also were permitted to train on duty twice a week for two hours during warrant duty, but for a number of years prior to the lawsuit, they were not provided with any on-duty

---

111. *See* 29 C.F.R. § 785.28.
112. 124 F.3d 1380 (11th Cir. 1997).

physical training time while on warrant duty. SRT supervisors instructed officers to do whatever was necessary to maintain adequate cardiovascular and strength levels but never directed officers to engage in any specific off-duty routine or training. The county employer required only that the officers remain in adequate shape to perform SRT functions and pass a physical fitness exam. The method, location, and amount of off-duty training were left to the officers' complete discretion.[113]

In their lawsuit, the SRT officers alleged that the county violated the FLSA by refusing to compensate them for the hours they spent exercising off-duty to maintain their fitness. At trial, a jury found in favor of the officers, but the Eleventh Circuit reversed, finding that the off-duty time spent by the SRT officers maintaining their physical fitness standards was not compensable work within the meaning of the FLSA. The court found that

- the officers' off-duty fitness training was conducted outside of their regular working hours;
- the off-duty fitness training was not directly related to their jobs;
- the officers did not perform any productive work while conducting off-duty physical training, as they were not responding to SRT calls or serving warrants; and
- the officers' off-duty training satisfied the voluntariness requirement.[114]

The court explained its conclusion that the off-duty fitness training satisfied the voluntariness requirement and that the fitness training was *not* directly related to the officers' jobs as follows:

> The SRT supervisors required only that the officers pass the semi-annual fitness test. . . . [The officers] presented no evidence that they were required to spend a specific amount of time training or to perform certain exercise routines during their off-duty hours. Moreover, . . . [the officers] did not suggest that their employment would be adversely affected if they did not participate in any particular off-duty activities, as long as they could pass the fitness tests. In conducting off-duty exercise, SRT officers were free to train at any location, at any time, and for any duration. Given the freedom the officers enjoyed in selecting their off-duty activities, we conclude that the actual off-duty physical training performed by individual officers was voluntary within the meaning of the regulations.

> Finally, we conclude that the officers' off-duty physical training was not directly related to their SRT employment. In this case, the officers' physical fitness training was necessary to maintain a level of physical conditioning that each SRT officer already had attained. The County, by administering the semi-annual fitness exam, required only that the officers sustain the

---

113. *See id.* at 1382–83.
114. *See id.* at 1385.

level of physical fitness established during the SRT training school and further developed during the primary cycle's on-duty cardiovascular and strength training activities. The County did not require the officers to acquire or develop a skill unique to their employment as SRT officers. Although physical fitness training allows SRT officers to perform their core employment function of responding to emergency situations, such training also provides the individual officers with benefits that extend beyond their employment position. The mere fact that fitness training must be undertaken off duty in order to perform SRT functions is insufficient to establish that such activity is directly related to the employee's job. Because the SRT officers' off-duty fitness training satisfies all of the four criteria listed in the regulations, we conclude that the officers' off-duty training need not be counted as working time.[115]

The court went on to note that the conclusions reached by applying the training-time regulations—sections 785.27 and 785.28 of C.F.R. Title 29—to the facts of this case were identical to those it would reach if it were to apply the FLSA's primary benefit analysis or the rules applicable to pre-work and post-work activities to the facts. The court found that given the personal value of off-duty fitness training and the fact that the SRT officers could perform their off-duty fitness training at home, at a private gym, or at a county facility, the off-duty exercise could not be considered to have been performed predominately for the benefit of the county employer. Similarly, the court found that the off-duty training could not be considered an integral and indispensable part of the SRT officers' principal activity since they were not employed to conduct physical training or even to attain certain physical fitness standards. Rather, the court said, SRT officers were employed to provide rescue services during potentially life-threatening situations. The mere fact that a high level of physical conditioning was necessary to perform these services did not transform off-duty exercise into work for FLSA purposes.[116]

Training Directly Related to the Employee's Job

Whenever training is directly related to an employee's job it is compensable. The FLSA regulations explain that training is directly related to an employee's job if it is designed to make the employee handle his or her job more effectively.[117] Training the purpose of which is to prepare an employee for another job or to teach an employee a new or additional skill is not considered directly related to the employee's job. As the regulations explain:

> Where a training course is instituted for the bona fide purpose of preparing for advancement through upgrading the employee to a higher skill, and is not intended to make the employee more efficient in his present

---

115. *Id.*
116. *See id.* at 1386.
117. *See* 29 C.F.R. § 785.29.

job, the training is not considered directly related to the employee's job even though the course incidentally improves his skill in doing his regular work.[118]

The requirement that training be directly related to the employee's job before it can be compensable has been the basis of no small amount of litigation. One federal trial court held that any training that does not apply to a specific job but only to better performance in the workplace in general is not work directly related to an employee's job. In that case, the employer required its operating engineers, who were not required to have college degrees, to pass a series of foundational skills assessments. The time the employees spent studying for the assessments was found to be noncompensable since its only purpose was to make the engineers better educated generally.[119] In another case, the federal Eleventh Circuit Court of Appeals found that while the training at issue related to 10 percent of an employee's job duties, that was not enough to make it not directly related to his job.[120] Finally, DOL itself said in an opinion letter that where a job did not require proficiency in English, an employee's study of employer-provided written instruction in English outside working hours was not directly related to the employee's job. DOL agreed with the employer that while such instruction might enhance employee job satisfaction, improve morale at work, and provide employees with greater job opportunities generally, it did not help the employee perform his job more efficiently. The fact that the training may have had an indirect effect on an employee's current job (as greater facility in English surely would have) did not make it directly related to the job.[121]

Training That Is a Precondition of Employment

What if training of a certain kind is a precondition of employment but the employer will allow applicants to complete the training on their own time after they have begun work? In one case, *Chao v. Tradesmen International, Inc.,*[122] the federal Sixth Circuit Court of Appeals found that such time was not compensable. The employer, Tradesmen International, was a skilled tradesmen–leasing company that required all field employees to have completed a ten-hour Occupational Safety and Health Administration (OSHA) general-construction safety course. The company allowed applicants to complete the training post-hire, after regular working hours, with the understanding that it would terminate their employment if they did not complete the training course within a reasonable amount of time.

---

118. *Id.*

119. *See* Maynor v. Dow Chem. Co., 671 F. Supp. 2d 902, 991–21 (S.D. Tex. 2009) (question of material fact remained as to whether training helped employees perform their job better, precluding summary judgment).

120. *See* Price v. Tampa Elec. Co., 806 F.2d 1551, 1552 (11th Cir. 1987).

121. *See* U.S. Dep't of Labor, Emp't Standards Admin., Wage & Hour Div., Wage and Hour Administrator Opinion Letter, FLSA 2006-5 (Mar. 3, 2006), https://www.dol.gov/whd/opinion/FLSA/2006/2006_03_03_05_FLSA.pdf.

122. 310 F.3d 904 (6th Cir. 2002).

In determining whether the training time was compensable, the court did not look to the FLSA's training-time regulations but instead looked to the provisions of the Portal-to-Portal Act, the amendment to the FLSA that requires employers to compensate employees for pre-work and post-work activities that are integral and indispensable to the principal activities of their jobs.[123] The court found that the safety course, although required by the employer, was not an integral and indispensable part of the tradesmen's duties.[124] In a case involving members of a private campus police force, the federal First Circuit Court of Appeals found that the time officers spent in EMT training, which was a precondition to their hiring, was not an integral and indispensable part of their job duties.[125]

A Special Rule Applicable to Government Employers Only

The FLSA regulations, here as elsewhere, make a concession to the ways in which public-sector employment differs from private-sector employment. At Section 553.226 of C.F.R. Title 29, DOL identifies as noncompensable any time a state or local government employee spends outside of working hours in a class or training session that is required for certification before he or she can perform a particular job. Thus, time spent completing the training that the State of North Carolina requires for certification and recertification of paramedics and EMTs is not compensable time. This is true even if the local government employer is paying for the cost of the training (of course, the employer is not forbidden from treating the training time as compensable work; it is just not required to do so under the FLSA).

Suppose a local law enforcement officer is attending class at a law enforcement training facility or a firefighter is attending a fire academy and residence at the respective training facility is required. Because of Section 553.226, the hours not spent in class are not compensable, even where the participants are residing on-campus for the period of the training program. Although employees are not "home" and are not free to pursue their usual off-duty activities while at the training site, they may still use the hours not spent in class for their own purposes, e.g., reading, sleeping, surfing the Internet, or watching TV. One way to think about this is to remember that certifications are personal to employees. An employee with a law enforcement officer certification or a paramedic certification can take that certification with him or her to work for another local government employer.

Note that an employer that takes advantage of this special local government exception does not have to satisfy the general rules for compensating training time discussed above.

---

123. See pages 67 through 77 of this chapter for a discussion of pre-work and post-work activities.

124. *See Chao*, 310 F.3d at 911.

125. *See Bienkowski v. Ne. Univ.*, 285 F.3d 138, 139–43 (1st Cir. 2002).

When Employees Enroll in Classes or Training on Their Own Initiative

Employees sometimes enroll in training completely of their own accord or may voluntarily choose to take advantage of special employer-offered courses. When an employee enrolls in a course or college program at his or her own initiative, the time is not compensable—even if the coursework is directly related to the employee's job. Occasionally, an employer will offer a free class or training opportunity after working hours for the benefit of its employees. If attendance is not required and an employee's participation is voluntary, the time spent in such classes would not be considered hours worked.[126]

Travel Time

Employees travel for work-related reasons all the time. But to assume that all instances of "traveling for work" are compensable is off the mark. As with other issues of compensable time, travel time is generally compensable only when the time is spent primarily for the benefit of the employer. Travel time may be divided into two broad categories: travel from home to work and out-of-town travel (or travel away from the home community, to use the terminology of the U.S. Department of Labor (DOL)).

Travel from Home to Work

The travel time an employee spends during his or her normal commute from home to work is never compensable, not even when the travel is in an employer-issued vehicle. If an employee's job duties require travel from site to site during the course of the workday, the trip from home to the first work site is considered simply another instance of commuting time and is not compensable unless the employer has directed the employee to stop somewhere else first, such as at a central office, or unless the employee must stop to pick up an employer-owned vehicle for use during the workday.[127] Commuting time is analyzed as an instance of pre-work and post-work (preliminary and postliminary) activity.[128] As a general rule, commuting is not considered to be an integral and indispensable part of an employee's primary activity.[129] The FLSA has been amended twice since its passage to make that point clear, first, in 1947, in the Portal-to-Portal Act (FLSA Section 254), and later, in 1996, in the Employee

---

126. *See* 29 C.F.R. §§ 785.30, 785.31.

127. *See* 29 U.S.C. § 254(a); 29 C.F.R. § 785.38. *See also* Kavanagh v. Grand Union Co., Inc., 192 F.3d 269, 273 (2d Cir. 1999) (fact that geographical distance employee had to cover was substantial did not render time from home to first worksite stop compensable); Burton v. Hillsborough Cty., 181 F. App'x 829 (11th Cir. 2006) (picking up employer-owned vehicle).

128. See the discussion on pages 62 through 77 of this chapter.

129. *See* 29 U.S.C. § 254(a); 29 C.F.R. § 785.35. *See also* Adams v. United States, 471 F.3d 1321, 1323 (Fed. Cir. 2006).

Commuting Flexibility Act, which amended the Portal-to-Portal Act. As amended, Section 254(a) of the FLSA says that

> . . . no employer shall be subject to any liability or punishment under the Fair Labor Standards Act . . . on account of the failure of such employer to pay an employee minimum wages, or to pay an employee overtime compensation, for or on account of any of the following activities . . .
>
> (1) *walking, riding, or traveling to and from the actual place of performance of the principal activity or activities which such employee is employed to perform,* and
>
> (2) activities which are preliminary to or postliminary to said principal activity or activities, which occur either prior to the time on any particular workday at which such employee commences, or subsequent to the time on any particular workday at which he ceases, such principal activity or activities. For purposes of this subsection, *the use of an employer's vehicle for travel by an employee and activities performed by an employee which are incidental to the use of such vehicle for commuting shall not be considered part of the employee's principal activities if the use of such vehicle for travel is within the normal commuting area for the employer's business or establishment and the use of the employer's vehicle is subject to an agreement on the part of the employer and the employee or representative of such employee.*[130]

Public safety employees have nevertheless argued that (1) the expectation that they monitor an employer-issued communications radio while commuting to and from work turns what ordinarily would be unpaid travel time into compensable time and (2) the fact that canine officers transport their dogs back and forth from home to work turns their commutes into compensable time. The courts have not agreed with either argument.[131]

When an Employee Is Called Back to Work

Suppose an employer calls an employee back to work after the end of a scheduled workday to respond to an emergency. Is the back-to-work travel time compensable? Surprisingly, the answer turns on the location to which the employee is called back.

---

130. 29 U.S.C. § 254(a) (emphasis added).

131. *See, e.g.,* Aiken v. City of Memphis, 190 F.3d 753, 759 (6th Cir. 1999) (mere monitoring of police radio did not turn commute into compensable time); Reich v. New York City Transit Auth., 45 F.3d 646, 650 (2d Cir.1995) (commute of law enforcement dog-handlers not compensable except to the extent that actual duties of care, feeding, training, walking, or cleaning up of dog occurred during commute); Huffman v. City of Lake Jackson, No. H-08-1541, 2009 WL 3735467, at *4 (S.D. Tex. Nov. 4, 2009) (same); Bolick v. Brevard Cty. Sheriff's Dep't, 937 F. Supp. 1560, 1565 (M.D. Fla. 1996) (same); Andrews v. DuBois, 888 F. Supp. 213, 217–20 (D. Mass. 1995) (same). See also pages 112 through 116 of this chapter.

The travel-time regulation found at Code of Federal Regulations (C.F.R.) Title 29, Section 785.36 says that

> if an employee **who has gone home after completing his day's** work is subsequently called out at night to travel *a substantial distance* to perform an emergency job for one of his employer's customers all time spent on such travel is working time.[132]

If this regulation were to be applied to a public employer, this would mean that if a utility repairperson or a public works or public safety employee is called back to work and is directed to report to a location other than the place to which he or she usually reports, the travel time would be compensable if the employee had to travel "a substantial distance." What is a substantial distance? The regulations do not say nor are there any cases providing guidance. It is arguable that no city or county employee called back to perform emergency work is likely to travel a substantial distance because any location to which they would be directed would be within the employing jurisdiction's limits. To make matters more confusing, Section 785.36 says that DOL is taking *no* position on the compensability of travel time to an employee's regular place of work and back after hours to respond to an emergency. Thus, the regulations appear to say that time spent traveling to either an employee's regular worksite or to a different location when the employee is called back in after regular hours is not compensable time. Of course, employers may choose to compensate employees for all travel time when they are called back in after hours.

Out-of-Town Travel

What does it mean when we speak of "out-of-town" travel? The term "out of town" is not mentioned in the text of the FLSA or in the FLSA regulations. Instead, the regulations speak of "travel that is all in a day's work," "travel away from the home community," and "home to work on special one-day assignment in another city."[133] "Travel away from the home community" is defined as overnight travel.[134] Regular "out-of-town" travel that involves travel to another city or county where the employee returns home at the end of the day is "travel that is all in a day's work."[135] "A special one-day assignment in another city" involves the employer's "special request to meet the needs of the particular and unusual assignment"—in another words, something not ordinarily contemplated as part of the employee's job duties.[136]

Although this organization of concepts may appear confusing, the regulations may be boiled down to four basic rules that govern whether time spent traveling for work must be compensated.

---

132. 29 C.F.R. § 785.36 (emphasis added).

133. The regulations governing compensation of travel time may be found at 29 C.F.R. §§ 785.37–.41.

134. *See* 29 C.F.R. § 785.39.

135. *See* 29 C.F.R. § 785.38.

136. *See* 29 C.F.R. § 785.37.

1. Travel time must be paid when it occurs during the employee's regularly scheduled hours.
2. Time spent traveling away from home on otherwise non-working days that involves an overnight stay must be paid when the travel itself occurs during what would be working hours on a regular workday.
3. Time spent traveling away from home outside of regular working hours as a passenger in a car or on an airplane, train, or bus does not have to be paid.
4. Time spent traveling outside of regular working hours as the driver of an automobile must be paid.

Travel during an Employee's Workday

Travel time is always compensable when it takes place during an employee's regularly scheduled hours of work. The easiest way to think about this is to remember that here, the employee is simply substituting travel for other duties. It doesn't matter whether the employee is traveling from worksite to worksite, as a building inspector might do, or to a meeting across town or across the country. The employee is entitled to be paid for the time.[137]

Travel during a Non-Workday

The rule governing time spent traveling on a non-workday is less intuitive than the rule that applies to travel during the workday because (1) the rule only applies to travel that involves an overnight stay and (2) the rule makes a distinction between travel that occurs during the hours that an employee would be scheduled to work if it were a workday and the hours that an employee would be off duty if it were a regular workday.

Imagine that Phil and Patti, both FLSA nonexempt employees, drive from Paradise, N.C., to Chapel Hill on late Sunday afternoon. They are attending a class in public employment law at the School of Government and need to be there by 9 a.m. on Monday. Since it is a good five-hour drive from Paradise to Chapel Hill, they need to leave the day before. They set out at 3 p.m. Patti drives. Phil sits in the passenger seat and sings along to the radio to entertain Patti.

Patti and Phil's regular hours are Monday to Friday, 9 a.m. to 5 p.m. Section 785.39 of C.F.R. Title 29 directs that Phil be paid for two hours of work on that Sunday, from 3 p.m. to 5 p.m. His employer does not have to pay him for the additional three hours he spends in the car from 5 p.m. to 8 p.m. Patti, on the other hand, gets paid for the entire trip, from 3 p.m. to 8 p.m.

Why the difference?

To start with, Section 785.39 provides that travel away from home (when it involves an overnight stay) is compensable when it occurs on a non-working day during what would be working hours on a workday. In other words, if an employee regularly works from 9 a.m. to 5 p.m. from Monday through Friday, travel time between 9 a.m. to

---

137. *See* 29 C.F.R. § 785.39.

5 p.m. on Saturday or Sunday is compensable time. So, both Phil, who is the passenger, and Patti, who is the driver, are paid for the hours between 3 p.m. and 5 p.m.

But different rules apply to the roles of driver and passenger. Section 785.41 of C.F.R. Title 29 provides that anyone who is driving is considered to be working while traveling. Being a passenger is different. Section 785.39 makes clear that DOL will not "consider as worktime that time spent in travel away from home outside of regular working hours as a passenger on an airplane, train, boat, bus, or automobile." That is why Patti is paid for the hours from 5 p.m. to 8 p.m. and Phil is not. Had more of their trip taken place between the hours of 9 a.m. to 5 p.m., Phil would have been paid more for the trip.

Working on an Employer Project While a Passenger in an Automobile

What if Phil owed the city manager a report first thing upon his return from Chapel Hill and, instead of regaling Patti with songs and jokes, he worked on his report on his laptop during the entire car ride? In that case, Phil would be paid for the entire trip—from 3 p.m. to 8 p.m.—because he was performing work for the employer's benefit during that time. It isn't any different than if Phil were sitting on his couch at home working on the report. The time would be compensable. Any time an FLSA nonexempt employee performs work at the direction of and for the benefit of the employer, the time must be paid, whether on-site or at home, whether in town or traveling.[138]

Gap Time

What is "gap time"? The term does not appear in either the text of the FLSA or in the regulations. It is, however, a term used by human resources and payroll professionals and it appears in a number of Administrator Opinion Letters from the U.S. Department of Labor (DOL). "Gap time" refers to the hours that fall between a nonexempt employee's regularly scheduled hours and the number of hours that an employee must work before becoming entitled to overtime. When an employee is scheduled to work forty hours per week, there is no gap time. But employees may be scheduled for fewer than forty hours. It is common for a regular workweek to be thirty-seven and one-half hours per week, for example. In that case, gap time is time worked between thirty-seven and one-half and forty hours. Do nonexempt employees get paid for working during gap time?

Imagine four local government employees: Susan, a nonexempt helpdesk support specialist in the City of Paradise's information technology (IT) department; Will, who is a nonexempt planner in the planning and zoning department; Jared, who is a nonexempt sergeant in the Paradise police department; and Nora, who is a nonexempt firefighter in the Paradise fire department. Some of these employees will get gap time, others will not.

---

138. *See* 29 C.F.R. §§ 785.7, .11.

Nonexempt Hourly Employees: The Case of Susan

Susan's position as an IT support specialist requires her to work from 8 a.m. to 4 p.m. Monday through Friday, with a half-hour unpaid lunch break, for a total of 37.5 hours per week. Susan is paid on an hourly basis at the rate of $20 per hour. She earns a total of $750 during a normal workweek. What happens when Susan works forty hours in a workweek? Is she paid for the additional time she works? What if Susan works forty-five hours in a workweek? How much she is paid depends on what agreement the city and Susan have about how she will be paid when she works more than her scheduled number of hours.

Suppose that the IT director asks Susan to stay late one day to help with a software installation. She stays until 6:30 p.m. that night, which brings the total number of hours she works that week to forty. If Susan is paid an additional $50 for the two and one-half additional hours she works that week ($20 per hour x 2.5 hours), all is well and good from Susan's perspective.

But suppose Susan isn't paid anything for the extra two and one-half hours she has worked. She is simply paid her regular $750 for the regularly scheduled hours she has worked ($20 per hour x 37.5 hours). Susan thinks that there has been a mistake. Her supervisor tells her that it is the city's policy not to pay employees for gap time—the time between their regularly scheduled hours of thirty-seven and one-half hours per week and forty hours (after which overtime rules would apply). "Whaat?" yells Susan.

If Susan and the city agreed at the outset of her employment that she would not be compensated for gap-time hours—whether that was part of her employment contract, written or oral, express or implied—the city will **not** be in violation of the FLSA when it does not provide her with additional compensation for the extra hours she worked. That's because of a little-known hole in FLSA coverage.

The Loophole That Permits the Gap-Time Exception

Given its power over the American workplace, the Fair Labor Standards Act is surprisingly compact. The core requirements of the law may be found in only three sections: Section 206 establishes the minimum wage; Section 207 establishes the maximum hours a nonexempt employee may work without being paid overtime premium pay; and Section 213 sets forth exemptions from the overtime rule. Section 206(a)(1)(c) provides simply that "every employer" shall pay wages at the rate of no less than $7.25 an hour. Most of the regulations dealing with compensable time derive from Section 207, which sets forth the basic overtime rule in subsection (a)(1):

> Except as otherwise provided in this section, no employer shall employ any of his employees . . . for a workweek longer than forty hours unless such employee receives compensation for his employment in excess of the hours above specified at a rate not less than one and one-half times the regular rate at which he is employed.

Section 213 is not relevant here.

The FLSA regulations do not address the situation in which Susan finds herself. Both DOL (in its Wage and Hour Administrator Opinion Letters) and the federal courts have interpreted this silence to mean that an employer may structure the terms of employment to provide that employees will receive their stated hourly rate for all of their regularly scheduled hours, but that for extra hours that do not cause the employee to exceed the forty-hour maximum, no additional compensation has to be paid. This may seem shocking, but such a practice does not violate the FLSA if the employee's total compensation for the week (that is, the compensation for the regular schedule) remains above the minimum wage when it is divided by the total number of hours worked (the regular schedule plus the additional hours).[139]

To return to Susan, if we take her compensation for her regular schedule, namely, $750 per week ($20 per hour x 37.5 hours), and divide it by the total number of hours she has worked that week (forty), we get an average hourly wage of $18.75, well above the minimum wage. Compare Susan's situation with that of an employee earning only $7.50 per hour. That employee's weekly earnings would be $281.25 for a regular thirty-seven-and-one-half-hour-per-week schedule. If the employee were to work forty hours this week without receiving any additional compensation for the gap time, his average hourly wage would be $7.03 per hour. Under these circumstances, the city would be violating the FLSA by not compensating the employee for the gap-time hours worked, but only because the average hourly wage falls below the federal minimum, not because the city failed to pay the difference between thirty-seven and one-half and forty hours of work.

An Agreement Not to Pay for Gap Time

In this hypothetical, the city's ability to not compensate Susan for those extra two and one-half hours ultimately depends on whether Susan has agreed to this arrangement. "Agreement" is a relative term here: the issue is whether Susan knew in advance that she would not be compensated for the gap-time hours and worked them anyway. About "agreement," the Fourth Circuit has said:

> Where the parties' actions and the circumstances demonstrate that the plaintiff was aware of a particular condition of employment, the employee's acceptance of, and continued, employment manifests acceptance of the condition. However, if the employee contemporaneously protests, there is no implied agreement to the condition.[140]

---

139. For the leading Fourth Circuit case on this issue, see *Monahan v. County of Chesterfield*, 95 F.3d 1263 (4th Cir. 1996). See also the following opinion letters from DOL's Employment Standards Administration, Wage and Hour Division: WAGE & HOUR OPINION LETTER, FLSA 2004-14 (Oct. 8, 2014), https://www.dol.gov/whd/opinion/FLSA/2004/2004_10_08_14_FLSA_GapTime .pdf; WAGE & HOUR OPINION LETTER, FLSA 2004-10 (Sept. 20, 2004), https://www.dol.gov/whd/ opinion/FLSA/2004/2004_09_20_10_FLSA_CompTime.pdf. See the discussion of the concept of "agreement" under the FLSA at pages 120 through 121 of this book.

140. *See Monahan*, 95 F.3d at 1275, *citing* Bodie v. City of Columbia, 934 F.2d 561, 566 (4th Cir. 1991).

If the city's policy not to pay for gap time is set forth in an employee handbook, and if Susan has received a copy of that handbook and gave a written acknowledgement of having read it, a court would likely say that Susan has impliedly agreed to its terms. Even if there is no written policy, a court will likely find that an employee agreed to a policy not to pay for gap time if, in actual practice, the city does not pay for gap time and employees like Susan work gap-time hours without pay. On the other hand, if no one ever told Susan that this policy was part of the terms and conditions of her employment, and if Susan complains about not being paid for gap-time hours, a court will not find that Susan agreed to those terms. Under those circumstances, Susan would be owed compensation for the two and one-half gap-time hours at her regular $20-per-hour rate.

Unpaid Gap-Time Claims Must Be Brought in State Court

Here's another FLSA fact that is not well known: even if Susan is owed gap-time compensation (because she did not agree to unpaid gap time), she cannot bring a claim for those unpaid hours under the FLSA. The FLSA is violated only when an employer (1) fails to pay an average of the minimum wage for all straight-time hours worked (a violation of FLSA Section 206), (2) fails to pay time-and-one-half the employee's regular rate for hours worked over forty hours (a violation of Section 207), or (3) fails to compensate the employee through the provision of compensatory time off (also a violation of Section 207). (See chapter 4, page 120, for further discussion of "comp time.") The statute does not authorize a lawsuit to recover unpaid gap-time wages. Further, the failure of an employer to live up to any other promises it has made about wages is not a violation of the FLSA. An employer's promises about wages may be enforced only by bringing a breach of employment contract lawsuit in state court. It is there that Susan will have to seek back pay.

May the City Compensate Susan Anyway?

If the city is not required by the FLSA to pay Susan for gap-time hours, could it compensate her with hour-for-hour paid time off for the hours between thirty-seven and one-half and forty? The answer to this question is "yes." The fact that the city does not have to pay Susan for gap-time hours does not mean that it cannot compensate her for that time, either by paying her regular hourly rate, a lower hourly rate, or by giving her paid time off.

Non-Overtime versus Overtime Workweeks

What happens if Susan works overtime one week? Suppose Susan works forty-five hours one week instead of her regularly scheduled thirty-seven and one-half. Must she be paid for the gap-time hours under these circumstances? It just doesn't seem logical for her to be paid for the first thirty-seven and one-half hours worked, to be paid nothing for hours worked between thirty-seven and one-half and forty hours, then to be paid time-and-one-half her regular rate for the five hours of overtime she works.

DOL addressed this issue in a 2004 opinion letter in which it said that in an overtime workweek, an hourly employee must be paid the agreed-upon hourly rate for all straight-time hours worked, as well as the premium due for all overtime hours, before an employer can be said to have paid the overtime compensation due.[141] In an overtime workweek, gap-time hours must be paid in cash and cannot be compensated with FLSA compensatory time off (comp time). This is true whether overtime hours are paid in cash or with FLSA comp time, which gives an employee one and one-half hours of paid time off for every hour worked over forty hours.

Although DOL did not cite to a specific regulation in its opinion letter, the regulation found at C.F.R. Title 29, Section 778.315 sets forth the principle that gap-time hours count toward overtime and must be paid at the regular hourly rate in any week in which an FLSA nonexempt employee works overtime.

> In determining the number of hours for which overtime compensation is due, all hours worked (see § 778.223) by an employee for an employer in a particular workweek must be counted. Overtime compensation . . . must be paid for each hour worked in the workweek in excess of the applicable maximum hours standard. This extra compensation for the excess hours of overtime work under the Act cannot be said to have been paid to an employee unless all the straight time compensation due him for the non-overtime hours . . . has been paid.

In dicta in its 1996 decision in *Monahan v. County of Chesterfield*, the federal Fourth Circuit Court of Appeals agreed with DOL on this point.[142] So Susan could file a complaint with DOL or bring a lawsuit in federal court under the FLSA to recover compensation for gap-time hours worked in an overtime workweek.

Nonexempt Salaried Employees: The Case of Will

Susan, as we have seen, is paid strictly on an hourly basis. Is the result any different when an FLSA nonexempt employee is paid on a salary basis rather than on an hourly basis? Consider the example of Will, who works as a planner for the City of Paradise. Although Will is a nonexempt employee, the city pays him on a salary basis for a thirty-seven-and-one-half-hour workweek. He earns $960 per week. In other words, Will earns $960 each week for as many hours as he works, up to and including thirty-seven and one-half hours. Like any nonexempt employee, Will earns time-and-one-half premium pay when he works more than forty hours in a workweek. But with one of the other planners out on Family and Medical Leave Act leave, Will lately finds himself working more than thirty-seven and one-half hours per week

---

141. *See* DOL, Wage & Hour Opinion Letter, FLSA 2004-10, *supra* note 139.

142. *See Monahan*, 95 F.3d at 1273. The only other federal appeals court decision on this issue, the 2013 decision from the Second Circuit, *Lundy v. Catholic Health System of Long Island, Inc.*, 711 F.3d 106, 116 (2d Cir. 2013), expressly disagreed with the Fourth Circuit and held that compensation for gap time could not be recovered under the FLSA even when an employee had worked overtime.

more often than not. Some weeks he works no more than forty hours, but in others he works overtime hours.

Whether Will is entitled to compensation for gap-time hours when he works between thirty-seven and one-half and forty hours depends on whether his salary is meant to compensate him for a fixed thirty-seven-and-one-half-hour workweek or for as many hours as he works in any given week. If Will's salary is meant to cover a fixed workweek, then he must be compensated at his hourly rate for any additional non-overtime hours he works. (Note that like Susan, Will would have to file a breach of contract suit in state court to recover unpaid gap-time compensation.) If Will has expressly or impliedly agreed to work for $960 per week for all non-overtime hours worked, he is not entitled to additional compensation for any hours worked between thirty-seven and one-half and forty hours.[143]

Sometimes employers fail to make clear whether a nonexempt employee's salary is meant to cover a fixed workweek or a variable workweek. In such cases, courts will look to workplace practice to determine the terms of the employee's employment contract. The Fourth Circuit has exhibited little sympathy for employees claiming after the fact that they did not understand that their salaries covered all non-overtime hours, saying in the *Monahan* case,

> . . . we do not find that the FLSA places the burden on the employer to hold an employee's hand and specifically tell him or her that the salary "fully compensates him or her up to the overtime threshold," if that fact can be easily gleaned from employment policies, practices and procedures.[144]

If Will does not complain the first time he is paid only his regular salary for weeks in which he works gap-time hours, and if he continues to work the gap-time hours, a court would likely find that he has agreed to a fixed salary for a variable-hour workweek.

None of this changes when Will works overtime hours. If his salary is only meant to cover thirty-seven and one-half hours of work time, the city must pay Will his gap-time hours at the pro-rated hourly rate.[145] If his salary is meant to cover all of the hours he might work up to forty hours, however many they might be from week to week, then he is not owed any additional compensation for gap-time hours (although he is due time-and-one-half for hours after forty hours). This was the factual scenario underpinning the *Monahan* case, which was brought by police officers working on a salary basis, where the Fourth Circuit held that,

> . . . if the mutually agreed upon terms of an employment agreement do not violate the FLSA's minimum wage/maximum hour mandates and provide compensation for all nonovertime hours up to the overtime threshold, there can be no viable claim for straight gap time under FLSA if all hours

---

143. *See* 29 C.F.R. §§ 778.322, .323.
144. *Monahan*, 95 F.3d at 1275 (footnote omitted).
145. *See* 29 C.F.R. § 778.322.

worked above the threshold have been properly compensated at a proper overtime rate.[146]

The determining factor is "agreement of the parties as to what the salary is intended to compensate."[147]

Section 207(k) and Salaried Nonexempt Employees: The Case of Jared

Jared is an FLSA nonexempt sergeant in the Paradise police department. The city pays all of its law enforcement officers on a salary basis and schedules them to work 161 hours during a 28-day work period under the 207(k) exemption. Under this exemption, overtime kicks in after a law enforcement officer works 171 hours. Jared's weekly salary is $865. Does Jared get paid for the gap time between his scheduled 161 hours and the statutory maximum of 171 hours, after which he must be paid overtime?

The analysis here is exactly the same as that applicable to Will's right to gap-time pay. If Jared's salary is meant to compensate him for a fixed 161 hours, then the city will owe him his pro-rata hourly wage for each of the hours he works between 161 and 171 hours in a workweek. If his salary is meant to compensate him for all non-overtime hours, then the city does not owe him any additional compensation. The use of the 207(k) exemption does not do anything other than (1) allow the work schedule to be between seven and twenty-eight days and (2) set a higher maximum-hour threshold for overtime premium pay rules to apply. Indeed, the Fourth Circuit has found the notion that an employee like Jared might be entitled to gap-time pay to be illogical, saying about a Virginia county where law enforcement officers worked a 24-day cycle with a 147-hour overtime threshold that

> . . . if the County had scheduled the officers for all hours up to the 147 hour threshold per cycle, Plaintiffs would not be before us today because there would be no "gap time" issue, but the officers would be working three to twelve more hours per pay cycle and approximately 135 more hours per year for the same salary amount.[148]

Section 207(k) and Hourly Nonexempt Employees: The Case of Nora

Nora is a nonexempt firefighter. While the City of Paradise schedules its firefighters using the 207(k) exemption, it uses a fourteen-day, rather than a twenty-eight-day, schedule. Paradise firefighters, unlike its law enforcement officers, are paid on an hourly basis. Nora's hourly rate is $17 per hour. She is scheduled to work a rotating schedule of forty-eight hours one week and twenty-four hours the following week, for a total of seventy-two hours in a two-week period. Under Section 207(k), Nora would earn overtime only when she works more than eighty-six hours in a two-week period.

---

146. *See Monahan*, 95 F.3d at 1283.
147. 29 C.F.R. § 778.323.
148. *See Monahan*, 95 F.3d at 1276.

By now, the answer of how to treat Nora's gap-time hours should be clear. If the city's policy is not to pay nonexempt employees for gap-time hours in non-overtime workweeks, the city does not have to pay Nora any more than her usual $1,224 per work period ($17 multiplied by her usual seventy-two hours per two-week period), even during work periods where she works as many as eighty-five or eighty-six hours in the work cycle. That is because even during fourteen-day work periods where Nora works eighty-six hours, her average hourly rate is still approximately double the minimum wage. On the other hand, if the city has told Nora that she will be paid $17 per hour for each hour she works up to the overtime threshold of eighty-six hours, then it must pay her for gap-time hours in a non-overtime workweek.

The rule is clearer in overtime work cycles. As was the case with Susan, who was also paid on an hourly basis, Nora must be paid her regular hourly rate for all straight-time hours she works in an overtime work cycle (in other words, she must be paid for all of her gap-time hours), in addition to the time-and-one-half her regular rate that she is due for hours over eighty-six.

Caring for K-9s

Law enforcement canine officers generally have twenty-four-hour care responsibility for the dogs assigned to them (called K-9s). The dogs live at home with the officers and the officers are responsible for all aspects of the dogs' care, including grooming, walking, feeding, bathing, and ensuring that the dogs received proper veterinary care. Canine-care time is not a subject directly addressed in the FLSA regulations, but numerous courts have held that the time canine officers spend at home caring for their dogs is compensable.[149]

Public employers have two options when it comes to compensating officers for canine-care time. The first is to have officers record and describe all off-duty time spent on the various aspects of canine care and to compensate them for this care as the employer would for time spent on any work matters outside regularly scheduled hours. Because the nature of canine-care duties are different from the officer's primary job duties, the after-hours canine-care work may be compensated at a lower rate. When the time spent on canine care pushes an officer's hours over the overtime threshold, the officer must be compensated with overtime (cash or FLSA compensatory time off). Overtime may be calculated at a blended rate.[150]

The second option is for the employer to enter into an agreement with its canine officers that sets a flat rate of pay for canine care. This sounds simpler than it sometimes is. The applicable regulation—which is general and not specific to canine care—addresses situations where it is difficult to determine the exact hours an employee

149. See Truslow v. Spotsylvania Cty. Sheriff, 783 F. Supp. 274, 279 (E.D. Va. 1992).
150. For more on this topic, see chapter 4, specifically, pages 146 through 147.

spends on work done at home or after hours. It requires that the compensation rate be reasonable and take into account all the relevant facts.

> An employee who resides on his employer's premises on a permanent basis or for extended periods of time is not considered as working all the time he is on the premises. Ordinarily, he may engage in normal private pursuits and thus have enough time for eating, sleeping, entertaining, and other periods of complete freedom from all duties when he may leave the premises for purposes of his own. *It is, of course, difficult to determine the exact hours worked under these circumstances and any reasonable agreement of the parties which takes into consideration all of the pertinent facts will be accepted . . . .*[151]

The U.S. Department of Labor (DOL) and the courts have interpreted this regulation to cover the compensation of canine police officers for the off-duty time they spend caring for their dogs.[152] As the regulation makes clear, there are two key components to making successful use of this exception from the FLSA's standard rules about compensation of nonexempt employees: first, there must be an actual agreement between the employer and employee; second, the agreement must be reasonable.[153]

Agreement on the Canine-Care Rate

"Agreement" means different things in different FLSA contexts. In the context of compensatory time off or "comp time," agreement means that employees have been given notice before working overtime that they will be compensated with compensatory time off. Employees who do not wish to work overtime under this arrangement may seek employment elsewhere. In the context of deductions from pay for sleep time, agreement means that firefighters have voluntarily agreed to a sleep-time deduction without fear of losing their jobs if they do not agree.

In the context of canine care, agreement means that the arrangement is not imposed on officers unilaterally and that they affirmatively consent to the method of compensation. In a leading case from the federal Second Circuit Court of Appeals, a canine officer claimed that he spent up to forty-five off-duty hours per week working with his assigned police dog. His employer instructed the officer to fill out a weekly overtime slip requesting two hours' pay rather than calculate the actual amount of time he spent caring for the dog. The court held that there was no "agreement"

---

151. 29 C.F.R. § 785.23 (emphasis added).

152. See the following opinion letters from DOL's Employment Standards Administration, Wage and Hour Division: WAGE & HOUR OPINION LETTER, FLSA 2006-10 (Mar. 10, 2006), https://www.dol.gov/whd/opinion/FLSA/2006/2006_03_10_10_FLSA.pdf; WAGE & HOUR OPINION LETTER, FLSA (Aug. 11, 1993), 1993 WL 901171. *See also* Krause v. Manalapan Twp., 486 F. App'x 310, 312 (3d Cir. 2012) (four hours per week of "comp time" for off-duty care of K-9s was reasonable); Letner v. City of Oliver Springs, 545 F. Supp. 2d 717, 723–24 (E.D. Tenn. 2008) and the extensive list of cases cited therein.

153. *See* Leever v. Carson City, 360 F.3d 1014, 1018 (9th Cir. 2004).

between the employee and the employer because the two-hour overtime limit was imposed on the employee unilaterally.[154] DOL has said that whether the required agreement has been reached depends upon all of the facts of a particular case.[155]

Reasonableness of the Rate for Canine Care

For an agreement about compensation for a canine officer's off-duty provision of canine care to be reasonable, it must take into account the number of hours the officer actually spends on canine care.[156] DOL Wage and Hour Opinion Letters emphasize that requiring parties to approximate the number of hours worked when forming an agreement pursuant to Section 785.23 of Title 29 of the Code of Federal Regulations (C.F.R.) is consistent with the purpose of the FLSA, which is to ensure that employees are paid for "all hours worked."[157]

Examples of Reasonable and Unreasonable Rates

In *Leever v. Carson City*,[158] the federal Ninth Circuit Court of Appeals held that a salary differential for canine care paid by the employer city was unreasonable where (1) it was unclear upon what factors it was based and (2) the number of hours the officer alleged that she spent caring for her K-9 would easily have entitled her to compensation far in excess of the salary differential. The city presented no evidence that, when negotiating the canine-care compensation agreement, it had made any inquiry into the number of hours spent by the officer on canine care or the number of hours that were reasonably required to be spent by its canine officers on dog care. Indeed, the city admitted that it had no idea how much time the plaintiff officer spent caring for her K-9 during her off-duty hours. Rather, the city relied only on what it called a "comprehensive parity study," which summarized the pay provided by other law enforcement agencies to their canine officers. Unfortunately, the "study" was no more than handwritten notes of telephone inquiries to neighboring jurisdictions. The court found that based on the officer's wage rate and what would have been her overtime rate based on her regular rate of pay, the salary differential approximated one hour of overtime pay per week. Regardless of whether the officer spent the twenty-eight off-duty hours for which she claimed she was due compensation actually working with her K-9, the court concluded that the one hour per week for which the city was

---

154. *See* Holzapfel v. Town of Newburgh, 145 F.3d 516, 520 (2d Cir. 1998). *See also* Huffman v. City of Lake Jackson, No. H-08-1541, 2009 WL 3735467, at *5 (S.D. Tex. Nov. 4, 2009) (evidence insufficient to support allegation that canine-care compensation agreement was unilaterally imposed).

155. *See* DOL, Wage & Hour Opinion Letter, FLSA 2006-10, *supra* note 152.

156. *See Leever,* 360 F.3d at 1018–20; *Holzapfel,* 145 F.3d at 526–27 (two hours of overtime per week was unreasonable where the employer knew that the officer worked at least seven overtime hours per week on canine care).

157. See the following opinion letters from DOL's Employment Standards Administration, Wage and Hour Division: Labor Wage & Hour Opinion Letter, FLSA (Aug. 11, 1993), *supra* note 152; Wage & Hour Opinion Letter, FLSA (Feb. 3, 1981), 1981 WL 179033.

158. 360 F.3d 1014.

compensating her was clearly an insufficient amount of time for the tasks involved in off-duty care of a K-9.[159]

The federal Second Circuit Court of Appeals has observed that the individual traits and needs of officers and animals preclude any easy determination as to what is a "reasonable time" for a canine officer to take care of his or her dog.[160] The variety of kinds of canine-care compensation agreements that courts have found to be reasonable is testimony to the accuracy of that observation. In *Huffman v. City of Lake Jackson*,[161] for example, a city's canine officer agreed to a canine-care compensation arrangement in which he was given four paid hours off per week and a $100-per-month stipend in exchange for caring for his K-9, with the city paying for the dog's food, medical care, and training expenses. The city also provided the officer with a canine-equipped police cruiser and a portable outdoor doggy enclosure for use at work and at home. After resigning from his employment with the city, the officer brought suit, claiming that the agreement was unilaterally imposed and unreasonable. The district court found that the agreement was a mutual one and reasonable under C.F.R. Title 29, Section 785.23.[162]

In *Brock v. City of Cincinnati*,[163] the district court found unreasonable the parties' agreement that city canine officers were to be paid straight-time compensation for approximately seventeen minutes per day, seven days a week for off-duty care of their K-9s. On appeal, however, the Sixth Circuit found the agreement reasonable because while the seventeen minutes per day of compensatory time far under-approximated the actual amount of FLSA "work" performed by the officers, the city provided non-monetary support to the officers in the form of a take-home cruiser, taxpayer-provided dog food, veterinary care, a kennel, travel to competitions, and on-duty training days.[164] The Sixth Circuit concluded that

> [t]he actual amount of time spent in FLSA "work," if reliably ascertained, is a reference point for a range of reasonable agreements, a range that is widened by a variety of non-monetary costs and benefits. The City's package was comprehensive; that it included a relatively small amount of paid time does not, by itself, render the agreement unreasonable.[165]

Section 785.23 agreements ensure that canine officers are reasonably compensated for all hours worked in circumstances where it is laborious and difficult to determine the exact number of off-duty hours involved in dog care each day. But these

---

159. *See id.* at 1020–21.
160. *See Holzapfel*, 145 F.3d at 526. *See also* Rudolph v. Metro. Airports Comm'n, 103 F.3d 677, 681 (8th Cir. 1996) ("Dog care—feeding, grooming, cleaning cages or pens, and exercising—may take more time on one day than on others").
161. No. H-08-1541, 2009 WL 3735467 (S.D. Tex. Nov. 4, 2009).
162. *See id.* at *5.
163. 236 F.3d 793 (6th Cir. 2001).
164. *See id.* at 806–07.
165. *Id.* at 807.

agreements also benefit employers in that officers who agree to a reasonable set of terms cannot later bring claims for unpaid overtime based on hours worked in excess of the agreement. In the case *Rudolph v. Metropolitan Airports Commission*,[166] the canine-care contract between an airport authority and its two canine officers provided that the officers would be paid for one-half hour of canine care each day and that they were to get prior approval for any additional time they thought necessary to properly care for their dogs. The officers had affirmatively agreed to these terms following mediation during negotiations for a new collective bargaining agreement. They nevertheless claimed that they had spent substantially more time on off-duty canine care than the agreement provided for and sued for back overtime pay. The officers claimed that the airport authority knew or had reason to know that this additional work was being performed for its benefit and that it was therefore liable for overtime wages notwithstanding the agreement. The court was not receptive to the officers' argument, finding that since the terms of the contract required them to receive permission for any additional canine-care time, any additional work the officers performed was neither "suffered nor permitted" by their employer. The court held that the airport authority was entitled to rely on the officers following the clear terms of the agreement and was not liable for any additional compensation for time spent caring for the K-9s.[167]

Bottom Line

Employers of canine officers may avoid the uncertainty and irregularity of the number of hours of off-duty work officers engage in by negotiating canine-care agreements with them. The law requires that the amount of canine-care compensation agreed upon must reasonably approximate the amount officers would have earned if they had recorded the exact amount of time they worked, including any overtime. One way to reach a reasonable agreement would be to have officers periodically record the amount of time they spend on off-duty canine care, being sure to have them describe in detail what they are doing in each instance. A dog lover—officer or civilian—could spend an inordinate amount of time on dog care. The employer has the right to limit the time spent to what is objectively and minimally necessary for the care of a dog. An employer could also consult an independent expert, such as a veterinarian, on the minimal requirements of dog care. What is important is that the amount to which the parties agree be based on some objective standard, rather than be pulled out of the air. Finally, as the cases teach, not all of the compensation need be in the form of wages. Use of an employer vehicle, employer-paid improvements to the officer's home or property, or additional paid leave are among the ways a law enforcement agency can compensate its canine officers for their off-duty canine-care responsibilities.

---

166. 103 F.3d 677 (8th Cir. 1996).
167. *See id.* at 683–84.

Chapter 4

Overtime Compensation

The Basic Overtime Rule

The Fair Labor Standards Act (FLSA) requires an employer to pay an employee one-and-one-half his or her regular rate of pay for all hours over forty that employee works in a given week, unless the employee satisfies the FLSA's salary tests *and* one of the executive, administrative, or professional duties tests.[1] Employees who meet the requirements of these tests are called "exempt employees"—that is, exempt from the FLSA's overtime requirements—and need not be paid overtime if they work more than forty hours in a week.

Overtime pay, like straight-time compensation, must be paid on the next regular payday for the pay period in which it is earned.[2] That does not mean that it must be paid on the day on which the pay period ends—no requirement exists that wages be paid simultaneously with the end of the pay period. Rather, both straight-time and overtime compensation must be paid within a reasonable amount of time following the end of the pay period.[3] Where the amount of overtime earned cannot be calculated in time for overtime to be paid on the next regular payday—for example, when employees have not turned in their timesheets on time—an employer may delay the payment of overtime compensation until after the amount owed is calculated, but it must be paid no later than the next payday after the amount of overtime is determined.[4]

---

1. Chapter 1 of this book covers how to determine whether an employee is exempt or nonexempt under the FLSA and includes a fuller discussion of these tests.

2. Martin v. United States, 117 Fed. Cl. 611, 618 (2014) (payment of straight-time and overtime wages two weeks after regular payday violates the FLSA, even where delay was caused by a shutdown of the federal government), *citing* Biggs v. Wilson, 1 F.3d 1537, 1540 (9th Cir. 1993); Olson v. Superior Pontiac–GMC, Inc., 765 F.2d 1570, 1579, *modified*, 776 F.2d 265 (11th Cir. 1985); Atl. Co. v. Broughton, 146 F.2d 480, 482 (5th Cir. 1944); Birbalas v. Cuneo Printing Indus., 140 F.2d 826, 828 (7th Cir. 1944).

3. Benavides v. Miami Atlanta Airfreight, Inc., 322 F. App'x 746, 747 (11th Cir. 2009) (payment in arrears for seven or eight days—the time between the end of the pay period and employer's regular payment date—is not unreasonable, untimely, or in violation of the FLSA).

4. *See* 29 C.F.R. § 778.106.

Exceptions to the Basic Rule

There are a number of exceptions to the basic overtime rule that requires an employer to pay FLSA nonexempt employees at the rate of time-and-one-half their regular rates of pay for all hours over forty worked in a given week. First—and perhaps most important to government employers—is the compensatory time-off rule, an alternative method to paying cash compensation for overtime. The compensatory time-off (or "comp time") rule allows a public employer to provide an employee with paid time off in lieu of cash overtime. When an employer uses comp time instead of cash overtime, the time off must be credited to the employee at the rate of one and one-half hours of compensatory time for each hour of overtime work.[5]

Another exception important to local government employers is found in FLSA Section 207(k), which (1) allows public employers to calculate overtime compensation for law enforcement and fire service employees on the basis of work periods longer than one week and (2) increases the numbers of hours that law enforcement and fire service employees must work before becoming eligible for overtime.[6]

Additional exceptions to the basic overtime rule include the *fluctuating workweek method*, the exception for employees of seasonal recreation establishments, the *special detail/assignment rule*, and the *fewer-than-five rule* for law enforcement officers and firefighters.

The fluctuating workweek method of calculating overtime allows an employer (1) to pay nonexempt employees whose hours fluctuate from week to week an unchanging salary that compensates them for all hours worked in a week regardless of whether they work fewer or greater than forty hours a week and (2) to pay overtime hours at a rate of one-half the employee's regular rate of pay.[7]

The seasonal recreation exception allows public employers who operate recreation facilities such as beaches, ice skating rinks, or parks that are physically separate from other government worksites and are open seven or fewer months a year to exempt the nonexempt employees from overtime pay.[8]

Under the special detail/assignment exception, employing departments may facilitate the hiring of law enforcement and fire service employees employed by a separate and independent employer without the hours worked by these employees on this special assignment counting toward overtime with the public employer.[9]

Finally, under the fewer-than-five rule, if a local government employs fewer than five law enforcement officers or fewer than five firefighters in any given workweek, those positions will be exempt from overtime during that workweek.[10]

---

5. *See* 29 U.S.C. § 207(o); 29 C.F.R. § 553.20.
6. *See* 29 U.S.C. § 207(k); 29 C.F.R. §§ 553.201, .220, .221, .224, .230, .231.
7. *See* 29 C.F.R. § 778.114(a).
8. *See* 29 U.S.C. § 213(a)(3); 29 C.F.R. § 779.23.
9. *See* 29 C.F.R. § 553.227.
10. *See* 29 U.S.C. § 213(b)(20); 29 C.F.R. § 553.200.

The FLSA also has separate rules for when an employee takes a second job with the same employer on a regular basis on one hand, and on an occasional and sporadic basis on the other. There is also a special rule allowing public employers and employees to arrange shift substitutions that avoid overtime. All of these exceptions to and variations on the basic overtime rule will be discussed in more detail in this chapter.

Compensatory Time Off or Comp Time

Section 207(o) of the Fair Labor Standards Act (FLSA) allows government employers an alternative way to compensate nonexempt employees for hours worked in excess of forty that it does not allow private-sector employers: by using *compensatory time off* or, as it is more commonly known, *comp time*. Comp time allows public employers to provide paid time off in lieu of cash overtime. When a government employer uses compensatory paid time off instead of cash overtime, **the time off must be credited at the rate of one and one-half hours of compensatory time for each hour of overtime work**—just as the cash rate for overtime is calculated at the rate of one and one-half times the regular rate of pay. **It is a violation of the FLSA for an employer to compensate a nonexempt employee for overtime hours with hour-for-hour comp time.**[11]

Deciding to Use Comp Time

Public employers may use comp time instead of cash overtime for all of their nonexempt employees or only for some. For example, employers may use comp time in lieu of cash for all overtime worked by a given employee or group of employees or only in connection with certain assignments, such as weather emergencies or public festivals. An employer must meet only one prerequisite before using comp time: before any overtime hours are worked on this basis, the employer must secure the *agreement* of any employee who is to be compensated with comp time instead of cash overtime.[12]

What "agreement" means in this context is something less than what we might ordinarily understand the term to mean. An employer may make receipt of comp time in lieu of cash overtime an express condition of employment at the time of hiring. It may, for example, provide either oral or written notice of its decision to use comp time to affected employees and ask each of them for written acknowledgment.[13] An employer does not have to ask for written acknowledgment, however, and may simply assume lack of objection from the fact that an employee has reported for work and worked assigned overtime hours after notification.[14] Where there is no formal

---

11. *See* 29 C.F.R. § 553.20.

12. *See* 29 U.S.C. § 207(o)(2)(A)(ii); 29 C.F.R. §§ 553.23(a), (c)(1); Moreau v. Klevenhagen, 508 U.S. 22, 35 (1993).

13. *See* Cheek v. City of Greensboro, No. 1:12-CV-981, -1311, 2015 WL 4210835, at *4 (M.D.N.C. July 10, 2015) (signed acknowledgments of city policy of compensating overtime with compensatory time off established agreement "without dispute").

14. *See* 29 C.F.R. § 553.23(c)(1). *See also* Jacksonville Prof'l Fire Fighters Ass'n Local 2961 v. City of Jacksonville, 685 F. Supp. 513, 523 (E.D.N.C. 1987).

written comp-time agreement, the FLSA regulations require that "a record of its existence must be kept" nonetheless—presumably through some form of documentation that the employee has been notified or through a provision of the employer's personnel policy.[15]

Although the relevant regulation, Section 553.23 of Title 29 of the Code of Federal Regulations (C.F.R.), stresses that an employee's agreement to receive compensatory time off must be freely and voluntarily made,[16] the reality is that where receipt of comp time is a condition of employment, an employee who is unwilling to receive time off in lieu of cash has only one option—to find another job.

Cap on the Number of Comp Time Hours That May Be Accrued

The regulations specify that employers may allow nonexempt employees to accrue only 240 hours of comp time, with the exception of employees working "in a public safety activity, an emergency response activity, or a seasonal activity," who may accrue up to 480 hours.[17] Note that employers may only apply the 480-hour limit to employees engaged in public safety and emergency response activities and only if those activities are a regular part of the employees' work. Thus, law enforcement officers, firefighters, emergency medical personnel, as well as 911 dispatchers and telecommunicators may be subject to the higher limit. Employees whose regular work does not involve public safety or emergency response but who undertake such duties during the course of a public emergency remain subject to the lower cap of 240 hours.[18] If employees work more than 240 or 480 hours of overtime—as they often do in emergency situations—employers must either begin to pay out overtime hours in cash or send employees home to use their paid time off (although in emergencies, that is not generally an option).[19]

For law enforcement officers and firefighters who are scheduled under an FLSA Section 207(k) 28-day work cycle (discussed below on page 133), the statutory limit on comp-time accrual is still 480 hours. Employers using the 207(k) 28-day work cycle may use comp time to compensate officers and firefighters at a rate of one and one-half hours paid time off for every hour worked over 171 and 212, respectively.[20]

Using Accrued Comp Time

A public employer must allow an employee to use his or her accrued comp time "within a reasonable period after making the request if the use of the compensatory time does not unduly disrupt the operations of the public agency."[21] Most employers

---

15. *See* 29 C.F.R. § 553.50.

16. *See* 29 C.F.R. § 553.23(c)(1).

17. *See* 29 C.F.R. § 553.21.

18. *See* 29 C.F.R. § 553.24.

19. *See* 29 U.S.C. § 207(o)(3)(A).

20. *See id.*; 29 C.F.R. §§ 553.201(b), .231. For a discussion on the lawful use of a "gap-time" exception to the FLSA's compensable-time rules, see chapter 3, page 105, of this book.

21. *See* 29 U.S.C. § 207(o)(5); 29 C.F.R. § 553.25.

find this easier said than done. One reason that employees accrue comp time in the first place is that there is generally more work to be done or shifts to be covered than there are people or regularly scheduled hours in which to do the work. Allowing employees to take time off may only make the problem worse. Nevertheless, an employer must allow an employee who has requested the use of accrued comp time to take time off absent an undue hardship.

Lawsuits arising out of denials of an employee's request to use comp time are among the most common comp-time lawsuits. Not surprisingly, given the number of overtime hours their work requires, the majority of these cases involve law enforcement agencies and their need to maintain minimum staffing requirements. Consider the following hypothetical.

> *The Paradise police department requires officers to enter requests to use comp time in a log book. They are to enter the dates on which they wish to use their comp time, as well as the date on which they make the request. Requests to use comp time on a particular day are granted unless the number of officers who have already requested to use comp time on that day, when combined with officers on approved leave, leaves the police department below or in danger of falling below minimum staffing levels.*

Does this policy satisfy the comp-time provisions of the FLSA? It certainly seems like it should, as it is biased toward granting leave except where the department's ability to carry out its mission would be compromised. Let's take a closer look.

In analyzing a comp-time policy's compliance with the FLSA and its regulations, an employer must pay close attention to two key concepts: "within a reasonable period" and "unduly disrupt." The regulations themselves define "reasonable period" this way:

> Whether a request to use compensatory time has been granted within a "reasonable period" will be determined by considering the customary work practices within the agency based on the facts and circumstances in each case. Such practices include, but are not limited to (a) the normal schedule of work, (b) anticipated peak workloads based on past experience, (c) emergency requirements for staff and services, and (d) the availability of qualified substitute staff.[22]

The regulations define "unduly disrupt" as follows:

> When an employer receives a request for compensatory time off, it shall be honored unless to do so would be "unduly disruptive" to the agency's operations. Mere inconvenience to the employer is an insufficient basis for denial of a request for compensatory time off . . . . For an agency to turn down a request from an employee for compensatory time off requires

---

22. 29 C.F.R. § 553.25(c)(1).

that it should reasonably and in good faith anticipate that it would impose an unreasonable burden on the agency's ability to provide services of acceptable quality and quantity for the public during the time requested without the use of the employee's services.[23]

In the hypothetical, the Paradise police department's policy limits its discretion in denying requests to use comp time to circumstances that most courts accept as "unduly disruptive" to a law enforcement agency—namely, when the use of comp time would leave the agency understaffed.[24] The policy is, on its face, flexible in that it does not limit the number or percentage of officers who make use of comp time but instead speaks only of minimum staffing requirements, which implies that the department will consider its needs on a day-by-day basis. Implemented that way, the policy as applied would likely satisfy the "unduly disruptive" standard for denying a request to use comp time.[25]

But what about the "reasonable period" standard? Does the city have the obligation to affirmatively offer an alternative date to an employee whose proposed use of comp time it denies? The answer to that question is unclear. In a 2009 case, the federal Seventh Circuit Court of Appeals found that a public employer's practice of turning down requests to use comp time without anything more (or at least without evidence showing it had done anything more) violated the requirement that leave be granted within a reasonable time.

> [T]he City does not treat a police officer's request as beginning a reasonable time within which the Police Department must provide compensatory time off. [The City] receives written requests that it either grants or denies; if a request is not granted immediately then the form is returned—without reasons, without recourse, and without any effort to schedule leave within a "reasonable time." Now it may be that, by submitting one request after another, most officers can secure some leave within a reasonable time of the initial request. But [the City] does not keep records to show that this occurs . . . .[26]

It would be better practice to provide a mechanism whereby an employee denied the use of comp time is offered an alternate date or dates or is actively given an opportunity to request another day.

---

23. 29 C.F.R. § 553.25(d).

24. *See, e.g.,* Houston Police Officers' Union v. City of Houston, 330 F.3d 298, 306–07 (5th Cir. 2003); Cole v. City of Port Arthur, No. 1:13-CV-176, 2014 WL 3513366, at *8 (E.D. Tex. July 16, 2014). *See also* Hellmers v. Town of Vestal, 969 F. Supp. 837, 847–48 (N.D.N.Y. 1997) (genuine issue of material fact remained as to whether defendant employer's restrictions on the use of compensatory time were necessary to prevent an undue disruption of police operations).

25. *See, e.g., Cole,* 2014 WL 3513366, at *5.

26. Heitmann v. City of Chicago, 560 F.3d 642, 646–47 (7th Cir. 2009). *See also Houston Police Officers' Union,* 330 F.3d at 303 ("the language [i.e., reasonable time] offers a span of time to the employer, the beginning of which is the date of the employee's request").

Suppose Paradise were to adopt the same policy regarding comp-time use in a department other than the police department. Interestingly, as of the date of publication, there have been no reported cases on the denial of comp-time use arising in other types of departments. It seems reasonable to conclude, however, that for departments where minimum staffing is mission-critical, such as fire departments, emergency medical services agencies, telecommunicator agencies, and certain divisions of public works departments, policies such as the one in the hypothetical would pass muster. For other departments, especially those where the work is of a more long-term or ongoing nature, a minimum staffing requirement may be less likely to qualify as "unduly disruptive" to the employer than in the case of departments expected to respond immediately.

May an employer deny the use of comp time on the grounds that it would require calling in an employee from another division or shift or asking another employee to work overtime? The position of the U.S. Department of Labor (DOL) on this question has in the past been that the fact that an employer can accommodate a request to use comp time only by having another employee work overtime is not enough to make the request unduly disruptive. In the preamble commentary found in the Federal Register when the comp-time regulations were first published, DOL asserted the following.

> The Department recognizes that situations may arise in which overtime may be required of one employee to permit another employee to use compensatory time off. However, such a situation, in and of itself, would not be sufficient for an employer to claim that it is unduly disruptive.[27]

In a 1994 Opinion Letter, the DOL's Wage and Hour Administrator reaffirmed this position, noting that even where there is a collective bargaining agreement with a provision prohibiting the use of comp time where the employer would be forced to incur overtime costs, an outright ban on the use of comp time in such circumstances would violate FLSA Section 207(o)(5).[28] DOL's interpretation was cited as the basis for a Wisconsin federal district court's decision finding that a collective bargaining agreement violated the FLSA by providing that the city employer could deny the use of comp time if it would require the city to call in another police officer to work overtime or call in an officer from another location.[29]

Yet both DOL and the Wisconsin court recognized that requiring other officers to work overtime in order to honor another employee's request to use comp time could be unduly disruptive in some circumstances.[30] In the 1987 preamble

---

27. Application of the Fair Labor Standards Act to Employees of State and Local Governments, 52 Fed. Reg. 2012-01, pmbl. at 2017 (Jan. 16, 1987).

28. *See* U.S. Dep't of Labor, Emp't Standards Admin., Wage & Hour Div., Wage & Hour Opinion Letter, FLSA (Aug. 19, 1994), 1994 WL 1004861.

29. *See* DeBraska v. City of Milwaukee, 131 F. Supp. 2d 1032, 1037 (E.D. Wis. 2000).

30. *See id.* at 1037.

commentary to the FLSA regulations, DOL acknowledged the case-by-case nature of such a determination:

> The legislative history to the 1985 Amendments specifically clarifies that the term "unduly disrupt" means something more than mere inconvenience . . . . The [legislative] Reports provide an example that a request by a snow plow operator in Vermont or Maine to use compensatory time in February would probably be unduly disruptive even if the request were made well in advance. On the other hand, the same request by the same employee for compensatory time in June probably would not be unduly disruptive. As stated in the proposed rule, for an agency to refuse an employee's request for compensatory time off, it must be clear that the granting of such compensatory time off must result in an unreasonable burden on the agency's ability to provide services of acceptable quality and quantity. . . . it should be noted that *the legislative history . . . states that for those employees where the problem of disruption of services to the public is persistent, compensatory time should not be the preferred method of compensation for overtime work.* The Department believes the proposed rule accurately mirrors the legislative intent.[31]

It is clear that a blanket prohibition against the use of comp time when it would result in requiring another employee to work additional or overtime hours violates the FLSA, as least under DOL's interpretation of the law. It is also clear that mere inconvenience to the employer is not a sufficient basis on which to deny use of comp time. Can an employer achieve any more certainty than that in administering comp-time use? The answer to this question is yes. If an employer includes specific conditions on the use of comp time—conditions that do not include a blanket prohibition—in an agreement that it enters into with employees, DOL and the courts will generally honor the agreement.

Incorporating Restrictions on the Use of Comp Time into the Employer's Comp-Time Policy or Agreement

As discussed above, before a public employer can avail itself of the compensatory time-off alternative, it must reach an agreement with employees as to its use—even if, from the employee's perspective, the employer has all of the bargaining power. One way in which an employer can obtain certainty is by incorporating the conditions under which comp time may be used into the agreement itself, whatever form the agreement takes.

> The use of compensatory time in lieu of cash payment for overtime must be pursuant to some form of agreement or understanding between the employer and the employee . . . reached prior to the performance of the

---

31. 52 Fed. Reg. 2012-01, pmbl. at 2017 (emphasis added).

work . . . . To the extent that the . . . conditions under which an employee can take compensatory time off are contained in an agreement or understanding as defined in [29 C.F.R.] § 553.23, the terms of such agreement or understanding will govern the meaning of "reasonable period".[32]

DOL does not have to review the terms of such agreements prospectively.[33]

The U.S. Supreme Court has not had occasion to address the legal constraints on policies governing the use of comp time. In *dicta* (a discussion of a point not necessary to the holding), the Court has said that Section 207(o)(5) of the FLSA should be read as a minimal guarantee that an employee will be able to make some use of compensatory time when he or she requests to use it. Federal appeals courts, however, have addressed the issue. Some courts have found that even policies that are relatively inflexible when it comes to the use of comp time are valid provided that they are clearly part of an agreement between the employer and its employees. In the federal Fifth Circuit Court of Appeals case *Aiken v. City of Memphis*,[34] for example, a collective bargaining agreement provided that the reasonable period for requesting the use of accrued comp time began thirty days prior to the requested date and ended when the number of officers requesting the use of comp time on the given date would bring the precinct's staffing levels below the minimum necessary for efficient operation. The necessary result of this policy was that the city did not pay replacement officers overtime pay to permit other employees to use their accrued comp time. In *Aiken*, the Fifth Circuit found nothing in the agreement that violated any requirement of the FLSA and therefore found no reason to interfere with the agreement because the comp-time regulations give express authorization to enter into agreements that define the scope of a reasonable period for the use of comp time.[35] In a case with similar facts, the federal Ninth Circuit Court of Appeals also found no violation of the FLSA in a leave policy that (1) allowed the county employer to deny comp-time use on a specific date if all of a predetermined number of leave openings had already been filled but (2) guaranteed an officer the opportunity to use leave within one year of the request.[36]

Some Final Considerations

As the regulations and cases that discuss the meaning of "reasonable period" and "unduly burden" make clear, an employer's ability to condition the terms under which employees may use comp time does not depend upon whether the parties' agreement on the issue is one entered into through collective bargaining (unlawful for public

---

32. 29 C.F.R. § 553.25(c)(2).

33. 52 Fed. Reg. 2012-01, pmbl. at 2017 ("The Department, however, believes that some parties may choose to include in their agreement or understanding the conditions or terms regarding the taking of compensatory time off. No useful purpose would be served in the Department's view, by providing for some further review under the FLSA of the appropriateness of the agreed upon terms.").

34. 190 F.3d 753 (5th Cir. 1999).

35. *See* 29 C.F.R. § 553.25(c)(1). *See also Aiken*, 190 F.3d at 755–57, citing that regulation.

36. *See* Mortensen v. Cty. of Sacramento, 368 F.3d 1082, 1086–90 (9th Cir. 2004).

entities in North Carolina) or through individual written or oral agreements.[37] What is important is that the conditions attached to comp-time use are set out clearly and understood by employees before they begin to work their overtime hours. Employers should avoid taking a short cut by specifying a specific number or percentage of employees who may use comp time on any given day, as the few courts that have considered this approach have not been well-disposed toward it.[38]

Managing Large Accruals of Comp Time

One way in which employers can manage accrued comp time is to send any employee with accrued comp time home, even at a time when the employee has not requested its use, for example, when an employee's department or section is experiencing slower work periods. Employees may not object to being sent home since they are not being sent home without pay—comp time is *paid* time off.[39] Employers may also adopt policies that either allow or require employees to use comp time before they use accrued paid sick or vacation leave. Similarly, either an employer or an employee may require that accrued comp time run concurrently with FMLA leave, turning unpaid leave into paid leave.[40] Finally, employers can set limits lower than 240 hours, or 480 hours for public safety employees, on the amount of comp time employees may accrue. They will necessarily have to pay overtime in cash once the lower limit is reached, but there will be fewer days of compensatory time off that require accommodation.

Accrued Comp Time That Remains at Separation

Comp time may only be used in the manner authorized by the FLSA itself and by the DOL's FLSA regulations. **Accrued FLSA comp time may not be made subject to a "use it or lose it" policy, nor may it be converted to sick or vacation leave**; neither the statute nor the regulations authorize its use in this way. Comp time accrues indefinitely until the statutory maximums of 480 hours for public safety employees and 240 hours for all other nonexempt employees are reached. At that point, the accrued hours remain credited to the employee indefinitely until used or paid out in cash, and any additional overtime hours that the employee works must be paid out in cash.

---

37. *See* 29 C.F.R. §§ 553.23(a), .25(c)(2). In fact, the majority of cases arise in the collective-bargaining context.

38. *See supra* note 12.

39. *See* Christensen v. Harris Cty., 529 U.S. 576, 583 (2000) (section of FLSA requiring public employer to honor employee's reasonable request to use compensatory time did not prohibit employer from forcing employees to use accrued compensatory time).

40. *See* 29 C.F.R. § 825.207.

The text of the FLSA is clear that upon separation from service, whether because of retirement, a voluntary departure for a position with another employer, or involuntary termination, employers must pay out any accrued comp time

> at a rate of compensation not less than—
> (A) The average regular rate received by such employee during the last 3 years of the employee's employment, or
> (B) the final regular rate received by such employee,
> whichever is higher.[41]

Overtime or Comp Time for FLSA Exempt Employees

The preceding discussion of comp time concerned employees who are not exempt from the overtime requirements of the FLSA. For exempt employees, the statute does not require payment of overtime at all, of course. Yet the FLSA regulations expressly allow employers to pay exempt employees additional compensation for hours worked beyond what is expected without jeopardizing the employee's exemption from overtime pay. The rules allow such additional compensation to be paid on any basis, including paid time off.[42] North Carolina local government employers typically refer to this additional or bonus time off for exempt employees as a form of "comp time," or compensatory time off, although they would be wise to give it another name in order to avoid confusion. For this reason, this book will refer to additional paid time off for exempt employees as "bonus time off."

Although comp time for nonexempt employees must be granted on the basis of one and one-half hours off for every hour worked in excess of forty hours, bonus time off for exempt employees may be structured in whatever way the local government employer chooses. Bonus time off may be granted to exempt employees when they have worked in excess of forty hours (or some other number), in excess of their scheduled hours, or in excess of a certain number of hours per month. The time off may be calculated on the basis of one and one-half hours off for each extra hour worked, on an hour-for-hour basis, or even on the basis of a half-hour off for each extra hour worked. Because this is a benefit that is not required by law, employers may structure it however they choose.

Unlike comp time for nonexempt employees, which cannot accrue in excess of 240 hours (480 hours for public safety employees), bonus time off for exempt employees may accrue without limit. Employers may restrict the carry-over of accrued bonus time off for exempt employees from year to year, in contrast with comp time for nonexempt employees, which remains on the books indefinitely. There is no requirement that bonus time off for exempt employees be paid out to employees when they leave or retire from the employer's service.

---

41. 29 U.S.C. § 207(o)(4); 29 C.F.R. § 553.27.
42. *See* 29 C.F.R. § 541.604.

Nonexempt Employee Comp Time in a Nutshell

1. Comp time is accrued at the rate of one and one-half hours paid time off for every hour of overtime that is worked.

2. For a comp-time policy to be lawful under the FLSA, employees must have an "agreement" with the employer about the policy.

3. When an employer uses comp time instead of cash overtime, it may not allow employees to accrue more than 240 hours of comp time (or 480 hours if the employee works in public safety). Once an employee accrues 240 (or 480) hours, any additional overtime must be paid in cash.

4. An employer must allow an employee to use accrued comp time within a reasonable time after the employee requests the comp time.

5. An employer may send employees home, at times of the employer's choosing, and may require employees to use comp time before sick or vacation leave.

6. Unused comp time never goes away. Upon separation, it must be paid out.

7. An employer may award *exempt* employees who work a greater number of hours than scheduled with paid time off. In contrast to FLSA comp time for nonexempt employees, exempt employee bonus time off may be credited at any rate and subject to any conditions the employer chooses.

The Fluctuating Workweek Exemption to the Overtime Rule

The fluctuating workweek is a second exception to the basic overtime rule. Consider the following hypothetical.

> John is an emergency medical services (EMS) dispatcher whose hours vary unpredictably from week to week. He always works at least forty hours per week, but some weeks he works forty-two hours, other weeks he works forty-eight hours, and occasionally he works close to sixty hours. Ellen is a water-plant operator whose weekly hours vary as well, but they vary on a scheduled basis. Ellen works thirty-two hours every first and third week of the month and forty-eight hours every second and fourth week. Both John and Ellen are FLSA nonexempt employees. The city for which John and Ellen work pays cash overtime instead of using compensatory time off. Yet neither John nor Ellen earns overtime at the rate of time-and-one-half. Without violating the FLSA, the city pays both John and Ellen at just one-half their regular rate of pay for each hour over forty that they work in a given work week.

How can that be? The answer is that the city uses the fluctuating workweek.

Requirements for Using the Fluctuating Workweek Alternative

The text of the FLSA itself says nothing about fluctuating workweeks, but the DOL regulations implementing the FLSA set out an entire section explaining the circumstances under which employers may use this alternative method of calculating overtime when employees work hours that fluctuate from week to week.[43] This method is called the "fluctuating workweek method." It provides for (1) the payment of an unchanging salary that compensates the employee for all hours worked in a given week regardless of whether the employee works fewer or greater than forty hours a week and (2) payment for overtime hours at a rate of one-half the employee's regular rate of pay.

To use the fluctuating workweek method of payment, five requirements must be met:

1. the employee must work hours that fluctuate from week to week;
2. the employee must be paid a fixed salary that serves as compensation for all hours worked;
3. the fixed salary must be large enough to compensate the employee for all hours worked at a rate not less than the minimum wage;
4. the employee must be paid an additional one-half of the regular rate for all overtime hours worked; and
5. there must be a "clear *mutual* understanding" that the fixed salary is compensation for however many hours the employee may work in a particular week, rather than for a fixed number of hours per week.

Let's look more closely at each of these requirements.

1. The Employee Must Work Fluctuating Hours

Section 778.114 says that this method of payment may be used for employees with "hours of work which fluctuate from week to week" and that it is "typically" used to pay "employees who do not customarily work a regular schedule of hours."[44] Nevertheless, nothing in the regulation *requires* that the employee's hours be unpredictable or unknowable in advance. Two federal Fourth Circuit Court of Appeals decisions involving North Carolina public employers make that clear. In both *Flood v. New Hanover County* and *Griffin v. Wake County*, the court found that a work schedule in which the plaintiff employee's hours varied on a regular, predictable basis satisfied the requirement that the employee's hours fluctuate from week to week.[45]

In addition, nothing requires that the fluctuation include some weeks where the hours worked are fewer than forty and some where the hours worked are greater than forty. All the regulation requires is that the employee's hours fluctuate from week

---

43. *See* 29 C.F.R. § 778.114.

44. *Id.* at (a), (c).

45. Flood v. New Hanover Cty., 125 F.3d 249, 253 (4th Cir. 1997); Griffin v. Wake Cty., 142 F.3d 712, 715 (4th Cir. 1998).

to week. In the *Flood* case, the Fourth Circuit held that the employer could use the fluctuating workweek method to compensate employees working a rotating schedule of 48.3, 56.3, 64.45, and 72.45 hours per week.[46] The Seventh Circuit Court of Appeals reached a similar conclusion in the case *Condo v. Sysco Corp.*[47] Putting this together, it is clear that in the example above, both John (who works unpredictable hours but always more than forty hours per week) and Ellen (whose schedule varies on a regular basis) may be compensated using the fluctuating workweek method of payment.

2. The Employee Must Be Paid a Fixed Salary

The fluctuating workweek method of payment requires that the employer pay the employee a fixed salary each week. The amount cannot vary based on the number of hours worked. In the example above, John, the EMS dispatcher, is paid $675 per week, while Ellen, the water-plant operator, is paid $800 per week. John is paid $675 whether he works forty-two, forty-eight, or fifty-seven hours in a given week. John's weekly salary would still be $675 if, during a particular week, he worked only thirty hours. Ellen is paid $800 whether she is working one of the thirty-two-hour weeks or one of the forty-eight-hour weeks on her schedule.

3. The Rate Must Be at Least Minimum Wage

The salary used to compensate an employee under the fluctuating workweek method can be of any amount, with only one proviso: the salary must be large enough that the regular rate—the amount found by dividing the employee's fixed salary by the total number of hours worked in any week—is at least equal to the minimum wage. The regular rate of pay will vary from week to week because the hours that the employee works fluctuate from week to week. Even in a week where John the EMS dispatcher works fifty-seven hours, his regular rate of pay remains above the current minimum wage of $7.25 per hour ($675 ÷ 57 = $11.85/hour). If John somehow worked so many hours that his regular rate dipped below minimum wage, the city would have to raise his salary for that week so that he earned minimum wage.

4. Overtime Hours Are Compensated at One-Half the Regular Rate

Under the fluctuating workweek method, the fixed salary is defined as compensation for **all** hours that an employee has worked in any workweek. That is, the payment of the salary is compensation at the regular rate of pay for all of the hours the employee works in that week, including overtime hours. For the hours below forty, the employee is compensated by his or her fixed salary. For hours over forty, the employee is compensated for the "time" in "time-and-one-half" by the fixed salary. Since the employer has already paid the employee the regular rate for all of the hours he or she has worked (including the hours over forty) by payment of the salary, the employer owes the employee just one-half of the regular rate for the hours over forty.

---

46. *See Flood*, 125 F.3d at 253.

47. 1 F.3d 599, 603 (7th Cir. 1993) (where employee's hours fluctuated above but not below forty hours per week, employer could choose to compensate employee pursuant to system set forth in 29 C.F.R. § 778.114).

Thus, if John the EMS dispatcher works forty-nine and one-half hours one week, his employer must pay him his fixed salary of $675 and nine and one-half hours of overtime pay at one-half his regular rate of pay for that week. On weeks during which Ellen the water-plant operator works thirty-two hours, she receives her fixed salary of $800—no more and no less. On weeks during which Ellen works forty-eight hours, her employer must pay her fixed salary of $800 and eight hours of overtime pay at one-half her regular rate of pay.

5. The Employer and Employee Must Have a "Clear, Mutual Understanding" that the Salary Is for All Hours Worked, Not for a Specified Number of Hours

Usually, when an employer pays an FLSA nonexempt employee on a salaried basis, the employer and employee understand that the salary is meant to compensate the employee for a regular schedule with a fixed set of hours: "We will pay $800 for a forty-hour week." But it is different when an employer uses the fluctuating workweek. An employer may use the fluctuating workweek method only if it has made two points clear to the employee before the employee starts work under this payment method: first, that the fixed salary will be compensation for however many hours the employee works in a week and that the salary will not increase in weeks in which the employee works a greater number of hours and second, that any hours over forty will be compensated at one-half the regular rate for that week. Employees do not have to "agree"—in the sense of "consent"—to the use of the fluctuating workweek method. They merely have to be told about its use.[48] Reporting to work implies consent.

Why Use the Fluctuating Workweek Method?

For most employers, the primary reason for using the fluctuating workweek method is to reduce overtime costs. DOL and the federal courts take pains to emphasize that the fluctuating workweek method is not an exception to the overtime rule (although this book treats it as one) but is, rather, merely an alternative method of paying overtime. Theoretically, an employer using the fluctuating workweek method is already paying some of the costs of overtime up front in the fixed salary, and neither the employer nor the employee is receiving a break or being cheated.

In reality, however, employers pay only one-third (one-half of the regular rate) of the additional amount that must be paid to a nonexempt employee working more than forty hours a week. Where overtime hours are unpredictable, this reduces the amount of potentially unbudgeted overtime liability. Because the regular rate is calculated anew each week based on the total number of straight and overtime hours worked that week, the cost of each hour of overtime to the employer goes down the greater the number of overtime hours an employee works.

From an employee's perspective, it looks like the greater the number of hours worked, the less the employee is paid. Not surprisingly, the fluctuating workweek is not popular among employees who work a substantial amount of overtime. For those employees who work fewer than forty hours a week on a recurring basis, however, the fluctuating workweek can provide a more predictable income.

---

48. *See Griffin*, 142 F.3d at 715–17.

The Bottom Line on the Fluctuating Workweek

Local government employers with employees whose hours vary from week to week may choose to use the fluctuating workweek method of payment, but they do not have to do so. This method may be used to compensate dispatchers, emergency medical services personnel, law enforcement officers and firefighters, water- and wastewater-plant operators, and any other positions where operating needs require scheduling that results in workweeks in which the number of hours worked changes from week to week. It may not be used for employees (law enforcement officers and firefighters) who are being compensated under the Section 207(k) exemption (discussed in more detail below).

Overtime Pay Exceptions for Law Enforcement and Firefighting Employees: The Section 207(k) Exemption

Law enforcement officers and firefighters present a bookkeeping and payroll challenge because they frequently work shifts of twelve or twenty-four hours and may be scheduled to work these shifts several days in a row, accumulating a lot of hours quickly. One might say that law enforcement officers and firefighters work the ultimate fluctuating workweek. In addition to the fluctuating workweek method, the FLSA offers an additional overtime option to public employers: the Section 207(k) exemption for law enforcement officers and firefighters. While the fluctuating workweek method, discussed above, may be used for any employee whose hours fluctuate, the 207(k) exemption, in contrast, is limited to law enforcement officers and firefighters as those positions are defined in the statute. This exemption is called the 207(k) exemption because it is found at Section 207(k) of Title 29 of the U.S. Code (it is sometimes called the 7(k) exemption after its location in the original bill). The 207(k) exemption is well-liked by law enforcement agencies and fire departments because it makes calculating the overtime of their employees more efficient and because it reduces overtime costs in a small, but real, way.

How the 207(k) Exemption Works

The 207(k) exemption allows public employers to figure overtime compensation for law enforcement and fire employees on the basis of work periods longer than the standard one-week work period that applies to all other employees. The work period can be as long as twenty-eight days. The employer still maintains whatever payroll schedule it prefers—weekly, bi-weekly or monthly—and law enforcement officers and firefighters still get paid on that schedule. But overtime premium pay for law enforcement officers and firefighters is determined and paid out at the end of the 207(k) work period. Employers do not have to schedule all of their law enforcement or firefighting employees using the 207(k) exemption. They may choose to limit the use of the 207(k) exemption to those categories, ranks, or shifts of employee for which the exemption would be most useful. Employers may also use 207(k) work periods of different lengths for different categories of law enforcement or firefighting employees.[49] For example, a city police department might choose to keep its detectives on a regular forty-hour, seven-day workweek and not avail itself of the 207(k) exemption because the detectives generally keep Monday through Friday, 9 a.m. to 5 p.m. hours. It might put its patrol officers on a twenty-eight-day work schedule but have its sergeants work on a fourteen-day schedule. The department does not need to have any special justification for using different work schedules. If it finds scheduling its nonexempt law enforcement personnel in this way advantageous, it may do so.

When a law enforcement agency uses the longest possible work period—28 consecutive days—law enforcement officers earn time-and-one-half overtime pay only after they have worked 171 hours within that 28-day work period. For firefighters on a 28-day work schedule, overtime is earned only after 212 hours.[50] The FLSA regulations allow law enforcement agencies and fire departments to use the 207(k) exemption for work periods of **any** length between seven and twenty-eight days and to prorate accordingly the number of hours that must be worked before overtime pay is required.[51] Most departments use work periods that are multiples of seven. Those multiples work out this way:

	Law Enforcement	Fire Protection
28 days	171 hours	212 hours
14 days	86 hours	106 hours
7 days	43 hours	53 hours[52]

Employers do not have to align their duty schedules with the 207(k) schedule. In other words, an officer's or firefighter's shift or tour of duty could span the end of one 207(k) work period and the beginning of another.[53] Employers do not have to alter their pay schedules to align with a 207(k) work period.[54] Consider the following example.

The City of Paradise uses the 207(k) exemption and a twenty-eight-day work schedule for both its law enforcement and firefighting employees. The city pays its employees on a weekly basis. For the first three paydays in the twenty-eight-day cycle, employees receive their regular straight-time rate for all of the hours they have worked the preceding week. Then, on the fourth payday, they receive their regular straight-time compensation and any overtime due for the entire twenty-eight-day pay period.

The situation is a little bit different in Paradise County. As in the city, law enforcement and firefighters work a twenty-eight-day schedule, but the

49. *See* 29 C.F.R. § 553.224(b).
50. *See* 29 C.F.R. § 553.201(a).
51. *See* 29 C.F.R. §§ 553.230(a), (b).
52. *See* 29 C.F.R. § 553.230(c).
53. *See* 29 C.F.R. § 553.224(a).
54. *See id.*

county pays its employees on a bi-weekly basis. Here, employees working under the 207(k) exemption receive their regular straight-time rate for all of the hours they have worked during the first two weeks on the first bi-weekly pay period of the twenty-eight-day cycle. They receive their regular straight-time compensation for the second two weeks and any overtime due for that twenty-eight-day pay period on the second bi-weekly pay period of that cycle.

The 207(k) Exemption and Comp Time

Employees scheduled in accordance with Section 207(k) may be compensated for overtime hours worked with compensatory time off rather than with cash overtime pay, just like employees on a regular seven-day work period.[55]

Establishing the 207(k) Exemption

Law enforcement agencies and fire departments do not have to obtain permission from DOL and do not need the agreement of their employees to adopt a twenty-eight-day work schedule and use the 207(k) exemption. The FLSA regulations merely say that the 207(k) work period must be "established" and "regularly recurring" for the exemption to apply.[56] Employers must also satisfy two recordkeeping requirements. First, the adoption of the schedule must be documented in the employer's payroll records, along with the length of the work period (that is, twenty-eight days, fourteen days, or whatever it is) and the starting date and time of each work period. Second, the payroll notation should state that the schedule has been adopted pursuant to Section 207(k) of the FLSA and 29 C.F.R. Part 553.[57]

The burden of proof that the employer has actually established a 207(k) schedule is on the employer.[58] Public safety personnel have sometimes argued that the adoption of the 207(k) exemption must be made by a public announcement of some sort, but that argument has been routinely rejected by the courts.[59] The courts have held, for example, that an inter-office memorandum from a city manager to staff announcing the adoption of the use of the 207(k) exemption, plus the actual use of a twenty-eight-day schedule was sufficient proof that the city had established the exemption.[60] In fact, public employers do not even have to express a specific intent to use the 207(k)

---

55. *See* 29 C.F.R. §§ 553.201(b); 553.231.

56. *See* 29 C.F.R. § 553.224(a).

57. *See* 29 C.F.R. § 553.51.

58. *See* Birdwell v. City of Gadsden, 970 F.2d 802 (11th Cir. 1992); Barefield v. Vill. of Winnetka, 81 F.3d 704, 709 (7th Cir. 1996); Lamon v. City of Shawnee, 972 F.2d 1145, 1151 (10th Cir. 1992) (finding that even though city had never used the work period it had previously adopted, it still qualified for the 207(k) exemption).

59. *See, e.g.,* Calvao v. Town of Framingham, 599 F.3d 10, 18 (1st Cir. 2010); Spradling v. City of Tulsa, 95 F.3d 1492, 1505 (10th Cir. 1996).

60. *See* Milner v. Hazelwood, 165 F.3d 1222, 1223 (8th Cir. 1998).

exemption in order to use it.[61] An employer's actual practices can suffice as proof that it has established a 207(k) work schedule.[62]

Who Qualifies as a Law Enforcement Officer or Firefighter for 207(k) Purposes?

Not every employee of a law enforcement agency or fire department may be compensated using the 207(k) exemption. The exemption is limited to sworn law enforcement officers and to those with the legal authority to fight fires.

Law Enforcement Officers

For purposes of the 207(k) exemption, the FLSA regulations define law enforcement officers as

- "uniformed or plainclothed member[s] of a body of officers,"
- who have the statutory power to enforce the law,
- who have the power to make arrests, and
- who have participated in a special course of law enforcement training.[63]

Employees engaged in law enforcement activities may not spend more than 20 percent of their time on work that does not qualify as a law enforcement activity or as work incidental to such an activity, although they may engage in occasional or sporadic work of a different kind, just like any other nonexempt employee.[64]

The regulations provide that an unsworn jailer counts as a law enforcement officer for 207(k) purposes, but other civilian employees of the police or sheriff's department do not.[65] Also not included in the definition of law enforcement officer for 207(k) purposes are inspectors and compliance officers, such as building and health inspectors, animal control officers, and building guards who are not sworn law enforcement officers.[66]

Firefighters

A firefighter is defined for 207(k) purposes as an employee, including a firefighter, paramedic, emergency medical technician, rescue worker, ambulance personnel, or hazardous materials worker, who—

- is trained in fire suppression,
- has the legal authority and responsibility to engage in fire suppression, and
- is employed by a fire department of a municipality, county, fire district, or State; and

---

61. *See Rosano v. Twp. of Teaneck*, 754 F.3d 177, 188 (3d Cir. 2014); *Barefield*, 81 F.3d at 710.
62. *See* Singer v. City of Waco, 324 F.3d 813, 819 (5th Cir. 2003); Wood v. City of Elgin, No. 07 C 05418, 2008 WL 4545334, at *3 (N.D. Ill. Oct. 9, 2008) (city's practices established use of 207(k) work schedule even where collective bargaining agreement said otherwise).
63. 29 C.F.R. § 553.211(a).
64. 29 C.F.R. § 553.212(a). *See also* 29 U.S.C. § 207(p)(2); 29 C.F.R. § 553.30.
65. *See* 29 C.F.R. §§ 553.211(f), (g).
66. *See* 29 C.F.R. § 553.211(e).

- is engaged in the prevention, control, and extinguishment of fires or response to emergency situations where life, property, or the environment is at risk.[67]

No other employees of a fire department may be compensated using the 207(k) exemption.[68]

Ordinarily, fire inspectors and fire marshals do not qualify for the 207(k) exemption. Notwithstanding the fact that fire marshals and investigators indirectly work to prevent fires by investigating the causes of fires, identifying arsonists, and engaging in public education about fires, such activities do not qualify as being directly engaged in the prevention of fires.[69] As with law enforcement employees, employees engaged in fire protection activities may engage in occasional or sporadic work of a different kind, just like any other nonexempt employee.[70] Unlike law enforcement personnel, however, firefighters are not subject to the 20 percent limitation on time spent on work that does not qualify as a fire protection activity or one incidental thereto. As explained below, fire protection activities can include responding to emergency situations where life is at risk, bringing dual-function firefighters/emergency medical personnel within the exemption's ambit.[71]

Emergency Medical Services Personnel and the 207(k) Exemption

Section 207(k) and its implementing regulations are clear that so long as an employee meets the definition of an employee engaged in law enforcement activities or in fire protection activities, that employee qualifies for the 207(k) exemption. That can include emergency medical services (EMS) employees in some instances. No doubt because EMS is frequently housed within a fire department, the FLSA regulations explicitly say with respect to an employee engaged in fire protection activities that a "paramedic, emergency medical technician, rescue worker, [or] ambulance personnel"

---

67. 29 C.F.R. § 553.210(a) (numbered subsections omitted).

68. *See* 29 U.S.C. § 203(y); 29 C.F.R. § 553.210(a).

69. *See* Lockwood v. Prince George's Cty., 217 F.3d 839, at *3 (4th Cir. 2000) (per curiam) (holding that fire investigators are not "employees engaged in fire protection activities for purposes of [section] 207(k)").

70. *See* 29 C.F.R. § 553.212(b).

71. In 1999, Congress amended the FLSA at 29 U.S.C. § 203 by adding a new subsection (y) to define the term "employee in fire protection activities." DOL, however, did not amend the FLSA regulations to reflect the change in the definition of "employee engaged in fire protection activities" until 2011. In amending 29 C.F.R. §§ 553.210 and 553.212, DOL deleted the reference to "employees engaged in fire protection" from § 553.212(a), which had allowed covered employees to spend up to 20 percent of their time on work not related to law enforcement *or fire protection* activities, but kept the 20 percent limitation for employees engaged in law enforcement activities. DOL also deleted former § 553.215, which provided for the inclusion of emergency medical personnel employed in other public agencies in the 207(k) exemption under certain circumstances. *See* Updating Regulations Issued Under the Fair Labor Standards Act, 76 Fed. Reg. 18,832, pmbl. at 18,837 (Apr. 5, 2011). These changes rendered the Fourth Circuit's decisions in *Adams v. City of Norfolk*, 274 F.3d 148 (2001), *Roy v. County of Lexington*, 141 F.3d 533 (1998), and *West v. Anne Arundel County*, 137 F.3d 752 (1998), no longer applicable to the question of when dual-function firefighter/paramedic positions qualify for the 207(k) exemption.

may qualify for the exemption if he or she is *cross-trained* to engage in fire protection work, has the legal authority and responsibility to fight fires, and is employed by a municipal, county, or state fire department.[72] The FLSA does not require that the employee actually engage in fire suppression work on a regular or even on an occasional basis. It requires only that employees be engaged either in fire prevention and suppression *or* in responding to "emergency situations where life, property, or the environment is at risk."[73]

There are a number of cases addressing the application of the 207(k) exemption to EMS personnel who are cross-trained in fire protection. Most focus on the issue of whether or not the EMS personnel in question have the *legal responsibility* to engage in fire suppression. DOL has cited with approval a six-factor test applied by the federal Ninth Circuit Court of Appeals for determining whether a dual-function firefighter/paramedic has "some real obligation or duty" to engage in fire suppression. The six factors are:

1. whether the paramedic ambulances carry firefighting equipment or breathing apparatuses;
2. whether dispatchers know whether the paramedics they are sending to a call are single- or dual-function paramedics;
3. whether paramedic ambulances are regularly dispatched to fire scenes or whether they are dispatched only when there appears to be a need for advanced life-support medical services;
4. whether dual-function paramedics are expected to wear fire-protective gear;
5. whether dual-function paramedics are dispatched to a variety of incidents, such as vehicle accidents or crime scenes, at which they are expected to perform only medical services, and
6. whether there is evidence that a dual-function paramedic has ever been ordered to perform fire suppression.[74]

Where dual-function paramedics were thoroughly cross-trained to fight fires and had the legal authority to do so, wore fire protection gear and carried breathing apparatus, were ordered to all fire scenes, and were routinely ordered to perform fire suppression duties, DOL concluded that they qualified as employees engaged in fire protection activities and thus were eligible for the 207(k) exemption.[75] Conversely, where paramedics were not expected to wear fire protective gear and paramedic

---

72. *See* 29 C.F.R. § 553.210(a).

73. *See* 29 U.S.C. § 203(y); 29 C.F.R. § 553.210(a). *See also* U.S. Dep't of Labor, Emp't Standards Admin., Wage & Hour Div., Wage & Hour Opinion Letter, FLSA 2006-20 (June 1, 2006), https://www.dol.gov/whd/opinion/FLSA/2006/2006_06_01_20_FLSA.pdf.

74. *See id., citing* Cleveland v. City of Los Angeles, 420 F.3d 981, 990, *cert. denied*, 126 S. Ct. 1344 (2006). *See also* Gonzalez v. City of Deerfield Beach, 510 F. Supp. 2d 1037, 1040–42 (2007).

75. *See* U.S. Dep't of Labor, Emp't Standards Admin., Wage & Hour Div. (DOL), Wage & Hour Opinion Letter, FLSA 2006-20, *supra* note 73. See also the following opinion letter

ambulances did not carry firefighting equipment, dispatchers did not know whether they were dispatching straight paramedics or dual-function paramedic/firefighters, paramedic ambulances were dispatched to fire scenes only when there was a need for medical services and were regularly dispatched to many different kinds of emergencies, and there was no evidence that a dual-function paramedic was ever ordered to engage in fire suppression, the Ninth Circuit found that the so-called dual-function paramedics did not have the responsibility to fight fires.[76] The federal Eleventh Circuit Court of Appeals, on the other hand, found that the term "responsibility" did not, by itself, require that dual-function paramedics had to actually engage in fire suppression to satisfy the requirement that they have "legal authority and responsibility to engage in fire suppression." The court reasoned that the accepted definition of "responsibility" referred to a duty that a person might or might not ever be called upon to perform.[77] So where dual-function paramedics had advanced firefighting training, were equipped with "turn-out" gear, were sent regularly to fire scenes, and were required to be available to assist with fire suppression if needed and had fire suppression included among their listed job duties, the Eleventh Circuit found them to have a responsibility to fight fires, even if they had never been called upon to do so.[78]

The federal Fourth Circuit Court of Appeals has not addressed this issue. The cases discussed above seem to turn not on whether cross-trained EMS employees actually engaged in firefighting but on whether they were routinely put in positions where they could be asked to assist in fire suppression by being regularly summoned to the scene of fires and by being required to carry fire equipment and turn-out gear.

Other Public Safety Employees

As discussed above, some jurisdictions place emergency medical personnel under the supervision of a law enforcement agency or fire department. This arrangement is lawful and makes organizational sense for some cities and counties. But as the preceding sections discuss, an employee whose primary job duty is the provision of emergency medical services does not qualify for the 207(k) exemption unless he or she meets the statutory and regulatory definitions of either a law enforcement officer or a firefighter. Several North Carolina local governments cross-train and cross-utilize their public safety personnel in this way, but most do not.

The positions of telecommunicator and public safety dispatcher, as well as emergency medical personnel who are not cross-trained, are positions that local governments typically place within one of their public safety agencies. But despite being part of a law enforcement or fire agency, these positions are not engaged in law

---

from DOL: Wage & Hour Opinion Letter, FLSA 2005-9NA (Sept. 9, 2005), https://www.dol.gov/whd/opinion/FLSANA/2005/2005_09_09_9NA_FLSA.htm.

76. See Cleveland, 420 F.3d at 990.

77. See Huff v. DeKalb Cty., 516 F.3d 1273, 1280–81 (11th Cir. 2008).

78. See id. at 1281–82.

enforcement or firefighting activities, and their employers may not schedule them under the 207(k) exemption. This is true even where a sworn officer or a firefighter is serving as a telecommunicator or dispatcher.[79]

Special Rules for Compensable Time for 207(k) Employees

With two exceptions, law enforcement and firefighting employees working under a 207(k) work schedule are subject to the same rules with respect to determining which activities and what work time are compensable as are nonexempt law enforcement or fire employees working a normal forty-hour, seven-day workweek.[80] The exceptions apply to meal times and sleep times.

Bona Fide Meal Periods for 207(k) Law Enforcement Officers

Although the meal-period rules for officers scheduled under the 207(k) exemption are set forth separately from the general rule governing the compensability of meal periods, the rules are the same substantively. Employers may exclude meal periods of at least thirty uninterrupted minutes from the compensable time of law enforcement officers on a tour of either exactly twenty-four or fewer than twenty-four hours[81] or on a tour of more than twenty-four hours.[82] An officer's meal period cannot be excluded if the officer is on call.[83]

Bona Fide Meal Periods for 207(k) Firefighters

Employers may not exclude a 207(k) firefighter's meal periods from compensable time, even if they are thirty minutes in length and uninterrupted, if that firefighter is on duty for either exactly twenty-four hours or fewer than twenty-four hours.[84] When a firefighter is on duty for more than twenty-four hours, meal periods may be excluded from compensable time if they are at least thirty minutes long and the firefighter has been completely relieved of duties.[85] The meal period cannot be excluded if the firefighter is on call.[86]

Sleep Time for Both 207(k) Law Enforcement Officers and 207(k) Firefighters

For 207(k) personnel, a shift or tour of duty must be more than twenty-four hours long for sleep time to be excluded from compensable time. The following requirements must also be met.

1. no more than eight hours of sleep can be excluded from compensable time,
2. the employee must have given either express or implied agreement to the exclusion,

---

79. *See, e.g.*, U.S. Dep't of Labor, Emp't Standards Admin., Wage & Hour Div., Wage & Hour Opinion Letter, FLSA 2006-36 (Sept. 28, 2006), https://www.dol.gov/whd/opinion/FLSA/2006/2006_09_28_36_FLSA.pdf.

80. *See* 29 C.F.R. § 553.221.

81. *See* 29 C.F.R. §§ 223(a) & (b), 785.19, .22.

82. *See* 29 C.F.R. § 553.223(d).

83. *See* 29 C.F.R. § 785.19(a).

84. *See* 29 C.F.R. § 553.223(c).

85. *See* 29 C.F.R. §§ 553.223(d), 785.19, .22.

86. *See* 29 C.F.R. § 785.19(a).

3. the employer must provide adequate sleeping facilities, and
4. the employee must be able to get at least five hours of uninterrupted sleep. [87]

On 207(k) shifts that are exactly twenty-four hours long or are fewer than twenty-four hours long, sleep time may not be excluded from compensable time. This is different from the regular sleep-time rule, which allows for shifts of exactly twenty-four hours to be excluded.[88]

Special-Detail Assignments for Law Enforcement and Fire Protection Personnel

Under the "special-detail assignments" provision of the FLSA regulations, employees who engage in law enforcement or fire protection activities as defined by the FLSA may agree to work so-called special-detail assignments for **separate and independent employers** without the hours worked on such special-detail assignments counting toward overtime with their primary public employers.[89] Examples of special-detail assignments include law enforcement officers hired to provide security for a concert or sporting event at a privately-owned arena or firefighters engaged as stand-by first responders for a traveling carnival or hired to spring into action should anything catch fire at a private fireworks display. **The employee must accept the special-detail assignment voluntarily for the exemption to apply.** If the law enforcement or fire agency assigns an employee to special-detail duty as a requirement of the employee's primary employment, the exemption is not available and the hours worked will count toward overtime with the primary agency.[90] A public employer may maintain a list of employees available to work special detail and may choose the employees to work individual special-detail assignments from that list.[91]

Wages for a special-detail assignment may either be paid directly to a participating employee by the separate and independent employer or may be made to the employing agency and processed through the local government's payroll. The local government may negotiate with the separate and independent employer about the rate the law enforcement officers or firefighters will receive for the special detail. The employing agency may also charge an administrative fee to the separate and independent employer.[92] The employing agency may require that employees on a special-detail assignment observe normal standards of conduct and may take disciplinary action against those who fail to do so.[93] Finally, the fact that public employers may facilitate special-detail work does not mean that they must do so. Employers may also prohibit or restrict outside work of this kind by their law enforcement and firefighter employees.[94]

---

87. *See* 29 C.F.R. § 553.222(c).
88. *See* 29 C.F.R. §§ 553.22(b)(2), 785.21.
89. *See* 29 U.S.C. § 207(p)(1); 29 C.F.R. § 553.227(a).
90. *See* 29 U.S.C. § 207(p)(1); 29 C.F.R. §§ 553.227(b), (g).
91. *See* 29 U.S.C. § 207(p)(1); 29 C.F.R. § 553.227(d).
92. *See* 29 U.S.C. § 207(p)(1); 29 C.F.R. § 553.227(d).
93. *See* 29 U.S.C. § 207(p)(1); 29 C.F.R. § 553.227(d).
94. *See* 29 U.S.C. § 207(p)(1); 29 C.F.R. § 553.227(h).

Managing special-detail assignments is generally a straightforward matter when the separate employer is a private entity. But things can get complicated when the special-detail assignment involves work at facilities owned by or affiliated with the local government employer itself. A private entity or individual may lease an event space owned by the government employer for a charity event, concert, wedding, party, or conference. Public housing complexes managed by a city or county housing authority may also engage law enforcement officers for security work. Whether or not these facilities are in fact separate and independent from the city or county, as required to qualify for the overtime exemption, is not always clear.

According to the special-detail work regulation, whether two employers are, in fact, separate and independent can only be determined on a case-by-case basis.[95] Neither the text of the FLSA nor the regulations define what a "separate and independent employer" is for the purposes of the special-detail exemption. A 1986 Wage and Hour Administrator opinion letter identifies six factors that DOL considers relevant to determining whether two or more agencies of the same unit of government may be considered to be separate and independent employers,[96] and courts that have considered the issue have applied these factors.[97] They are as follows: whether the government employer and the special-detail employer

1. maintain separate payrolls,
2. deal with other employers at arms' length concerning the employment of any individual,
3. have separate budgets,
4. have separate retirement systems,
5. are independent entities under state law, and
6. can sue and be sued in their own names.[98]

---

95. See 29 C.F.R. § 553.227(c).

96. See U.S. Dep't of Labor, Emp't Standards Admin., Wage & Hour Div. (DOL), Wage & Hour Opinion Letter, FLSA (Oct. 10, 1985), 1985 WL 1087362 (employment of meat cutter by state department of corrections and state-funded community college was employment by two separate and independent agencies).

97. See, e.g., Clark v. City of Fort Worth, 800 F. Supp. 2d 781, 787–88 (N.D. Tex. 2011) (licensees of city-owned facilities were separate and independent employers); Baltimore Cty. FOP Lodge 4 v. Baltimore Cty., 565 F. Supp. 2d 672, 678–80 (D. Md. 2008) (denying summary judgment because there was substantial evidence on both sides of the issue of whether the county and the school board were separate and independent employers); Murphy v. Town of Natick, 516 F. Supp. 2d 152, 157–58 (D. Mass. 2007) (finding that city and its constituent departments are not separate and independent employers, even if they have separate budgets and management); Barajas v. Unified Gov't of Wyandotte Cty., 87 F. Supp. 2d 1201, 1207–08 (D. Kan. 2000) (denying summary judgment because question of whether city/county government and housing authority were separate and independent employers was a genuine issue of material fact). See also Nolan v. City of Chicago, 125 F. Supp. 2d 324, 337–38 (N.D. Ill. 2000) (applying the factors without citation and finding that the city, the city housing authority, and the city transportation authority were separate and independent employers).

98. See the following DOL opinion letters: Wage & Hour Opinion Letter, FLSA (Oct. 10, 1985), cited supra note 96; Wage & Hour Opinion Letter, FLSA 2006-21NA (Oct. 5, 2006),

As long as a city or county employer can satisfy all or most of these factors, the special-detail employer will likely be found to be separate and independent, and the work on the special-detail assignment will not count toward the employee's overtime hours with the home agency. For example, in each of the following cases, the special-detail employer was found to be separate and independent from the city or county primary employer when the six-factor test was satisfied, even though

- the downtown development authority was defined by state statutes as a body corporate and an agency of the city with designated municipal functions;[99]
- the city (primary employer) contributed 10 percent of the operating budget and appointed the board of directors of the non-profit city convention center authority;[100]
- a state law or local ordinance required the presence of law enforcement officers or firefighters at certain events or under certain circumstances;[101] and
- the local government employer provided workers' compensation coverage for officers working special detail assignments at the convention center and coliseum.[102]

The language of the agreement pursuant to which a local government employer facilitates its law enforcement or fire employees' special-duty work is an important piece of evidence in establishing that the secondary employer qualifies as a separate and independent employer. In the federal Eighth Circuit Court of Appeals case *Specht v. City of Sioux Falls*,[103] an agreement between the city of Sioux Falls and the state of South Dakota provided that the city would facilitate the voluntary assistance of city firefighters to state crews battling wildfires. The city thought the contract was

---

https://www.dol.gov/whd/opinion/FLSANA/2006/2006_10_05_21NA_FLSA.pdf (city and a state-controlled police board are separate and independent entities); WAGE & HOUR DIVISION OPINION LETTER, FLSA (July 1, 1993), 1993 WL 901149 (county law enforcement officers not working for separate and independent employer while performing special-detail work at county vocational and technical school).

99. *See* U.S. DEP'T OF LABOR, EMP'T STANDARDS ADMIN., WAGE & HOUR DIV., WAGE & HOUR OPINION LETTER, FLSA 2002-3 (June 7, 2002), https://www.dol.gov/whd/opinion/FLSA/2002/2002_06_07_3_FLSA.pdf.

100. *See* U.S. DEP'T OF LABOR, EMP'T STANDARDS ADMIN., WAGE & HOUR DIV., WAGE & HOUR OPINION LETTER, FLSA 2007-12 (Dec. 31, 2007), https://www.dol.gov/whd/opinion/FLSA/2007/2007_12_31_12_FLSA.pdf.

101. *See* 29 C.F.R. § 553.227(e); Specht v. City of Sioux Falls, 639 F.3d 814 (8th Cir. 2011); U.S. DEP'T OF LABOR, EMP'T STANDARDS ADMIN., WAGE & HOUR DIV., WAGE & HOUR OPINION LETTER, FLSA 2006-13 (Apr. 28, 2006), https://www.dol.gov/whd/opinion/FLSA/2006/2006_04_28_13_FLSA.pdf.

102. *See Clark*, 800 F. Supp. 2d at 788; DOL, WAGE & HOUR OPINION LETTER, FLSA 2006-13, *supra* note 101 (employment of off-duty police officers by entertainment services company managing city-owned coliseum was a special-detail assignment involving separate and independent employers).

103. 639 F.3d 814.

establishing a special-duty assignment with a separate and independent employer. The Eighth Circuit, however, thought otherwise. Although the court found that the firefighters were under the direct control of the state while engaged in fighting wildfires, it nonetheless found strong evidence that the city remained the employer of the firefighters during these assignments. The terms of, and the language used in, the agreement between the city and the state were crucial to the court's decision to deny summary judgment and order a trial on the issue of whether the state was a separate and independent employer. The court considered that

1. the agreement called the city a "contractor" and provided that the state was to reimburse it for all wage expenses it incurred, including overtime;
2. the agreement referred to the firefighters as the city's employees; and
3. the agreement indemnified the state for any damages or liability incurred by the city in providing services.[104]

The very nature of public-safety duties can lead to confusion about which entity is an officer's or firefighter's employer during special-duty hours. When a security or crowd-control detail turns into a situation in which law enforcement officers exercise their powers of arrest, for example, they act by virtue of their employment by the city or county. While there are no cases addressing whether such time counts toward overtime with the local government employer, it seems that it should. An officer has no powers of arrest, for example, by virtue of being a security guard for the special-detail employer. Similarly, if a secondary employer arranges for the presence of a fire truck at an event, such as a private fireworks display, and a fire breaks out that must be suppressed by the firefighters present, they engage in that activity only by virtue of their employment by the local government. The time spent suppressing the fire should therefore be considered work time for the government employer.

Law enforcement officers on special detail providing crowd control and security at special events or locations are generally not engaging the regular duties they perform for their local government employers. But what about officers who are engaged as security officers by public housing authorities? Sometimes, the work performed in the special-duty capacity looks a lot like regular law enforcement work performed for the city or county. Consider the case *Johnson v. Unified Government of Wyandotte County/Kansas City*.[105] Members of the city police department agreed to work during their off-duty hours as security officers at public housing complexes managed by the city housing authority. The officers wore their city police uniforms, as is common on special-detail assignments, but they were also required to report to and maintain contact with the city police dispatcher. The officers performed some services not otherwise performed by city police officers, such as enforcing housing authority no-trespassing policies and lease provisions, but the agreement between the city and the housing authority provided that the officers were also to investigate or handle

104. *See id.* at 823–24.
105. 127 F. Supp. 2d 1181 (D. Kan. 2000).

calls that would require the dispatch of city police officers to the housing complex, unless they were otherwise tied up with housing authority matters. In addition, on at least some occasions, officers on special-duty assignment were instructed to assist in the investigation of serious crimes that did not occur on housing authority property. These are some of the reasons the court denied a motion for summary judgment, finding the question of whether the work for the housing authority was actually a special detail a disputed issue of material fact.[106]

Law Enforcement and Fire Departments with Fewer than Five Employees

If a local government employs fewer than five law enforcement officers or fewer than five firefighters in any given workweek, those positions will be exempt from overtime during that workweek.[107] Law enforcement positions and fire-protection positions are considered separately for the purposes of this exemption, which applies to very small municipalities. For example, if a local government employs fewer than five employees in fire-protection activities but five or more employees in law enforcement activities, it may claim the exemption for the fire-protection employees but not for the law enforcement employees.[108] No distinction is made between full-time and part-time employees or between employees on duty and employees on leave. All such categories must be counted in determining whether the department employs fewer than five employees.[109] Volunteer firefighters and auxiliary police officers who provide services on a volunteer basis in order to maintain their law enforcement certification do not count in the calculation of the number of law enforcement officers a town employs in a workweek.[110]

The FLSA regulations do not expressly say that certified law enforcement officers and firefighters who are exempt employees under the executive or administrative duties tests[111] are to be counted in determining whether a department has fewer than five employees, but that must surely be the case. The fewer-than-five rule is fairly detailed and provides no exceptions from being counted for any person who works in law enforcement or fire-protection activities. Exempt employees in a law enforcement or fire department who meet the FLSA's definition of law enforcement officer or fire protection employee fall under the plain language of section 553.200's explanation of which employees are to be counted when determining whether there are fewer than five engaged in these activities.[112] This makes sense. In a small department, or in a department with few employees but many volunteers, the police or fire chief will

106. See id. at 1188–89.

107. See 29 U.S.C. § 213(b)(2); 29 C.F.R. § 553.200.

108. See 29 C.F.R. § 553.200(b).

109. See id.

110. See id.; Cleveland v. City of Elmendorf, 388 F.3d 522 (5th Cir. 2004); Ebersbach v. Vill. of McArthur, No. 07-CV-1223, 2008 WL 2355838, at *3 (S.D. Ohio June 9, 2008).

111. See chapter 1 of this book for a fuller discussion of these tests used to determine exemption from the FLSA's overtime provisions.

112. See 29 C.F.R. §§ 553.200, .210, .211.

likely qualify for either the executive or administrative exemption. Many of them will regularly go out on calls given the small size of their departments and, even if they do not regularly go out, they will perform law enforcement or fire-protection activities when needed.

The fewer-than-five exemption applies on a workweek basis. It is therefore possible that employers may have to pay overtime for hours worked over forty hours in some weeks, but not in others. In those workweeks in which the employer has five or more law enforcement officers or five or more firefighters, it may schedule those employees using the 207(k) exemption.[113]

Second Job for the Same Employer

For purposes of the FLSA, *all* hours worked by a nonexempt employee for the same employer count toward assessing the employee's right to overtime in a given work-week. This is true even where the employee is working two completely unrelated jobs in different departments.[114]

An employer has two options for paying a nonexempt employee with a second nonexempt job. First, where a nonexempt employee performs two or more different kinds of work for two different straight-time hourly rates, the employer and employee may agree in advance that the employee will be paid time-and-one half of the bona fide regular rate of the job that is performed during the overtime hours.[115] Second, in the absence of such an agreement, the employee's regular rate for that week is the weighted average of such rates. This means, in the words of the regulations, that the employee's "total earnings . . . are computed to include his [or her] compensation during the workweek from all such rates, and are then divided by the total number of hours worked at all jobs."[116]

Of course, sometimes a nonexempt employee takes a second job that is exempt. In that case, the employee must still be compensated at a time-and-one-half overtime rate for any hours worked over forty hours. The salary must merely be converted to an hourly rate. Where an *exempt* employee takes a second job that is nonexempt, the hours worked at the second job are paid at the regular straight-time rate for that job, since an exempt employee does not earn overtime. The character of the employee's job duties in their full-time position is what determines whether or not overtime must be paid for hours worked in a second job for the same employer.[117]

---

113. *See* 29 C.F.R. § 553.200(c). *See* pages 133 through 141, *supra*, for more on this exemption.

114. *See* 29 C.F.R. § 778.103.

115. *See* 29 U.S.C. § 207(g)(2); 29 C.F.R. § 778.419.

116. 29 C.F.R. § 778.115.

117. *See, e.g.,* U.S. Dep't of Labor, Emp't Standards Admin., Wage & Hour Div., Wage & Hour Opinion Letter, FLSA 2005-29 (Aug. 26, 2005), https://www.dol.gov/whd/opinion/FLSA/2005/2005_08_26_29_FLSA.pdf.

The Occasional and Sporadic Second Job

What if an employee doesn't want a regular second job but is happy to work every now and then for the same employer? Where a local government employee works *occasionally or sporadically* on a part-time basis for the same public agency *in a different capacity* from his or her regular employment, the hours worked in the different job do not have to be counted for the purpose of overtime but may be paid at a straight-time rate.[118]

The terms "occasional" and "sporadic" have very specific meanings for purposes of this exemption from overtime. "Occasional or sporadic" means infrequent, irregular, or occurring in scattered instances.[119] The work can be recurring (an event held every fall or every holiday season, for example), but it cannot be regular (weekly or monthly according to a regular schedule). Examples of occasional and sporadic part-time work include

- taking tickets or providing security for special events, such as concerts, team sporting events, or lectures, at stadiums or auditoriums;
- officiating at special youth or other recreation and sporting events at public recreation and park facilities; and
- assisting in food or beverage sales at concerts, sporting events, or special events, such as county fairs.[120]

In order to exclude such hours from overtime, the occasional or sporadic work may not be within the same general occupational category as the employee's regular work. Most employers and employees will have an intuitive sense of what jobs are in the same general occupational category, but in deciding whether occasional and sporadic work is in a different capacity, DOL will consider (1) the duties and other factors contained in the definitions of the three-digit categories of occupations found in the DOL's Education and Training Administration's Occupational Information Network (O*NET) system as well as (2) all the facts and circumstances in a particular case.[121] DOL gives the following examples, involving employees of a city parks and recreation department, of occasional and sporadic activities that are performed in a different capacity from an employee's regular work:

- an employee of the department's finance division *occasionally* refereeing for an adult evening basketball league sponsored by the department;
- a bus driver assisting in crowd control at a winter festival;

---

118. *See* 29 U.S.C. § 207(p)(2); 29 C.F.R. § 553.30.

119. *See* 29 C.F.R. § 553.30(b)(1).

120. *See* 29 C.F.R. § 553.30(b)(3).

121. *See* 29 C.F.R. §§ 553.30(c)(1), (2). Section 553.30 refers to the "Dictionary of Occupational Titles," but that publication was last published by the Education and Training Administration in 1991; it has since been replaced by the O*NET system (see https://www.onetonline.org).

- an administrative assistant *substituting* as a coach for a youth basketball team; or
- a maintenance engineer providing instruction on auto repair as part of a single-day parks and recreation program.[122]

Examples of occasional and sporadic activities that would **not** be considered to be performed in a different capacity from an employee's regular work include

- a parks and recreation department employee who primarily engages in playground maintenance also from time to time cleaning an evening recreation center or
- public safety employees taking on any kind of security or safety function within the same local government (such assignments are **never** considered to be employment in a different capacity).[123]

Finally, in order to exclude occasional and sporadic work from overtime, an employer may not order or pressure employees to undertake the work. Employees must be working the occasional and sporadic assignment of their own free choice.[124]

One occasional and sporadic position that all North Carolina counties and many cities offer is that of elections poll worker. Poll workers work one long, single shift (usually twelve–fourteen hours) on a day on which an election is held. In most years, there are two elections, the primary and the general election. But where there is a need for a second primary or run-off election or a need for a special election, there could be as many as four elections in a single year. There is no requirement that poll workers be persons otherwise employed by the county, but in most counties, it is not unusual for the ranks of poll workers to include county employees from various departments who use a vacation day to cover their absences from their regular job duties and work the polls at whatever rate the county is paying poll workers generally. This employment meets the occasional and sporadic exception.

Consider the following hypothetical.

Linda is a nonexempt custodian for the county parks and recreation department. Her regular schedule is 7 a.m.–3:30 p.m., Monday through Friday, a forty-hour-per-week schedule. She makes $9 per hour. The Paradise County Board of Elections gives first dibs on poll worker positions, which pay $10 per hour, to county employees, and Linda usually gets a job as poll worker. On election day, Linda takes a vacation day and works the polls during a fifteen-hour shift. The hours she works on election day do not count toward overtime. Instead, Linda earns $288 ($9 for each of the thirty-two hours she works as a custodian that week) and $150 ($10 for each of the fifteen hours she works as a poll worker), for a total of $438. Her pay will also include

---

122. *See* 29 C.F.R. §§ 553.30(c)(4), (5).
123. *See* 29 C.F.R. § 553.30(c)(3).
124. *See* 29 C.F.R. §§ 553.30(a), (b)(2).

another $72 for the eight hours of paid vacation leave she took on election day in order to be free to work as a poll worker. The total amount she receives that week is $510. On a normal week, without the poll work, Linda makes $360.

It's easy to see why Linda might be happy to accept the poll work, even without its counting toward overtime. The occasional and sporadic exception makes it affordable for the county to provide its workers with this opportunity to earn extra money. If the exception were not available, the board of elections would no doubt hire all of its poll workers from outside of county government rather than pay county employees overtime.

What are the outer limits of occasional or sporadic secondary employment? For example, would employment as an *early voting* poll worker satisfy the exception? Early voting lasts for ten days as of this book's publication date and takes place twice—and sometime three times—a year: prior to primary elections, prior to the day of the general election, and sometimes prior to the day of a run-off election. It is reasonable to think that an employee who works during a single ten-day early-voting period is working that second job on an occasional or sporadic basis: once a year for ten consecutive days. What about an employee who regularly works early voting for both the primary and the general election? Does the fact that the employee works these two jobs every year make it regular rather than occasional or sporadic?

The occasional or sporadic regulation clearly states that the fact that the secondary employment opportunity occurs regularly does not disqualify it from exception from the overtime rules.

> Employment in such activity may be considered occasional or sporadic for regular employees of State or local government agencies even where the need can be anticipated because it recurs seasonally (e.g., a holiday concert at a city college, a program of scheduled sports events, or assistance by a city payroll clerk in processing returns at tax filing time). An activity does not fail to be occasional merely because it is recurring.[125]

So, the issue seems to be how many days of work would take secondary employment out of the occasional or sporadic exception? DOL has opined that full-time dispatchers and records clerks who worked a monthly average of two to three special-event details (parades, meetings, parking and security details requested by citizens) as special police officers would be employed on an occasional or sporadic basis because the work is infrequent and unpredictable and the events do not recur with regularity.[126] Contrast this with a 1990 Opinion Letter in which DOL advised that public works employees who also worked for the fire department did not work on an occasional or sporadic basis where the employees responded to between thirty-nine

---

125. 29 C.F.R. § 553.30(b)(3).
126. *See* U.S. Dep't of Labor, Emp't Standards Admin., Wage & Hour Div. (DOL), Wage & Hour Opinion Letter, FLSA (Dec. 6, 2001), 2001 WL 1870383.

and seventy-seven fire calls per year and regularly attended two one-half hour training sessions each month.[127]

Two 2015 cases, both naming the Houston (Texas) Independent School District as defendant, heard before two different federal district court judges, came to very different conclusions based on fairly similar facts. In one, the judge found that because payroll records showed that the plaintiff employees' secondary work varied from day to day, from month to month, and from year to year, and varied as well as in the length of each shift worked, the plaintiffs worked their second jobs on a "sporadic" basis. The judge found one employee's work to be occasional where he only performed the second job 8 percent of the time at issue. That is perhaps not so remarkable. But in the case of a second employee who worked his secondary job 23 percent of the time, the judge also found that the work was occasional.[128] In the second case, the plaintiffs' secondary work was substantially similar to that of the plaintiffs in the first case. All three worked second jobs for the school district's stadium complex, taking tickets, keeping time at athletic events, and providing security at the doors. One employee's payroll records showed that she worked her second job at least two days a week for at least eight hours a week in every month other than November and December. The judge in this second case concluded that the work was, in fact, regular and frequent.[129]

Where does this leave us with respect to the ability of counties to claim that a second job at an early voting site is occasional and sporadic when it occurs three times a year for ten days at a stretch—more than 10 percent of a year's working days? The work occurs on a regular, predictable basis, so it cannot be said to be sporadic. But is it occasional? The fact that the employment occurs three times during the year does not in and of itself disqualify it. Three times seems to fit squarely within the meaning of occasional. The issue instead seems to be whether the length of the assignment (in days) makes it frequent. Thirty days is fewer than the thirty-nine to seventy-seven calls per year that part-time firefighters averaged in DOL's 1990 opinion letter, and it is less than the 23 percent of the time in the first of the Houston school district cases. A reasonable argument can be made that secondary employment for as many as three separate occasions per year for a period of up to ten days each time could be considered occasional employment that constitutes an exception to the FLSA's overtime requirement.

Employees of City- or County-Owned Seasonal Amusement or Recreational "Establishments"

Here's another exception to the basic overtime rule: positions at seasonal amusement or recreational establishments are exempt from the FLSA's overtime provisions.[130] All hours worked by workers in these positions, no matter how many, may be paid at

---

127. *See* DOL, Wage & Hour Opinion Letter, FLSA (Feb. 27, 1990), 1990 WL 10536208.
128. Ford v. Houston Indep. Sch. Dist., 97 F. Supp. 3d 866, 896 (S.D. Tex. 2015).
129. Franklin v. Houston Indep. Sch. Dist., 92 F. Supp. 3d 582, 587 (S.D. Tex. 2015).
130. 29 U.S.C. § 213(a)(3).

straight time. This exemption applies to both the public and private sectors. But just what does "seasonal" and "establishment" mean? To be a "seasonal" establishment, the facility must be one that operates no more than seven months in any calendar year.[131] A position at an "establishment" means that the employee's duties must be performed at a facility that is "a distinct physical place of business" separate from the main administrative location of the organization.[132] Examples of public-sector facilities qualifying as establishments include beaches, golf courses, and swimming pools. Year-round employees who spend part of the year working at a seasonal amusement or recreational establishment and the other part of the year working at the city's or county's regular year-round operations are exempt from overtime for those months in which they work at the seasonal establishment, but they must be paid overtime during that part of the year they are working at the main facility.[133]

In some cases, local governments whose climates allow them to operate recreational establishments on a year-round basis (some North Carolina municipal and county golf courses operate year-round, for example) may be able to take advantage of this exemption from overtime for periods beyond the seven-month limit mentioned in the text above. The FLSA and the regulations provide an alternate definition of the term "seasonal" for the purposes of this exemption. First, the facility's operating costs must primarily be generated from admission fees or receipts of some kind. A government-operated amusement or recreational facility whose operating costs are met wholly or primarily from tax funds fails to qualify under this alternate basis for exemption.[134] Any year-round facility, such as a beach or a municipal golf course, that is free to residents will surely not be able to qualify for this exemption. But if a year-round recreational facility is primarily supported by fees and receipts and if, during the preceding calendar year, its average monthly receipts for the slowest six months were substantially less than one-third of average monthly receipts for its busiest six-month period, its employees will also be exempt from the overtime provisions of the FLSA.[135]

When One Nonexempt Employee Substitutes for Another on a Shift

Sometimes an employee who works on a scheduled shift for which full coverage is essential needs to switch shifts with another employee or have another employee substitute for him or her to cover an absence. Consider the following situation.

---

131. 29 C.F.R. § 553.32(e).

132. 29 C.F.R. § 779.23. *See also id.* § 779.385; U.S. Dep't of Labor (DOL), Emp't Standards Admin., Wage & Hour Div., Wage & Hour Opinion Letter, FLSA 2009-5 (Jan. 14, 2009), https://www.dol.gov/whd/opinion/FLSA/2009/2009_01_14_05_FLSA.pdf.

133. *See* 29 U.S.C. § 213(a)(3); 29 C.F.R. §§ 553.32(e), 779.385. *See also* DOL, Wage & Hour Opinion Letter, FLSA 2009-5, *supra* note 132.

134. *See* DOL, Wage & Hour Opinion Letter, FLSA 2009-5, *supra* note 132; DOL, Field Operations Handbook § 25j12 (Aug. 10, 2016), https://www.dol.gov/whd/FOH/FOH_Ch25.pdf.

135. *See* 29 U.S.C. § 213(a)(3); 29 C.F.R. §§ 553.32(e), 779.385. *See also* Hays v. City of Pauls Valley, 74 F.3d 1002 (10th Cir. 1996).

Regina and Gene are dispatchers for Paradise County 911. They each earn $20 per hour. Regina is scheduled to work four twelve-hour shifts next week, but she does not want to work her Thursday shift because her parents will be visiting from California. Gene is only scheduled to work thirty-six hours next week. Regina and Gene agree that Gene will work one of her shifts and that Regina will pay Gene $320 for substituting for her twelve-hour shift. When payday rolls around, for the week in question Paradise County pays Regina $1,040 ($20 per hour multiplied by forty hours plus $30 per hour—time-and-one-half her regular rate—multiplied by eight hours). Paradise County pays Gene $720 for the week ($20 per hour multiplied by his scheduled thirty-six hours). As agreed, Regina then pays Gene $320.

Can this be lawful under the FLSA? The answer is yes.

When switching or covering shifts is voluntary and done with the approval of management, each employee involved in the arrangement will be paid as if he or she had worked his or her normal work schedule for that shift. In other words, the hours worked by the substituting employee will be paid to the scheduled employee and will not count as hours worked by the substituting employee for the purposes of overtime. The scheduled employee is responsible for compensating the substituting employee at the rate to which the two privately agree.[136] This is true even when employees are scheduled to work overtime and obtain a substitute for one of their scheduled shifts that week (or during a 207(k) work period, if applicable). The scheduled employee is paid overtime as if he or she had worked all of the scheduled hours.[137] This is how Regina comes to be paid overtime despite the fact that she did not physically work more than thirty-six hours that week and how she came to pay Gene what he would have been paid by their employer had he been scheduled for forty-eight hours that week. By taking Regina's twelve-hour Thursday shift, Gene went from working his scheduled thirty-six hours to actually working forty-eight hours. So, he worked four additional hours at straight time (four x $20 = $80) and eight hours of overtime (eight x $30 = $240). That is why he and Regina agreed that she would pay him $320 to take her shift.

An employer is free to suggest that one employee substitute for another employee when a need arises, but each employee must be free to refuse to do so without fear of disciplinary action and without being required to explain or justify the decision. If an employer orders an employee to substitute or cover for another employee, then the

---

136. *See* 29 U.S.C. § 207(p)(3); 29 C.F.R. § 553.31. *See also* Senger v. City of Aberdeen, 466 F.3d 670, 672–74 (8th Cir. 2006); DOL, WAGE & HOUR OPINION LETTER, FLSA 2008-2 (Mar. 17, 2008), https://www.dol.gov/whd/opinion/FLSA/2008/2008_03_17_02_FLSA.pdf; DOL, WAGE & HOUR OPINION LETTER, FLSA 2004-23 (Nov. 23, 2004), https://www.dol.gov/whd/opinion/FLSA/2004/2004_11_23_23_FLSA_DonatingAndExchanging.pdf.

137. *See Senger,* 466 F.3d at 672–74. *See also* Application of the Fair Labor Standards Act to Employees of State and Local Governments, 52 Fed. Reg. 2012-01, pmbl. at 2045 (Jan. 16, 1987).

hours worked by the substituting employee count toward overtime for that employee. It is just as if the scheduled employee called in sick unexpectedly and the shift supervisor told another employee not scheduled to work at that time to stay later or come in and work overtime.

Note that although management must have notice of and approve any substitution before this exemption can apply, the employer is not required to keep records of the substitution. The easiest way for an employer to give employees more flexibility while limiting their own overtime costs is to adopt a policy that requires supervisor approval for any substitution. The rule allowing one employee to enter into a private substitution arrangement with another employee is limited to the public sector.[138]

No Offsets or Credits Against Overtime Wages

With three limited exceptions, the FLSA does not permit other payments to an employee to be offset or credited against overtime payments.[139] The three exceptions are (1) when an employer pays a bonus to employees working more than eight hours a day or more than their regularly scheduled workday; (2) when an employer compensates an employee with premium pay at a rate of one-and-one-half times their usual rate for working on the weekend, on a holiday, or on a day-off; or (3) when an employer compensates an employee at a rate of one-and-one-half times their usual rate for working more than their regular work day or regular workweek and the payment is made pursuant to an employment agreement.[140]

---

138. *See* 29 U.S.C. § 207(p)(3); 29 C.F.R. § 553.31.
139. *See* 29 U.S.C. § 207(h).
140. *See* 29 U.S.C. §§ 207(e)(5)–(7) & (h)(2).

Chapter 5

Calculating the Regular Rate

The Regular Rate

The basic overtime rule under the Fair Labor Standards Act (FLSA) is deceptively simple: employers must pay nonexempt employees[1] at the rate of time-and-one-half of their regular rate for all hours over forty worked in a given week. But a remarkably difficult concept is hidden in that rule, namely, the regular rate. What is the regular rate? When employees work only their regular non-overtime hours and get paid only their stated hourly rate, the answer is simple. The hourly rate and the regular rate are the same. This is the case for most employees most of the time. But Section 7(e) of the FLSA says that the "regular rate" at which an employee is employed "shall be deemed to include all remuneration for employment paid to, or on behalf of, the employee."[2] Any payment in addition to the stated hourly rate gets figured into the regular rate. When employees earn bonuses, are paid a stipend for noncompensable on-call time, earn longevity pay, or receive cash in lieu of health insurance—to list just a few examples—these additional payments must be factored into the calculation of the regular rate for the period during which they were earned. In those periods, the regular rate will be higher than the stated hourly rate, and overtime time-and-on-half pay will be correspondingly higher.

The principle on which the regular rate is based is one of the least-discussed aspects of overtime law, yet it dates back to the earliest days of the FLSA. In 1945, the U.S. Supreme Court addressed the calculation of the regular rate and emphasized that the amounts to be included are not subject to negotiation:

> The regular rate by its very nature must reflect all payments which the parties have agreed shall be received regularly during the workweek, exclusive of overtime payments. It is not an arbitrary label chosen by the parties; it is an actual fact. Once the parties have decided upon the amount of wages and the mode of payment the determination of the regular rate becomes a matter of mathematical computation, the result of which is unaffected by any designation of a contrary "regular rate" in the wage contracts.[3]

The Regular Rate of Nonexempt Employees Paid on an Hourly Basis

For nonexempt employees, "hourly" rate of pay and "regular" rate of pay are two different things. They are closely related, but they are different. The hourly rate is the stated rate of pay that an employee is promised for each hour of work. Imagine that paramedic Joe's hourly rate is $10 per hour. If Joe works forty hours in a week, he is paid $10 for each hour worked, or $400. If he works more than forty hours in a week, he is entitled to "time-and-one-half" pay as an overtime premium. But time-and-one-half of what? This is where things get tricky. It is time-and-one-half of Joe's

---

1. See chapter 1 of this book, "Who Is Exempt from Overtime? The Salary Tests and the Duties Tests," for a comprehensive discussion on the topic of FLSA exemption.
2. *See* 29 U.S.C. § 207(e).
3. Walling v. Youngerman-Reynolds Hardwood Co., 325 U.S. 419, 424–25 (1945).

"regular rate." In a week in which Joe is paid no payments of any kind other than pay for hours worked, the "regular" rate and the "hourly rate" are the same.

But say that Joe works forty-five hours one week. He receives no payments other than pay for time worked. Since he receives no other kinds of payment, his hourly rate and his regular rate are the same: $10 per hour. His time-and-one-half premium rate is $15 per hour. His pay for the week is $400 ($10 times forty) plus $75 ($15 times five), for a total of $475. That's easy.

But suppose now that Joe works out a deal with his employer. He agrees to be on call two nights a week every week for a straight payment of $27.50 per night. On a night when he is not called out, he gets the $27.50 and nothing more. On nights when he is called out, he gets the $27.50 plus he is paid by the hour at his hourly rate for the hours he works while called out. Now Joe is entitled to an extra $55.00 per week even if he is not called out while on call. Suppose that Joe works forty-four hours one week. He is entitled to $10 per hour for the first forty hours and time-and-one-half for the four overtime hours. Again, time-and-one-half of what? This time it is **not** time-and-one-half of $10. That is still his hourly rate, without question. But for this week it is not his "regular" rate. That is because this week Joe has received payments in addition to the pay for hours worked. He has received $55 for being on call for two nights. How, then, do we calculate his regular rate and figure out his time-and-one-half overtime rate?

The rule for calculating Joe's regular rate this week is set forth in Title 29, Section 778.110 of the Code of Federal Regulations (C.F.R.):

(a) Earnings at hourly rate exclusively. If the employee is employed solely on the basis of a single hourly rate, the hourly rate is the "regular rate." For overtime hours of work the employee must be paid, in addition to the straight time hourly earnings, a sum determined by multiplying one-half the hourly rate by the number of hours worked in excess of 40 in the week. Thus a $12 hourly rate will bring, for an employee who works 46 hours, a total weekly wage of $588 (46 hours at $12 plus 6 at $6). In other words, the employee is entitled to be paid an amount equal to $12 an hour for 40 hours and $18 an hour for the 6 hours of overtime, or a total of $588.

(b) Hourly rate and bonus. If the employee receives, in addition to the earnings computed at the $12 hourly rate, a production bonus of $46 for the week, the regular hourly rate of pay is $13 an hour (46 hours at $12 yields $552; the addition of the $46 bonus makes a total of $598; this total divided by 46 hours yields a regular rate of $13). The employee is then entitled to be paid a total wage of $637 for 46 hours (46 hours at $13 plus 6 hours at $6.50, or 40 hours at $13 plus 6 hours at $19.50).[4]

---

4. 29 C.F.R. § 778.110.

For any given workweek, the regular hourly rate of pay is determined by dividing an employee's **total** pay (not counting the overtime premium) by the total number of hours actually worked that week.

So how much does paramedic Joe earn this week, in which he worked forty-four hours and received $55 for being on call (but was not called in) for two nights of the week? The first step is to figure out Joe's total pay for the week. *Multiply Joe's hourly rate, $10 per hour, by the total number of hours he has worked,* that is, forty-four hours. You arrive at a sum of $440. *Add Joe's on-call bonus payment, which was $55, to that $440 and you get $495 in total compensation.* The next step is to *divide total compensation by the total number of hours Joe has worked,* namely, forty-four hours: $495 ÷ 44 = $11.25. Joe's regular rate is $11.25 per hour, even though his hourly rate is $10.00 per hour. His overtime is therefore calculated as time-and-one-half of $11.25. This week, *Joe is paid a total of $522.52.* That represents $400 in straight-time pay ($10 x forty) plus $55 for being on-call plus $67.52 in overtime—calculated by taking $16.88 (or time-and-one-half of Joe's $11.25 regular rate) and multiplying it by four hours of overtime.

The Regular Rate of Nonexempt Employees Paid on a Salary Basis

Things are more complicated when a nonexempt employee is paid on a salary basis. The rule governing the calculation of the regular rate for salaried nonexempt employees is set forth at C.F.R. Title 29, Section 778.113:

> (a) Weekly salary. If the employee is employed solely on a weekly salary basis, the regular hourly rate of pay, on which time and a half must be paid, is computed by dividing the salary by the number of hours which the salary is intended to compensate. If an employee is hired at a salary of $350 and if it is understood that this salary is compensation for a regular workweek of 35 hours, the employee's regular rate of pay is $350 divided by 35 hours, or $10 an hour, and when the employee works overtime the employee is entitled to receive $10 for each of the first 40 hours and $15 (one and one-half times $10) for each hour thereafter. If an employee is hired at a salary of $375 for a 40-hour week the regular rate is $9.38 an hour.[5]

For salaried, nonexempt employees, the regular rate is determined by dividing the weekly salary and any other monetary compensation that the employee earns by **the number of hours that the salary is intended to compensate**. Where employees are not regularly expected to work overtime hours, the number of hours that the salary is intended to compensate will usually be forty, although in a city or county where the standard workweek is thirty-seven and one-half hours, thirty-seven and one-half might be the number of hours the salary is intended to compensate.

Planner Elizabeth's earnings illustrate this principle. Elizabeth is a *salaried FLSA nonexempt* employee. She is *paid $456 per week for a thirty-seven-and-one-half-hour*

---

5. 29 C.F.R. § 778.113(a).

workweek. This means that *her hourly rate is $12.16 per hour* ($456 ÷ 37.5). This would be Elizabeth's regular rate during any week in which she received no other compensation. During a week at the end of October, however, Elizabeth earns *an additional $100 bonus* for working on Halloween. If she works only her regularly scheduled thirty-seven and one-half hours, *she will receive $556 that week* ($456 + $100). But what happens if Elizabeth works forty hours that week, more than her regularly scheduled thirty-seven and one-half but below the statutory minimum for overtime compensation. *If Elizabeth works forty hours during the week in which she receives her Halloween bonus, she will earn $586.40.* How do we reach that figure? In addition to her weekly salary of $456 for thirty-seven and one-half hours, Elizabeth needs to be compensated for the two and one-half hours between her regularly scheduled thirty-seven and one-half hours and the forty hours she actually worked. Her employer will pay her hourly rate, $12.16 per hour, multiplied by two and one-half hours, for a total of $30.40. To reach her total compensation for the week, add together $456 plus $30.40 plus $100 (Halloween bonus), for a total of $586.40.

Suppose, however, that Elizabeth works forty-two hours (that is, two hours of overtime) during the week in which she earns the Halloween bonus. The addition of the Halloween bonus to her compensation for that week *will change her regular rate for that week.* Why will it change the regular rate? Because the FLSA regulations provide that "[t]he regular hourly rate of pay of an employee is determined by dividing his *total remuneration* for employment (except statutory exclusions) *in any workweek* by the total number of *hours actually worked by him in that workweek* for which such compensation was paid."[6] So in Elizabeth's case, to get her regular rate we need to take the total amount she has earned for the week—her hourly rate of $12.16 multiplied by the total number of hours she actually worked plus her $100 Halloween bonus—and divide it by the total number of hours she worked, namely forty-two.

Here's how it works. Not counting the overtime premium (which is what we have to calculate), Elizabeth has earned $610.72 this week: $12.16 x forty-two (which equals $510.72) plus $100 in Halloween pay. We then *divide $610.72 by forty-two,* the total number of hours she worked that week, to get *a regular rate of $14.55.* Now that we finally have Elizabeth's regular rate, we can calculate her total compensation for the week. First, we multiply Elizabeth's straight-time hours by the regular rate: $14.55 x forty = $582. Then we calculate *time-and-one-half of the regular rate, which is $21.83.* Elizabeth has only worked two hours of overtime, so we multiply $21.83 by two and determine that Elizabeth is owed $43.66 as an overtime premium. *Elizabeth's total compensation for the week will be $582 (straight-time hours times regular rate) plus $43.66 (overtime premium), for a total of $625.66.* The same result may be reached by multiplying the regular rate of $14.55 by forty-two (the total number of hours worked), which is $611.10, and adding one-half of the regular rate (or $7.28) multiplied by two (the number of overtime hours Elizabeth worked).

---

6. *See* 29 C.F.R. § 778.109 (emphasis added).

What about Elizabeth's $100 Halloween bonus? Hasn't that been forgotten in calculating her total compensation for the week? No, it has not. The $100 bonus has been factored into the regular rate—that is why the regular rate is higher than the hourly rate this week.

> **How to Determine the Hourly Rate of Salaried Nonexempt Employees**
>
> 1. First, establish what the salary is meant to cover. Is the salary compensating the employee for a forty-hour workweek, a thirty-seven-and-one-half-hour workweek, or a forty-five- or fifty-hour workweek?
>
> 2. Alternatively, is the employee being paid a flat salary for however many hours he or she works in a week?
>
> 3. If an employee is being paid a salary based on thirty-seven and one-half hours, then the hourly rate is the salary divided by thirty-seven and one-half. If an employee is being paid a salary based on forty hours, then the hourly rate is the salary divided by forty, and so on.
>
> 4. If an employee is being paid a flat salary for however many hours he or she works in a week, the hourly rate will be different every week, as the hourly rate will be the salary divided by the number of hours worked in the particular week.
>
> 5. The hourly rate can never be less than the minimum wage.

Nonexempt Employees Compensated by Monthly or Bi-Weekly Salaries

Some government employers who pay their nonexempt employees on a salary basis pay them on a bi-weekly or monthly basis. Because overtime compensation generally must be calculated on a weekly basis, bi-weekly and monthly salaries must first be converted to weekly salaries to calculate the regular rate of these employees. A monthly salary can be converted to a weekly salary by multiplying the monthly salary by twelve (the number of months in a year) and dividing that figure by fifty-two (the number of weeks in a year). A bi-weekly salary can be converted by multiplying the bi-weekly salary by twenty-six and then dividing that figure by fifty-two. The regular rate can be determined from these converted salaries.[7]

What Kind of Additions to Wages Get Included in the Regular Rate?

Not every addition to a nonexempt employee's wages gets included in the regular rate. Although the FLSA says that "all remuneration for employment paid to, or on behalf of" an employee must be included in the regular rate, it also sets forth eight kinds of payments that do not count in the calculation of the regular rate. In other words, all money paid to an employee as compensation for services is included in the calculation of the regular rate unless a payment made on top of wages falls into one

---

7. See 29 C.F.R. § 778.113(b).

of the eight exceptions set forth in subsections 207(e)(1) through (8) of the statute.[8] The employer bears the burden of showing that an exception applies.[9]

Below are the exclusions set forth in FLSA Section 207(e) that impact public employment—that is, the payments that do not factor into the regular rate calculation.

1. sums paid as gifts, including payments in the form of Christmas gifts or gifts made on other special occasions, and payments made as a reward for service, the amounts of which are not measured by or dependent on hours worked, production, or efficiency;

2. payments made for occasional periods when no work is performed due to vacation, holiday, or illness, or due to the failure of the employer to provide employees with a sufficient amount of work;

3. reasonable payments for traveling expenses, or for other expenses, incurred by an employee as part of his or her employment and reimbursable by the employer, and other similar payments to an employee that are not made as compensation for his or her hours of employment;

4. sums paid in recognition of services performed during a given period, provided that both the fact that payment is to be made and the amount of the payment are determined at the sole discretion of the employer at or near the end of the period and not pursuant to any prior contract, agreement, or promise causing the employee to expect such payments regularly;

5. contributions irrevocably made by an employer to a trustee or third person pursuant to a bona fide employee benefit plan, such as retirement plans and life, accident, disability, or health insurance plans or similar benefits for employees;

6. overtime compensation itself, as well as any extra compensation paid at a premium rate for certain hours worked by an employee in any day of a workweek because such hours are in excess of the employee's normal or regular working hours, as the case may be;

7. extra compensation paid at a premium rate paid for work by an employee on Saturdays, Sundays, holidays, or regular days of rest (or on the sixth or seventh day of the established workweek), so long as the premium rate is at

---

8. Not all of the statutory exceptions are relevant to government employers. Subsection (e)(8), for example, provides for the exclusion of "any value or income derived from employer-provided grants or rights provided pursuant to a stock option, stock appreciation right, or bona fide employee stock purchase program, provided certain conditions are met." Similarly, subsections (e)(3)(b) and (c), which, respectively, allow for the exclusion of payments made pursuant to a profit-sharing plan and payments that are talent fees paid to performers, are of no relevance to public employers.

9. *See* Newman v. Advanced Tech. Innovation Corp., 749 F.3d 33, 36 (1st Cir. 2014); Acton v. City of Columbia, 436 F.3d 969, 976 (8th Cir. 2006); Madison v. Res. for Human Dev., Inc., 233 F.3d 175, 187 (3d Cir. 2000); White v. Publix Super Mkts., Inc., No. 3:14-cv-1189, 2015 WL 4949837, at *2 (M.D. Tenn. Aug. 19, 2015); Gonzalez v. McNeil Techs., Inc., No. 1:06cv204, 2007 WL 1097887, at *3 (E.D. Va. Apr. 11, 2007). *See also* Mitchell v. Ky. Fin. Co., 359 U.S. 290, 295 (1959).

least one and one-half times the employee's usual hourly rate established in good faith for like work performed in non-overtime hours on other days;

8. extra compensation paid at a premium rate paid to an employee under an applicable employment contract or agreement for work outside of the employee's regular hours established in good faith by the contract or agreement as the basic, normal, or regular workday (not exceeding eight hours) or workweek so long as the premium rate is not less than one and one-half times the rate established in good faith by the contract or agreement for like work performed during such workday or workweek (in other words, payment of time-and-one-half of the employee's hourly rate for hours fewer than forty but more than the established regular number of hours).[10]

Court cases interpreting these statutory exclusions explain that what distinguishes payments that must be included in the regular rate from those that may be excluded is that the former can generally be tied to compensation for hours worked or for performance of an employee's general or specific duties on behalf of the employer, while the latter cannot.[11]

But despite the existence of these eight exceptions, most additions to the weekly pay of public employees do get included in the regular rate. The following sections discuss the most common ones.

Bonuses

Some bonuses are included in the calculation of the regular rate and some are not. There are many different kinds of additions to wages that employers and employees call bonuses. For regular-rate purposes, the most important distinction is that between *discretionary* and *nondiscretionary* bonuses. Discretionary bonuses **do not** need to be included in the regular rate. They fall within the statutory exception to the regular rate under FLSA Section 207(e)(3), discussed above. Nondiscretionary bonuses, however, **must** be included in the regular rate. Discretionary bonuses are those which may or may not be given in the sole judgment of the employer. The FLSA regulations define a discretionary bonus thus:

> In order for a bonus to qualify . . . as a discretionary bonus . . . the employer must retain discretion both *as to the fact of payment and as to the amount until a time quite close to the end of the period for which the bonus is paid.* The sum, if any, to be paid as a bonus is determined by the employer *without prior promise or agreement.* The employee has no contract right, express or implied, to any amount. If the employer promises in advance to pay a bonus, he has abandoned his discretion with regard to it.[12]

---

10. *See* 29 U.S.C. §§ 207(e)(1)–(7).
11. *See, e.g., Acton,* 436 F.3d at 976.
12. 29 C.F.R. § 778.211(b) (emphasis added).

The FLSA regulations on the regular rate give several examples of the difference between a discretionary and a nondiscretionary bonus:

> [I]f an employer announces to his employees in January that he intends to pay them a bonus in June, he has thereby abandoned his discretion regarding the fact of payment by promising a bonus to his employees. Such a bonus would not be excluded from the regular rate . . . . Similarly, an employer who promises to sales employees that they will receive a monthly bonus computed on the basis of allocating 1 cent for each item sold whenever, if in his discretion, the financial condition of the firm warrants such payments, has abandoned discretion with regard to the amount of the bonus though not with regard to the fact of payment. Such a bonus would ***not*** be excluded from the regular rate. On the other hand, if a bonus such as the one just described were paid without prior contract, promise or announcement and the decision as to the fact and amount of payment lay in the employer's sole discretion, the bonus would be properly excluded from the regular rate.[13]

In order for a bonus payment to be considered discretionary and excluded from the regular rate, *all* of the following conditions must be met:

1. the employer must retain discretion as to whether payment will be made;
2. the employer must retain discretion as to the amount paid;
3. the employer must retain discretion as to the payment of the bonus until near the end of the period which it covers; and
4. the bonus must not be paid in accordance with a prior contract, agreement, or promise.[14]

Some examples of discretionary bonuses include payments for an employee's unique or extraordinary efforts (provided that the bonus is not awarded based on pre-established criteria), bonuses for overcoming stressful or challenging situations, and employee-of-the-month bonuses.[15] The regulations consider severance bonuses to be discretionary as well, but the North Carolina Constitution prohibits the payment of severance bonuses unless they are by contract, which makes them nondiscretionary and thus included in the regular rate.[16]

Bonuses that accrue to an employee automatically as a function of policy or ordinance are considered nondiscretionary bonuses, provided the employee meets a certain standard or satisfies a certain condition. These bonuses must be included

---

13. *Id.* (emphasis added).

14. 29 C.F.R. § 778.211(a). *See also* McLaughlin v. McGee Bros. Co., 681 F. Supp. 1117, 1133–34 (W.D.N.C. 1988), *aff'd sub nom.* Brock v. Wendell's Woodwork, Inc., 867 F.2d 196 (4th Cir. 1989); Abbey v. United States, 99 Fed. Cl. 430, 438 (2011).

15. *See* 29 C.F.R. § 778.211(d).

16. *See* Leete v. Warren Cty., 341 N.C. 116 (1995).

in the regular rate. Examples of nondiscretionary bonuses that must be included in the regular rate include

- bonuses that are announced to employees to induce them to work more steadily, more rapidly, or more efficiently or to remain with the organization;
- attendance bonuses;
- individual or group production bonuses;
- bonuses for quality and accuracy of work;
- bonuses contingent upon an employee's continuing in employment until the time the payment of the bonus is to be made.[17]

What these types of bonus payments have in common is that they are all tied either to hours worked or the performance of duties for the employer.

Some Further Examples

In government employment, it is usually the governing body—the city council or board of county commissioners, for example—that determines in its sole discretion whether or not to allocate money for employee bonuses. There are a number of different ways a public employer may grant bonuses, and the way in which they are granted will determine whether they are discretionary, and may be excluded from the regular rate, or nondiscretionary and must be included in the regular rate. Let's consider each scenario in turn.

As part of its annual budget, the Paradise City Council votes in June to give all employees a one-time across-the-board bonus of 2 percent of each employee's annual salary or straight-time pay. Employees will receive the bonus in their July paychecks. The award of a bonus is a pleasant surprise to Paradise employees.

Is this bonus discretionary or nondiscretionary? The council has satisfied all four of the requirements for a bonus to be considered discretionary and therefore excludable from the regular rate. The council had discretion as to whether or not the bonus payment would be made, had discretion as to how much each employee would receive, retained discretion as to whether a bonus would be paid until near the time of payment, and paid the bonus of its own accord, without having made any previous promise to pay such a bonus.

But suppose the timing were different.

As part of its annual budget, the Paradise City Council votes in June to give all employees a one-time across-the-board bonus of 10 percent of each employee's annual salary or straight-time pay. Employees will receive the bonus in their December paychecks. The award of a bonus is a pleasant surprise to Paradise employees.

---

17. *See* 29 C.F.R. § 778.211(c).

Here, the bonus is nondiscretionary because, in deciding in June to budget money for a bonus payable in December, the council has given up its discretion as to whether or not to award a bonus, as well as its discretion as to the amount of the bonus each employee will receive. All an employee need do to receive the bonus is remain employed with the city until December.[18]

What if the city council made the determination of whether to award a bonus on a year-to-year basis, at the time it adopts its annual budget, but has, in fact, given its employees a bonus payable in July in every one of the past fifteen years? In this situation, the budget seems discretionary in form, but nondiscretionary in fact. At least two courts have found that a bonus that is routinely given may give rise to the level of an implied contract for the bonus and that such a bonus must then be included in the regular rate.[19] Would it make any difference if the way in which the bonus is calculated varied from year to year? Probably not. For a bonus to be excluded from the regular rate, it must meet all four of the criteria set forth above. Even if the city council retains discretion as to how much an employee's bonus will be in a given year, if it has given up its discretion as to whether or not to offer a bonus, the bonus is nondiscretionary and must be included in the regular rate.

> The Paradise County Board of Commissioners has decided against giving permanent pay raises in the coming year and has instead set aside a sum in next year's budget for one-time employee bonuses. The board directs the county manager and those department heads with independent hiring, firing, and supervisory authority (such as the sheriff, register of deeds, and the directors of human services departments) to determine the amount to be paid to each employee within the amount budgeted to them. The board advises the manager and the department heads that no employee has a right to a bonus because of length of service or time in a particular position. Instead, bonuses are to be determined by a performance evaluation based on the following factors: quality of work, quantity of work, job knowledge, attitude, dependability, and attendance.

Is this bonus discretionary or nondiscretionary? Once again, the answer depends on timing. The FLSA says that sums "paid in recognition of services performed during a given period" may be excluded from the regular rate "if either . . . both the

18. *See, e.g.*, Mata v. Caring For You Home Health, Inc., 94 F. Supp. 3d 867, 876 (S.D. Tex. 2015) ("The fact is that Defendants made the decision to pay a bonus to their attendants as part of their wages and communicated that decision to them. In doing so, Defendants lost the requisite discretion to properly classify it as a bonus excluded from the regular rate.").

19. *See* Gilbertson v. City of Sheboygan, 165 F. Supp. 3d 742, 749–50 (E.D. Wis. 2016) (employees entitled to summary judgment on claim that bonuses subject to annual budget approval were nonetheless nondiscretionary and part of the regular rate); Wang v. Chinese Daily News, Inc., 435 F. Supp. 2d 1042, 1055–56 (C.D. Cal. 2006), *aff'd*, 623 F.3d 743 (9th Cir. 2010), *judgment vacated on other grounds*, 565 U.S. 801 (2011) (finding that bonus payments that were based on objective criteria and routinely granted were to be included in the regular rate).

fact that payment is to be made and the amount of the payment are determined at the sole discretion of the employer at or near the end of the period and not pursuant to any prior contract, agreement, or promise causing the employee to expect such payments regularly."[20] So if Paradise County's board decides in June to award bonuses in July and tells county management to determine which employees deserve bonuses based on their subjective evaluation of objective criteria, the bonus would appear to satisfy the FLSA's criteria for exclusion from the regular rate. Whether or not an individual employee receives a bonus is, in this version of the example, entirely at the discretion of the employer.

The FLSA regulations also say that "bonuses which are announced to employees to induce them to work more steadily or more rapidly or more efficiently or to remain with the firm are regarded as part of the regular rate of pay."[21] If the Paradise Board of Commissioners sets aside the bonus money in the budget in June and instructs management to award it at the end of the year based on the stated criteria, the bonus would likely be an incentive bonus and would be included in the regular rate.[22]

Other Types of Bonuses or Extra Payments

Gifts and Special-Occasion Payments

The FLSA expressly provides that gifts and payments marking special occasions such as career or years-of-service milestones, or payments made in recognition of a holiday such as Christmas or New Year's Day, do not have to be included when calculating the regular rate, so long as the amount of the payment is not tied to the number of hours employees have worked or how productively or how efficiently they have worked. Consider the following two hypotheticals.

1. *The City of Paradise decides to give a holiday "gift" of $100 to the ten nonexempt employees who have taken the fewest sick days during the previous twelve months.*

2. *Paradise County decides to give all of its employees a $25 Amazon gift card as a holiday "gift."*

Which of these "gifts" must be included in the regular rate?

---

20. *See* 29 U.S.C. § 207(e)(3).

21. 29 C.F.R. § 778.211(c).

22. *See* Walling v. Harnischfeger Corp., 325 U.S. 427, 432 (1945) (employees who received incentive bonuses in addition to their guaranteed base pay earned a greater regular rate than the minimum base rate as a matter of law, and employer's failure to pay them for overtime based on the increased rate violated the FLSA, notwithstanding contract designation of base rate as the regular rate); McLaughlin v. McGee Bros. Co., 681 F. Supp. 1117, 1133–34 (W.D.N.C. 1988), *aff'd sub nom.* Brock v. Wendell's Woodwork, Inc., 867 F.2d 196 (4th Cir. 1989) (incentive-type bonuses given pursuant to an understanding as a reward for specific employee behavior must be included in the regular rate); *Gilbertson*, 165 F. Supp. 3d at 749–50 (same).

The city must include the $100 it pays the ten employees who have taken the fewest sick days in the regular rate calculation of each of the employees receiving the gift. "Taking the fewest sick days" is just one of several alternate measures of tracking which nonexempt employees have worked the most. Because it is tied to the amount of work an employee has done, it may not be excluded from the regular rate. The gift card, on the other hand, is a true gift, since it is being given to all employees without reference to the quality or quantity of work performed. It is not being given in return for anything. As such, it does not need to be included in the regular rate.

Straight-Fee Payment for Noncompensable On-Call Time

When employees are on call after regularly scheduled working hours or on a weekend or holiday, they must be paid for all of the time during which they actually work in response to a call or emergency. As discussed in chapter 3, on pages 77 through 81, *supra*, time spent on call during which employees are free to go about their own business subject only to a requirement that they respond to a call or text is generally not compensable time. Nevertheless, many government employers pay on-call employees a set fee for on-call shifts that is in addition to compensable on-call time and that is paid whether an employee is called back into work during the shift or not. Straight-fee payments for on-call shifts are a type of nondiscretionary bonus. An employee automatically receives the bonus payment whenever he or she is on call. The bonus is not subject to the discretion of the manager or department head. As such, straight-fee payments for on-call shifts must be included in the regular rate.[23]

Employers may be tempted to argue that payments for noncompensable on-call time can be excluded from the regular rate under the exception provided by FLSA Section 207(e)(2) for "similar payments to an employee which are not made as compensation for his hours of employment." After all, the argument would go, the time is noncompensable precisely because during this time, employees are free to do whatever they please for their own benefit. The United States Department of Labor (DOL), however, disagrees, explaining:

> For example, an employment contract may provide that employees who are assigned to take calls for specific periods will receive a payment of $5 for each 8-hour period during which they are "on call" in addition to pay at their regular (or overtime) rate for hours actually spent in making calls. If the employees who are thus on call are not confined to their homes or to any particular place, but may come and go as they please, provided that they leave word where they may be reached, the hours spent "on call" are not considered as hours worked. Although the payment received by such employees for such "on call" time is, therefore, not allocable to any specific hours of work, it is clearly paid as compensation for performing a duty involved in the employee's job and is not of a type excludable under section 7(e)(2). The payment must therefore be included in the employee's

---

23. *See* 29 C.F.R. § 778.223(b).

regular rate in the same manner as any payment for services, such as an attendance bonus, which is not related to any specific hours of work.[24]

Shift Differentials

When employees are paid a shift differential, they are being paid at a higher rate because of undesirable hours. The FLSA regulations governing the regular rate expressly state that shift differentials **must be included** when calculating the regular rate.[25]

Longevity Pay

Longevity pay is a plan under which employees receive additional wages based on the number of years of service. Whether longevity pay must be included in the regular rate depends on whether or not it is discretionary. Longevity pay is usually automatically awarded once an employee reaches a benchmark length of service. When it works that way, it is a nondiscretionary bonus. But what if the decision to award employees a longevity bonus is made each year at the discretion of the governing board or the manager? Isn't that a discretionary bonus?

In North Carolina, the longevity-pay plan for state employees has been adopted by the General Assembly and is codified in the North Carolina General Statutes. Among North Carolina local government employers, longevity-pay plans are usually adopted by the city council or the county board of commissioners as part of the personnel policy or personnel ordinance and are budgeted in advance. A longevity-pay plan that is adopted by statute or ordinance becomes a vested benefit to which individual employees are contractually entitled once they meet the minimum service requirement. (North Carolina state employees must have ten years of state service to qualify for longevity pay; most North Carolina local governments require five or ten years of service with the same local government employer.[26]) Under these circumstances and as long as the statute or ordinance remains in effect, longevity pay is never up

---

24. 29 C.F.R. § 778.223(b). *See also* Rudy v. City of Lowell, 716 F. Supp. 2d 130, 133 (D. Mass. 2010) (citing several U.S. Department of Labor opinion letters) ("[P]ayments received by employees for being 'on call,' while not allocable to any specific hours of work, are clearly paid as compensation for performing duties involved in the employees' jobs and are not of a type excludable under section 7(e)(2) of FLSA.").

25. *See* 29 C.F.R. § 778.207(b). *See also* Bay Ridge Operating Co. v. Aaron, 334 U.S. 446, 468–69 (1948) (footnote omitted) ("Where an employee receives a higher wage or rate because of undesirable hours or disagreeable work, such wage represents a shift differential . . . . Such payments enter into the determination of the regular rate of pay."); Featsent v. City of Youngstown, 70 F.3d 900, 904 (6th Cir .1995) (Section 7(e) of the FLSA does not exclude shift differentials from the regular rate); Reich v. Interstate Brands Corp., 57 F.3d 574, 578 (7th Cir. 1995) (same); Thomas v. Howard Univ. Hosp., 39 F.3d 370, 372 (D.C. Cir. 1994) (same); Cabunac v. Nat'l Terminals Corp., 139 F.2d 853, 854–55 (7th Cir. 1944) (same); Ramirez v. Riverbay Corp., 35 F. Supp. 3d 513, 530 (S.D.N.Y. 2014) (same); Scott v. City of N.Y., 592 F. Supp. 2d 386, 405–06 (S.D.N.Y. 2008) (same); Bell v. Iowa Turkey Growers Co-op., 407 F. Supp. 2d 1051, 1057 (S.D. Iowa 2006) (same).

26. For more on longevity pay generally, see DIANE M. JUFFRAS, EMPLOYEE BENEFITS LAW FOR NORTH CAROLINA LOCAL GOVERNMENT EMPLOYERS 166–68 (UNC School of Government, 2009). For a more detailed discussion of longevity pay as a vested benefit, see Diane M. Juffras,

to the discretion of the government employer—it is nondiscretionary and must be included in the regular rate.[27]

Employees do not have a contractual right to longevity pay when the longevity-pay plan is adopted by resolution and is funded on a year-to-year basis in the sole discretion of a governing board. Nevertheless, once longevity pay is funded in the annual budget and the length of service that is required for earning the longevity pay and the date and manner in which it will be paid out are established, longevity pay is no longer a discretionary bonus but has become nondiscretionary.[28] Thus, most of the time, longevity pay will be nondiscretionary at the time it is earned and so will have to be included in the regular rate. Since longevity pay increases an employee's regular rate of pay, and overtime is based on a percentage of the regular rate, public employers must recalculate the overtime paid during the previous year to account for the late longevity-related adjustment to the employee's regular rate.[29] A discussion on how to recalculate the regular rate to incorporate longevity pay is discussed on pages 179 through 180, *infra*.

Paid Vacation, Holiday, or Sick Days

Section 207(e) of the FLSA says that payments made for occasional periods when no work is performed due to vacation, holiday, illness, or failure of the employer to provide employees with sufficient work do not have to be included in the regular rate.[30] This means that in a week in which a nonexempt employee has used accrued paid leave—whether for one or more full days or for some portion of a workday—that portion of the employee's compensation for the week attributable to the use of paid leave does not have to be included in calculating the regular rate.[31] As a practical

---

When Can a Public Employer Reduce Employee Benefits? Pub. Emp't L. Bull. No. 30 (May 2004), at 14–16, https://www.sog.unc.edu/sites/www.sog.unc.edu/files/reports/pelb30.pdf.

27. For longevity pay that is a function of contract as nondiscretionary and includable in the regular rate, see *Wheeler v. Hampton Township*, 399 F.3d 238, 247 (3d Cir. 2005) (because longevity pay was provided for in collective-bargaining contract, it had to be included in the regular rate); O'Brien v. Town of Agawam, 350 F.3d 279 (1st Cir. 2003) (same); *Featsent*, 70 F.3d at 905 (same); Shepard v. City of Waterloo, No. 14-CV-2057-LRR, 2015 WL 9165915 at *13 (N.D. Iowa Dec. 16, 2015) *Scott*, 592 F. Supp. 2d at 405 (the regular rate must include longevity pay insofar as it is nondiscretionary); Theisen v. City of Maple Grove, 41 F. Supp. 2d 932, 937–38 (D. Minn. 1999) (inclusion of longevity pay in collective-bargaining contract means city had no discretion as to whether to make payments). *Contra* Moreau v. Klevenhagen, 956 F.2d 516 (5th Cir. 1992), *aff'd*, 508 U.S. 22 (1993) (longevity pay that plaintiff deputy sheriffs received each year was not part of their "regular rate of pay" for purposes of computing the rate of overtime pay under the FLSA because it was in the nature of a gift from the county commission, served no purpose other than to reward the plaintiffs for their time spent as county employees, and was not measured by/dependent on the hours the plaintiffs worked or their production or efficiency levels).

28. *See* Cheek v. City of Greensboro, 152 F. Supp. 3d 473, 486–87 (M.D.N.C. 2015).

29. *See* Schmitt v. Kansas, 844 F. Supp. 1449, 1463 (D. Kan. 1994).

30. *See* 29 U.S.C. § 207(e)(2).

31. *See* Szymula v. Ash Grove Cement Co., 941 F. Supp. 1032, 1039 (D. Kan. 1996), *citing* Boll v. Fed. Reserve Bank, 365 F. Supp. 637, 646–47 (E.D. Mo. 1973), *aff'd*, 497 F.2d 335 (8th Cir. 1974);

matter, employees will be unlikely to work more than forty hours and earn overtime pay in weeks in which they have used one or more full days of paid leave.[32] But it isn't impossible, especially if there is severe weather or another emergency that requires city or county employees to work more hours or days than usual.

Many employers allow employees to receive the cash value of their accrued but unused paid leave when they end their employment, whether the payment is made during or at the conclusion of employment. Whether or not this lump-sum payment needs to be included in the regular rate for the pay period in which it is paid depends upon whether the leave in question is vacation, sick, or personal leave on one hand, or accrued comp time on the other. Where an employer's personnel policy provides for payment of the value of accrued, unused vacation time at an employee's customary rate, the amount of the payment is **not included** in the regular rate. That is because the payment is not compensation for hours of work, just as compensation paid when an employee is actually on vacation is not payment for hours of work. In accordance with Section 207(e)(2) of the FLSA, payments that are not compensation for work should not be credited in the calculation of overtime pay.[33] The same holds true for paid sick leave and for paid time off that is denoted "personal leave."[34]

Compensatory Time Off

Compensatory time off, or "comp time," is another form of accrued paid leave the cash value of which, like that of accrued vacation and personal leave, is not entered into the regular-rate calculation. Comp time, however, is not included for a very different reason—namely, because it is a form of overtime compensation, and overtime compensation cannot be included in the calculation of the regular rate on which overtime compensation is based. Comp time is discussed in the section on the exception for overtime compensation in chapter 4 at page 120.

Holiday Pay

Whether or not to include holiday pay in the regular rate is a tricky question, as there are different forms of holiday pay and they are treated differently for regular-rate purposes. Paid holidays on which an employee performs no work are **not** included in the regular rate. For example, most local governments are closed on Thanksgiving Day and provide their employees with a full day of pay nonetheless. For those

---

York v. City of Wichita Falls, 763 F. Supp. 876, 884 (N.D. Tex. 1990).

32. *See, e.g.,* Joseph G. Moretti, Inc. v. Boogers, 376 F.2d 27, 28 (5th Cir. 1967) ("We especially point out that overtime for holidays . . . [is] due only for that time in any particular week in which the employee actually worked more than forty hours.").

33. 29 C.F.R. § 778.219(a). *See* Lemieux v. City of Holyoke, 740 F. Supp. 2d 246, 254 (D. Mass. 2010).

34. *See Lemieux*, 740 F. Supp. 2d at 254. For North Carolina public employers, the sick leave provision is not likely to matter because the North Carolina General Statutes allow employees to apply unused, accrued paid sick leave to creditable service in LGERS, TSERS, or one of North Carolina's other retirement systems for public employees.

employees who do not work on Thanksgiving but are paid as if they had, the amount of compensation represented by the paid holiday is not part of the regular rate for that week, just as paid vacation leave is not part of the regular rate. It is not compensation for time worked.

Other employees, primarily employees in public safety, public works, and utilities, may be scheduled to work on Thanksgiving or they may be on call. Jurisdictions handle these situations differently, but for the sake of example, assume that FLSA nonexempt employees working a full shift on Thanksgiving receive both the same holiday pay that non-working employees receive **and** their regular hourly rate for hours worked. In this case, too, the holiday pay is not included in the hourly rate, as it is not compensation for work.[35]

Another jurisdiction, however, might pay employees who must work on Thanksgiving time-and-one-half their hourly rate or double their hourly rate for hours actually worked but not pay them the holiday pay that their non-working colleagues receive. Where employees are paid a minimum of one-and-one-half times their regular hourly rate for work on a holiday, two things happen. First, the holiday premium (the "half" in "one-and-one-half" or half of the double time) is **not** included in the regular rate.[36] Only the usual hourly rate is included. Second, because the holiday premium is equal to—or even more than, in the case of double time—the overtime rate, the amount of the holiday premium may be credited toward any overtime the employee earns in that week.[37] For payments that may be used to offset overtime compensation, see chapter 4, page 153. Note that if an employer uses a holiday rate that is more than an employee's regular hourly rate but less than one-and-one-half times the hourly rate, the amount of the premium *is* included in the regular rate.[38]

Reimbursements for Travel and Tuition

FLSA Section 207(e)(2) provides that payments made to reimburse actual traveling expenses or other expenses incurred by an employee for the benefit of the employer may be excluded when calculating the regular rate.[39] We do not commonly think of

---

35. *See* 29 C.F.R. § 778.219(a)(2). *See also York*, 763 F. Supp. at 884 (court found that plaintiffs' vacation, holiday, and sick leave hours were not to be included as payable overtime hours unless these unscheduled hours were actually worked).

36. *See* 29 C.F.R. § 778.219(b). *See also* Bay Ridge Operating Co. v. Aaron, 334 U.S. 446, 468–69 (1948) (footnote omitted) ("Where an employee receives a higher wage or rate because of undesirable hours or disagreeable work, such wage represents a shift differential or higher wages because of the character of work done or the time at which he is required to labor rather than an overtime premium. Such payments enter into the determination of the regular rate of pay.)."

37. *See* 29 C.F.R. §§ 778.203, .219(b)(1) & (2).

38. *See* 29 C.F.R. § 778.203. *See also* Reich v. Interstate Brands Corp., 57 F.3d 574, 578 (7th Cir. 1995) ("So if a baker's regular weekday rate were $10 and the rate for Sunday work were $15, the Sunday premium would not be figured back into the 'regular rate,' and time-and-a-half pay for overtime during the week would remain at $15. But if the Sunday rate were $14, the extra pay would be included in the 'regular rate,' raising the overtime rate for both weekdays and Sundays.").

39. *See* 29 U.S.C. § 207(e)(2).

such payments as income, so it seems only natural that they would not be included in the regular-rate calculation. The pertinent FLSA regulation explains:

> Where an employee incurs expenses on his employer's behalf or where he is required to expend sums by reason of action taken for the convenience of his employer, section 7(e)(2) is applicable to reimbursement for such expenses. Payments made by the employer to cover such expenses are not included in the employee's regular rate (if the amount of the reimbursement reasonably approximates the expenses incurred). Such payment is not compensation for services rendered by the employees during any hours worked in the workweek.[40]

The regulation also provides examples:

> Payment by way of reimbursement for the following types of expenses will not be regarded as part of the employee's regular rate:
> (1) The actual amount expended by an employee in purchasing supplies, tools, materials, cell phone plans, or equipment on behalf of his employer or in paying organization membership dues or credentialing exam fees where relevant to the employer's business.
> (2) The actual or reasonably approximate amount expended by an employee in purchasing, laundering or repairing uniforms or special clothing which his employer requires him to wear.
> (3) The actual or reasonably approximate amount expended by an employee, who is traveling "over the road" on his employer's business, for transportation (whether by private car or common carrier) and living expenses away from home, other travel expenses, such as taxicab fares, incurred while traveling on the employer's business.[41]

Therefore, whenever an employer makes a per diem payment for reimbursement of an employee's work-related travel, that reimbursement is not considered part of the employee's regular wages for the purpose of calculating the regular rate and overtime compensation, provided that the reimbursement is reasonable. The term "living expenses away from home," referenced in subsection (3) of the regulation, set out in the text immediately above, includes the cost of meals away from home.[42] This is true even where an employer pays all employees the same set per diem regardless of their

---

40. 29 C.F.R. § 778.217(a).

41. 29 C.F.R. § 778.217(b)(1)–(3).

42. *See* U.S. Dep't of Labor, Emp't Standards Admin., Wage & Hour Div., Wage & Hour Opinion Letter, FLSA 2004-3 (May 13, 2004), https://www.dol.gov/whd/opinion/FLSA/2004/2004_05_13_3_FLSA.pdf. *See also* Sharp v. CGG Land (U.S.) Inc., 840 F.3d 1211, 1215 (10th Cir. 2016) ($35 per diem for meals while travelling is exempt—as a living expense—from being included in the employee's regular rate of pay; in determining whether an expense incurred by an employee constitutes a "travel expense," "traveling" must be read more broadly as time away from home, not just time in transit).

actual expenses.[43] The regulations warn that "if the amount paid as 'reimbursement' is disproportionately large, the excess amount will be included in the regular rate."[44]

Tuition Reimbursement

Whether tuition reimbursement (or payments made directly to an educational institution or a student-loan issuer) was included in the regular rate was for many years a subject of dispute. In its most recent revision of the regular-rate regulations in 2020, DOL expressly provides that the tuition reimbursement may be excluded from the regular rate.[45]

Cash in Lieu of Payment of Health Insurance Premiums

Sometimes an employee who is covered under a spouse's or parent's health insurance plan would like to opt out of his or her employer's health insurance plan and instead receive the cash value of the employer's contribution to premium costs under that plan. Some employers allow it. This practice is lawful (as opposed to the practice of giving employees a cash supplement to purchase individual insurance on the open market through the federal government's Health Insurance Marketplace, which is unlawful),[46] but it has consequences for the regular rate of nonexempt employees.

Where an employee does participate in his or her employer's health plan, as is usually the case, FLSA Section 207(e)(4) exempts the employer's contributions to the cost of premiums under group health insurance plans from the regular rate:

> (e) As used in this section the "regular rate" at which an employee is employed shall be deemed to include all remuneration for employment paid to, or on behalf of, the employee, but shall not be deemed to include--   . . .
>
> (4) contributions *irrevocably* made by an employer *to a trustee or third person* pursuant to a *bona fide plan* for providing old-age, retirement, life, accident, or health insurance or similar benefits for employees . . .[47]

The key terms to note in this statutory subsection are italicized: *irrevocably, to a trustee or third person, bona fide plan.* Generally speaking, employer contributions to a health insurer or to a third-party administrator of a self-insured plan cannot, once made, be taken back. Employer contributions therefore fall squarely within this exception and are not included in the regular-rate calculation. But a cash payment made in lieu of a health insurance contribution does not fall within the exception

---

43. *See* Berry v. Excel Grp., Inc., 288 F.3d 252 (5th Cir. 2002).

44. 29 C.F.R. § 778.217(c)(1).

45. *See* 29 C.F.R. § 778.224(b)(5).

46. *See* I.R.S. Notice 2013-54, Application of Market Reform and Other Provisions of the Affordable Care Act to HRAs, Health FSAs, and Certain Other Employer Healthcare Arrangements, *available at* https://www.irs.gov/pub/irs-drop/n-13-54.pdf. *See also* Diane M. Juffras, A Guide to the Affordable Care Act for Local Government Employers 76 (UNC School of Government, 2016).

47. 29 U.S.C. § 207(e)(4) (emphasis added).

because it is paid directly to the employee rather than to a trustee or third party or under the terms of a bona fide benefit plan. It simply does not satisfy the exception to the regular rate set forth in Section 207(e)(4).[48]

Employers have argued unsuccessfully that a cash payment in lieu of enrollment in the employer's health plan is exempted from the regular rate under Section 207(e)(2), which allows exclusion of payments not made as compensation for hours worked.

> (e) As used in this section the "regular rate" at which an employee is employed shall be deemed to include all remuneration for employment paid to, or on behalf of, the employee, but shall not be deemed to include -- . . .
>
> (2) payments made for occasional periods when no work is performed due to a vacation, holiday, illness, failure of the employer to provide sufficient work, or other similar cause; reasonable payments for traveling expenses, or other expenses, incurred by an employee in the furtherance of his employer's interests and properly reimbursable by the employer; *and other similar payments to an employee which are not made as compensation for his hours of employment . . .*[49]

Employers have argued that cash-in-lieu-of-benefits payments do not depend on when or how much the employee worked, and thus are similar to payments made for periods when no work is performed.[50] Therefore, they have argued, they should not be included in the regular-rate calculation. The courts have rejected this argument, finding that since the payments had been subjected to income and FICA withholding taxes as compensation for hours worked, those amounts should have been included in calculating the employee's regular rate for the purpose of overtime compensation.[51] The federal Ninth Circuit Court of Appeals noted in one such case that this argument, as asserted by the employer, was in direct contradiction to the interpretation of FLSA Section 207(e)(2) set forth by the U.S. Department of Labor (DOL) in the FLSA regulations, which says that a payment may not be excluded from the regular rate if it is generally understood as compensation for work, even though the payment

---

48. *See* Flores v. City of San Gabriel, 824 F.3d 890, 901–02 (9th Cir. 2016) (cash-in-lieu-of-benefits payments are not properly excluded from the regular rate under Section 207(e)(4)); Callahan v. City of Sanger, No. 14-cv-600-BAM, 2015 WL 2455419, at *8–9 (E.D. Cal. May 22, 2015) (same). *See also* Gilbertson v. City of Sheboygan, 165 F. Supp. 3d 742, 751 (E.D. Wis. 2016) (city stipulated that payments for opting out of health insurance must be included in the regular rate); Garcia v. R.J.B. Props., Inc., 756 F. Supp. 2d 911, 913–14 (N.D. Ill. 2010) (in decision about the award of attorney fees, the court noted its earlier, unpublished holding that payments in lieu of health insurance contributions must be included in the regular rate).

49. 29 U.S.C. § 207(e)(2) (emphasis added).

50. *See, e.g., Flores*, 824 F.3d at 898–99.

51. *See id.; Callahan*, 2015 WL 2455419, at *7, *citing* Retail Indus. Leaders Ass'n v. Fielde, 475 F.3d 180, 193 (4th Cir. 2007) ("Healthcare benefits are part of the total package of employee compensation an employer gives in consideration for an employee's service").

is not directly tied to specific hours worked by an employee.[52] The court noted that the examples given in Section 778.224(a) of payments that were not intended to be excluded, such as bonuses or the provision of room and board, are commonly considered to be compensation even though such payments do not fluctuate in accordance with the particular hours worked by an employee.[53] In contrast, DOL's examples of payments that do constitute "other similar payments" under Section 207(e)(2) and that may be excluded from the regular rate under that subsection—amounts paid to an employee for the rental of her vehicle; loans or advances made to the employee; and "[t]he cost to the employer of conveniences furnished to the employee such as parking space, restrooms, lockers, on-the-job medical care and recreational facilities" —are manifestly unlike payments made in place of health insurance contributions.[54]

How to Include Longer-Term Bonuses in the Regular Rate

As discussed above, where a bonus is for work that has been done within the pay period and the bonus is paid in that same pay period, then the amount of the bonus is merely added to the other earnings of the employee and the total is divided by the number of straight and overtime hours worked to get that week's regular rate. But bonuses such as lump-sum merit bonuses or lump-sum longevity payments are usually meant to compensate an employee for a period of time longer than a single workweek or work period. In that case, calculations of the bonus may necessarily be deferred over a period of time longer than a workweek. When that happens, the employer may disregard the bonus in computing the regular hourly rate until such time as the amount of the bonus can be ascertained. In those situations, an employer does not have to take the bonus into account in calculating the regular rate until the bonus is paid.[55] The employer simply pays compensation for overtime at one and one-half times the hourly rate paid to the employee, exclusive of the bonus. But once the amount of the bonus is known, *the regular rate for each week covered by the bonus period will have to be recalculated and the difference in overtime owed and overtime actually paid will have to be made up.* The employee will receive additional compensation—for each workweek that he worked overtime during the period covered by the bonus—equal to one-half of the hourly rate of pay allocable to the bonus for that week multiplied by the number of statutory overtime hours worked during the week.[56]

Note that some lump-sum bonuses are considered earned in an equal amount each week of the period to which the bonus related. Sometimes, however, a lump-sum bonus is considered to have been earned only in certain of the workweeks of the

---

52. 29 C.F.R. § 778.224(a).

53. *See Flores,* 824 F.3d at 898–99; 29 C.F.R. § 778.224(a). *See also Callahan,* 2015 WL 2455419, at *6–8.

54. *See Flores,* 824 F.3d at 898–901; 29 C.F.R. § 778.224(b).

55. *See* 29 C.F.R. § 778.209(a).

56. *See id.*

period to which it relates, in which case the amount of the bonus must be proportionately allocated to those weeks in which it was considered earned.

Making an Overtime Pay Adjustment to Include Longevity Pay in the Regular Rate

Most North Carolina jurisdictions that offer a longevity-pay bonus pay it out once a year, although they could pay it out more frequently if they wanted to. When it is clear that an employee has earned the longevity-pay bonus (by staying employed with the employer through the cut-off date) and that the amount of longevity pay can be calculated and credited to him or her, the longevity pay "must be apportioned back over the workweeks of the period during which it may be said to have been earned." As is the case with other bonuses earned over a period of time, the employer **must** retrospectively compensate employees for the difference between what the employees actually received in overtime compensation and what they would have received if the regular rate had included the pro-rata amount of longevity pay in those weeks that the employee worked overtime during the preceding year.

A Cautionary Note

At C.F.R. Title 29, Section 778.209(a), the FLSA regulations provide that bonuses that cannot be identified with a particular week's work may be divided into equal amounts of bonus for each of the weeks to which the bonus relates. At first blush, it would therefore seem appropriate to divide the amount of a longevity-pay bonus into fifty-two equal parts, representing the fifty-two weeks of the year for which the longevity pay is awarded. Do not do this. The amount of longevity pay is not tied to hours worked or weeks worked. It is tied to years of service, so this method of calculating the regular rate is not correct.

Although calculating back the overtime differential over the course of an entire year seems daunting at first, the task is not difficult if an employer follows the instructions set out by DOL in Section 778.209(b) of C.F.R. Title 29:

1. First, add together all of the hours, both straight-time and overtime hours, that the employee worked during the year covered by the longevity payment.
   - If an employer pays out a longevity bonus in the last week or last pay period of the longevity year, it won't know how many total hours the employee has worked in the year because it is possible that the employee will be needed to work overtime before this end-of-the-year week is through. In this case, the employer should wait until the next payday after the week in which the longevity is paid out to calculate the additional overtime.
   - If the employer waits until after the end of the year to pay out the longevity bonus, it will have no problem in calculating the total number of hours.

2. Once the total number of hours that an employee has worked in the year covered by the longevity payment has been determined, divide the total amount of the longevity payment by that number. This is the longevity rate of pay.

3. Now multiply the total number of overtime hours worked in the year by one-half of the longevity rate of pay. The result is the longevity overtime differential payout amount owed to the employee.

Why is the multiplier only one-half of the longevity rate of pay and not one-and-one-half times the rate? Because the calculation of the longevity rate of pay has already taken into account all of the straight hours worked (the "time" in "time-and-one-half").

Longevity Pay and the Regular Rate: The Example of Paramedic Joe

Let's look at an example. Recall paramedic Joe from the previous discussion of how to calculate the regular rate. Joe has an hourly rate of $10 per hour. In addition, he receives $55 each week as a bonus for being on call two nights per week. Let's assume he works four hours of overtime each week. In the example, we calculated his regular rate to be $11.25 per hour. That is higher than his hourly rate because the on-call pay must be added in to calculate the regular rate. So, with the calculation of the regular rate, Joe's four hours of overtime were paid at an overtime rate of $16.86. He earned a total of $67.50 in overtime pay, in addition to his weekly straight-time pay of $400 and his $55 on-call bonus.

Now, let's add a complication. This year, Joe earns a longevity bonus of $2,000. He still works four hours of overtime each week. He is something of a superman and has not taken a day of vacation or sick leave this year. That means that Joe has worked forty hours of straight time and four hours of overtime each of the fifty-two weeks of the year. *That's 2,080 hours of straight time and 208 hours of overtime. When all of his hours are added together, it turns out that Joe has worked a total of 2,288 hours*—straight-time and overtime hours combined—during the period represented by the longevity payment.

The complication is that the overtime that Joe was paid each week was based on a regular rate that, while it included the on-call bonus, did not include the longevity bonus. It did not include the longevity bonus because the longevity bonus had not been paid yet. So now Joe's employer must make a retroactive calculation of what he would have been paid in overtime if his longevity bonus had, in fact, been calculated into the regular rate. Nobody is at fault. There simply needs to be an adjustment to bring Joe's overtime payments over the past year up to where they should be, with the longevity bonus figured into the regular rate.

To determine Joe's longevity-differential payment, the employer must *divide the $2,000 longevity payment by Joe's 2,288 hours of work to get a longevity rate of pay of $.88* (yes, that's right, 88 cents). Finally, his employer must *multiply Joe's 208 hours of overtime by one-half of the longevity rate of pay, or $.44. Joe's employer*

owes him $91.52 to make up for the fact that longevity pay should have been included in his regular rate.

- 40 × 52 = 2,080 (straight-time hours)
- 4 × 52 = 208 (overtime hours)
- 2,080 + 208 = 2,288 (total hours worked)
- $2,000 longevity pay ÷ 2,288 hours worked = $.88 (longevity rate of pay)
- $.44 (one-half the longevity rate) × 208 hours of overtime = $91.52

Remember Joe's colleague planner Elizabeth, the salaried nonexempt employee? She, too, earns longevity pay. She's been around longer than Joe and is paid $2,600 in longevity pay. The same formula applies to both Elizabeth, a salaried nonexempt employee, and to Joe, an hourly nonexempt employee. Elizabeth has worked a total of 1,900 straight-time hours this year and has worked twelve hours of overtime each month. That's all her employer needs to know to figure out how much Elizabeth is owed to make up for the fact that longevity pay was not included in her regular rate. Here's the answer: Elizabeth's employer owes her $92.16. Can you apply the formula and get the correct amount? The answer is below.

Calculating Planner Elizabeth's Longevity-Pay Overtime Differential

1. Elizabeth is a salaried nonexempt employee. She is paid $456 per week for a thirty-seven-and-one-half-hour workweek.

2. To get Elizabeth's hourly rate, divide $456 by thirty-seven-and-one-half. Her hourly rate is $12.16 per hour.

3. Elizabeth is paid $2,600 in longevity pay at the end of the year.

4. Elizabeth has worked 12 hours of overtime each month, or 144 total hours of overtime, during the year. She has worked a total of 1,900 hours of straight time this year.

5. Add the total number of hours of straight time to the total number of hours of overtime to determine that Elizabeth has worked a total of 2,044 hours this year.

6. Divide the $2,600 of longevity pay by the 2,044 total hours Elizabeth has worked during the year to get an hourly longevity rate of $1.28.

7. Divide the hourly longevity rate of $1.28 by one-half and get $.64.

8. Multiply one-half of the longevity rate, or $.64, by 144, the number of overtime hours Elizabeth has worked during the year. This is the amount that Elizabeth's employer owes her to make up for the fact that her regular rate did not include her longevity pay. Elizabeth's employer owes her $92.16.

A Final Note on Calculating the Regular Rate

The regular rate of pay is based on the regular hourly rate or the regular salary before any non-statutory deductions are made. Deductions for salary advances, lost or damaged property, the recovery of training costs, or those made for disciplinary reasons cannot be taken into account in determining the regular rate. When a nonexempt employee works overtime hours, lawful deductions may be made from the employee's non-overtime hours but may not be taken into account in calculating overtime. For a full discussion of deductions from salary, see chapter 2 of this book.

The Regular Rate under the Fluctuating Workweek

The principles discussed above in regard to salaried nonexempt employees with traditional hours and pay schedules also apply to nonexempt employees whose number of hours vary from week to week and who are paid under the fluctuating workweek method.

Section 207(k) and the Regular Rate

The regular-rate rules applicable to salaried nonexempt employees with traditional hours also apply to hourly nonexempt law enforcement and fire protection employees who are subject to a higher hour threshold for overtime and generally work a work period longer than seven days pursuant to FLSA Section 207(k). The FLSA regulations say that when 207(k) law enforcement and firefighter overtime is being compensated with cash rather than with compensatory time off, the words "work period" should be substituted for the words "work week" wherever the regular rate is discussed.[57]

---

57. *See* 29 C.F.R. § 553.223.

Chapter 6

Are These People Employees? Volunteers, Interns, Independent Contractors, and the Special Case of Joint Employment

Local governments, like nonprofit organizations, are regular beneficiaries of community-minded people who are willing to perform services without pay—in other words, volunteers.[1] Some volunteers want nothing in return, but many government agencies and nonprofits offer reimbursement of expenses or a small cash gift both to thank their current volunteers and as an inducement to others to join their ranks. This is a lawful practice that benefits both sides. Sometimes, however, the compensation paid to volunteers creeps upward, and the government agency may find itself paying something close to the equivalent of minimum wage in return for volunteer services.

Local governments also benefit from the services performed by interns, who are generally students seeking to get exposure to and experience in the workings of government. Sometimes an intern receives no or only nominal compensation, in which case the intern is properly seen as a form of volunteer. But sometimes governmental employers think it appropriate to pay the intern a stipend—a fixed fee for the length of the internship. Local governments that pay stipends may not notice that, when divided by the average number of hours the intern works each week, "stipends" can start to look very much like wages at or above minimum wage.

---

1. Governments and nonprofit organizations may lawfully accept the services of unpaid volunteers. Private, for-profit employers, by contrast, must generally pay at least minimum wage—even to student "volunteers" (i.e., interns) who perform work useful to the private employers.

Is there a point at which the compensation paid to volunteers or interns turns them into employees? Are there other factors that enter into the analysis of whether a person performing services is actually an employee? May local governments treat volunteers and interns as independent contractors? How is an independent contractor different from an employee anyhow? And finally, what if a governmental employer supplements the ranks of its permanent employees with workers from a staffing agency? Are there pitfalls inherent in this joint employment relationship? These are the questions that will be addressed in this chapter.

Volunteers and Interns

We might think that a public employer would prefer that a person be classified as a "volunteer" rather than as an "employee." After all, an employer's obligations to a volunteer pale in comparison to its obligations to an employee: the employer owes employees retirement and health benefits and workers' compensation protection and must comply with the safeguards that the Fair Labor Standards Act (FLSA) and the Affordable Care Act provide employees. So where is the line between volunteer and employee? The *Merriam-Webster Dictionary* defines the adjective "voluntarily" as "acting or done of one's own free will without valuable consideration or legal obligation."[2] The FLSA definition of "volunteer" is consistent with this common usage and fleshes it out. For purposes of the FLSA, a person is a volunteer—and not an employee—when he or she

- "performs . . . service[s] for a public agency for civic, charitable, or humanitarian reasons, without promise, expectation or receipt of compensation for services rendered;"[3]
- does not, in fact, receive any compensation or is paid only "expenses, reasonable benefits, [or a] nominal fee[]"[4] to perform the services for which the individual volunteered;
- has offered their services "freely and without pressure or coercion, direct or implied, from an employer;"[5] and
- is not "otherwise employed by the same [local government] to perform the same type of services."[6]

As is usually the case with the FLSA, there is a lot to unpack here. How much can a government employer pay a volunteer and still have the compensation be considered "nominal"? What are "reasonable" benefits? Is there a limit on the kind of expenses

---

2. See the seventh variant (*voluntarily*) under *voluntary* in Merriam-Webster Dictionary online, https://www.merriam-webster.com/dictionary/voluntarily (last visited Oct. 3, 2019).
3. 29 C.F.R. § 553.101(a).
4. *Id.*
5. 29 C.F.R. § 553.101(c).
6. 29 C.F.R. § 553.101(d). *See also* 29 U.S.C. § 203(e)(4)(A).

that may be reimbursed or the amount of money that may be paid as a reimbursement? And in the case of employees who volunteer for their own employers, what would be the "same type of services"?

Compensating a Volunteer

Reimbursement of Expenses

A volunteer may be paid expenses, reasonable benefits, a nominal fee, or even a combination of the three without losing his or her status as a volunteer. Examples of expenses include a uniform allowance; reimbursement for reasonable cleaning expenses or for wear and tear on personal clothing;[7] reimbursement for out-of-pocket expenses incurred while providing volunteer services (such as payment for the cost of meals and transportation expenses); and reimbursement for tuition, transportation, and meal costs involved in attending classes intended to teach volunteers how to perform their services, as well as for books, supplies, or other materials essential to volunteer training.[8]

Nominal Fees

A volunteer may be paid a nominal fee and still retain his or her status as a volunteer. The U.S. Department of Labor (DOL) will consider the following factors in determining whether a given amount is nominal:

- the distance traveled by the volunteer to perform services;
- the time and effort expended by the volunteer;
- whether the volunteer has agreed to be available around the clock or only during certain specified time periods; and
- whether the volunteer provides services as needed or throughout the year (an individual who volunteers to provide periodic services on a year-round basis may receive a nominal monthly or annual stipend or fee without losing volunteer status).[9]

It is important to recognize that to be considered nominal, a fee may not be tied to hours worked or to a volunteer's productivity. Generally, one of the most important factors in assessing whether a payment to a volunteer is a substitute for wages is whether the amount paid varies depending on (1) the amount of time the volunteer spends on the activity or (2) the volunteer's productivity. Payments based on either hours worked or productivity are a signal that the individual is an employee rather than a volunteer. The federal Fourth Circuit Court of Appeals case *Purdham v. Fairfax County School Board*[10] is a good example of these principles as applied. The court there held that a school board's payment of a fixed stipend to a golf coach

---

7. *See* 29 C.F.R. § 553.106(b).
8. *See* 29 C.F.R. § 553.106(c).
9. *See* 29 C.F.R. § 553.106(e).
10. 637 F.3d 421 (4th Cir. 2011).

was a nominal fee where (1) the amount of the stipend did not change based on either how much time and effort the coach expended on coaching activities or how successful the team was and (2) the approximate hourly rate to which the coach's stipend could be converted was only a fraction (less than one-fourth) of the hourly wage he received as a full-time security assistant employed by the school board.[11] In contrast, in a case from the federal Sixth Circuit Court of Appeals, volunteer firefighters for a municipality were paid an hourly rate substantially similar to the hourly rates paid to full-time employed firefighters in neighboring areas. Although the firefighters in this case could choose whether to respond to a call (unlike the full-time firefighters), the court found that they were paid a substantial hourly wage for whatever time they chose to spend firefighting. The court found that they were employees, not volunteers.[12]

Nominal payments may be made on a "per call" basis to volunteer firefighters, law enforcement reserve officers, and emergency medical personnel, so long as the payment is tied to the volunteers' sacrifice rather than to their productivity.[13] In several opinion letters, DOL has said that a nominal volunteer fee is generally an amount that does not exceed 20 percent of the total compensation the employer would pay to have an employee in a full-time position performing similar duties or services.[14]

Employee-Like Benefits

The FLSA regulations provide that some level of employee-like benefits may be made available without turning a volunteer into an employee—even those sorts of benefits typically associated with employee status, such as participation in group insurance plans such as health insurance, disability plans, or coverage under workers' compensation insurance. But employers, including local government employers, should be cautious. Given that health insurance premiums are quite expensive, even as part of a group plan, it is probably better to read this regulation as allowing volunteers to participate in a local government's group health plan at their own cost or with nominal governmental contributions. Otherwise, a premium contribution on behalf of a volunteer will likely run afoul of the "reasonable" requirement because the value of the contribution would be more than nominal. In some instances, state law provides for modest retirement benefits for those volunteering in a public safety capacity. The FLSA regulations recognize this as a reasonable benefit.[15] As the regulations advise,

---

11. *See id.* at 433–34.
12. *See* Mendel v. City of Gibraltar, 727 F.3d 565, 571 (6th Cir. 2013).
13. *See* 29 C.F.R. § 553.106(e). *See also* U.S. Dep't of Labor (DOL), Emp't Standards Admin., Wage & Hour Div., Wage & Hour Opinion Letter, FLSA 2006-28 (Aug. 7, 2006), https://www.dol.gov/whd/opinion/FLSA/2006/2006_08_07_28_FLSA.pdf (volunteer firefighters).
14. See the following opinion letters from DOL: Wage & Hour Opinion Letter, FLSA 2006-28, *supra* note 13; Wage & Hour Opinion Letter, FLSA 2205-51 (Nov. 10, 2005), https://www.dol.gov/whd/opinion/FLSA/2005/2005_11_10_51_FLSA.pdf (school coaches and club advisors).
15. *See* 29 C.F.R. § 553.106(d).

however, the ultimate test can only be made on a case-by-case basis by examining the "total amount of payments made (expenses, benefits, fees) in the context of the economic realities of the particular situation."[16]

Other Types of Tangible Benefits

Sometimes law enforcement reserve officers and others in positions that require a minimum number of service hours to maintain certifications wish to volunteer without monetary compensation in return for being allowed to maintain their certifications. Although the language of the FLSA and the regulations seem to require that volunteers be motivated only by civic, charitable, or humanitarian purposes, the fact that a volunteer is motivated in part by the need to maintain a certification does not disqualify him or her from volunteer status.[17]

Employees as Volunteers: The Meaning of "Same Type of Services"

Here is a hard and fast rule: a volunteer may not provide services to a local government in a volunteer capacity if he or she is employed by that local government to provide the same kind of services. Section 553.101 of Title 29 of the Code of Federal Regulations (C.F.R.) states that

> [a]n individual shall not be considered a volunteer if the individual is otherwise employed by the same public agency to perform the same type of services as those for which the individual proposes to volunteer.[18]

To put it another way: an employee cannot volunteer to do his or her own job without compensation. This prohibition is designed to eliminate the possibility of an employer coercing an employee to perform unpaid work. As Section 785.44 of the FLSA regulations says,

> [t]ime spent in work for public or charitable purposes at the employer's request, or under his direction or control, or while the employee is required to be on the premises, is working time. However, time spent voluntarily in such activities outside of the employee's normal working hours is not hours worked.[19]

---

16. *See* 29 C.F.R. § 553.106(f). *See also Purdham*, 637 F.3d at 433.

17. *See* Cleveland v. City of Elmendorf, 388 F.3d 522, 527–28 (5th Cir. 2004) (motivations of maintenance of commissions and of gaining experience are not of significant consequence in determining volunteer status); Benshoff v. City of Va. Beach, 9 F. Supp. 2d 610, 623 (E.D. Va. 1998) (holding that firefighters motivated primarily, but not exclusively, by civic, charitable, and humanitarian reasons to serve uncompensated on rescue squads were volunteers; one firefighter joined rescue squad to learn more); Todaro v. Twp. of Union, 40 F. Supp. 2d 226, 230–31 (D.N.J. 1999) ("The regulatory definition does not require that the individual be exclusively, or even predominantly, motivated by 'civic, charitable, or humanitarian reasons'; therefore, the Court understands this phrase to be modified by an implied 'at least in part.'").

18. 29 C.F.R. § 553.101(d). *See also id.* § 553.104.

19. 29 C.F.R. § 785.44; DOL, Wage & Hour Opinion Letter, FLSA 2006-18 (June 1, 2006), https://www.dol.gov/whd/opinion/FLSA/2006/2006_06_01_18_FLSA.pdf.

For purposes of the FLSA, the phrase "same type of services" means *similar or identical services*. To determine whether services are of the same type, DOL will look to (1) the duties and other factors contained in the definitions of the three-digit categories of occupations in the DOL Education and Training Administration's Occupational Information Network (O*NET) system[20] and (2) whether, in the particular case, the volunteer service is closely related to the actual duties performed by or responsibilities assigned to the employee.[21]

The regulations give two examples of employee volunteers who *are* performing the "same type of services" as in their regular paid positions (meaning that the employer is violating the FLSA): (1) a nurse employed by a state hospital who volunteers to perform nursing services at a state health clinic and (2) employee firefighters in a mixed employee-volunteer fire department who volunteer for the same department in their off-duty hours.[22] The regulations also provide examples of employee volunteers who are **not** performing the "same type of services" as in their paid positions: (1) a city police officer who volunteers as a part-time referee in a city parks and rec basketball league, (2) an employee of the city parks department who serves as a volunteer city firefighter, and (3) an administrative assistant in the department of aging who volunteers with the Meals-on-Wheels program sponsored by the department for humanitarian and charitable reasons.[23] The examples given in the regulations are relatively straightforward and focus on employees whose volunteer work takes place in a department different than the one in which they regularly work.[24]

But what about employees who volunteer to perform different services in the same department or agency in which they are employed? The test, as a number of DOL opinion letters show, focuses on whether the work an employee does in a volunteer capacity is the same as the work performed in his or her paid position, not on whether the department or unit where the employee is providing services is the same. Consider the following situation.

> *An organization that provides programming services to at-risk youth is on occasion able to take their clients on cultural or sports-related field trips. The field trips require a greater number of chaperones than the organization has counselors. May employees of the organization serve as volunteer chaperones?*

---

20. 29 C.F.R. § 553.103 refers to the "Dictionary of Occupational Titles," but that resource was last published by DOL's Education and Training Administration in 1991 and has since been replaced by the O*NET system, which may be found at https://www.onetonline.org.

21. *See* 29 C.F.R. § 553.103(a).

22. *See* 29 C.F.R. § 553.103(b).

23. *See* 29 C.F.R. § 553.103(c).

24. *See also* DOL, Wage & Hour Opinion Letter, FLSA 2006-2 (Jan. 13, 2006), https://www.dol.gov/whd/opinion/FLSA/2006/2006_01_13_02_FLSA.pdf (code compliance officer may volunteer as reserve police officer).

In this scenario, DOL advised that any employee whose work did *not* involve supervising children could volunteer. Office and housekeeping staff and management, for example, could volunteer as chaperones who did not have to be paid. Counselors or others at the organization involved in the regular activities in which children participated could not serve as unpaid volunteer chaperones, even if the field trip took place on a non-workday.[25] Similarly, DOL advised a different employer that a paid fire captain could also serve as a volunteer chaplain for his employing jurisdiction, even if he were to be called upon to perform his services as chaplain in connection with the fire department. The reason: the two positions do not share the same job duties.[26]

In 2004, DOL gave two different counties opinions on whether paid detention officers in county jails could volunteer to perform patrol deputy work for the county sheriff. In the first county, detention officers were non-sworn, non-deputized civilian employees of the sheriff without the power of arrest. Their primary duties involved the processing, maintenance, and discharge of jail inmates. In contrast, special deputies were law enforcement officers who performed the same duties as full-time, sworn, state-certified deputies, just on an occasional and unpaid basis. In the second county, detention officers were themselves deputies who worked in jail security rather than out on patrol. Deputy sheriffs in the law enforcement division performed more diverse duties than did the detention officers because their responsibilities were for county-wide security.

In **both** instances, DOL opined that the detention officers could **not** perform patrol work on a volunteer basis, noting in one letter that, "while the specific duties of the two positions in question may be different in the particular daily tasks performed, the overall similarity and commonality of the jobs as variations of law enforcement outweigh these differences between them."[27] In both instances, DOL looked to the O*NET system and found that its description of duties for correctional officers and jailers on the one hand, and sheriffs and deputy sheriffs on the other, were similar and that, moreover, they were in the same job family and treated as related occupations.[28]

Volunteer Fire Departments and Emergency Medical Squads

Many firefighting and emergency medical agencies rely on volunteers for staffing, in whole or in part. Can a paid firefighter volunteer with another firefighting organization? Can a paid emergency medical technician (EMT) or paramedic volunteer with another emergency medical or rescue squad? These are questions of utmost importance for many agencies responsible for protecting the community. Happily, the answers are an unequivocal "yes." Firefighters just cannot volunteer to perform

25. *See* DOL, Wage & Hour Opinion Letter, FLSA 2006-18, *supra* note 19.
26. *See* DOL, Wage & Hour Opinion Letter, FLSA 2004-19 (Nov. 5, 2004), https://www.dol.gov/whd/opinion/FLSA/2004/2004_11_05_19_FLSA_FireCaptain.pdf.
27. *See* DOL, Wage & Hour Opinion Letter, FLSA 2004-26NA (Oct. 29, 2004), https://www.dol.gov/whd/opinion/FLSANA/2004/2004_10_29_26FLSA_NA_Deputy_Sheriff.htm.
28. *See id.*; DOL, Wage & Hour Opinion Letter, FLSA 2004-25NA (Oct. 22, 2004), https://www.dol.gov/whd/opinion/FLSANA/2004/2004_10_22_25FLSA_NA_Correction_officer.htm.

firefighting services with the same agencies that employ them. So, for example, a paid firefighter with the City of Paradise cannot volunteer with the city's fire department, even if the department is one that has both paid firefighters and volunteer firefighters. A paid *city* firefighter can, however, volunteer with the *county* fire department, with the fire department of *another municipality* or with a *strictly volunteer private nonprofit* fire agency. The same is true of EMTs and paramedics. Because the position of EMT and that of paramedic are separate and distinct, with different job duties, a local government with a mixed department of paid employees and volunteers might be tempted to allow paid paramedics to volunteer as EMTs. This, however, would be a mistake for the same reason that DOL opined against permitting detention officers to serve as deputies (see the discussion on page 188, *supra*): the positions are too similar. DOL's O*NET system classifies the two positions together, describing them both as involving assessing injuries, administering emergency medical care, and extricating trapped individuals, as well as transporting injured or sick persons to hospitals.[29]

What happens if a city firefighter volunteers with a private volunteer fire department and, during one of his volunteer shifts, the volunteer department is called to assist on a fire where the city department is the primary firefighting department? Nothing happens. While serving as a volunteer, the firefighter's hours are not intermingled with the main fire department, even though that firefighter is working alongside his employing department as a volunteer. The key distinction is that this firefighter is not working for his employing department at this fire; he is working in coordination with it. This is true even if the city department has operational control at the fire and the volunteer department takes direction from a city fire chief.[30] The same holds true for emergency medical employees who volunteer with neighboring but independent departments or squads.

Compensating an Intern

For FLSA purposes, what is an *internship*? An internship is a work experience offered by a unit of government, nonprofit organization, or business to individuals interested in gaining skills, knowledge, and hands-on experience in a given field. Interns are usually, but not always, students or recent graduates, and internships are usually temporary. Most internships require interns to perform services of some sort for the organization in return for which the student may receive lump-sum compensation known as a stipend or sometimes no compensation at all. From the student's perspective, a good internship gives him or her something that can be more valuable than money: practical experience that may lead to a real job in a particular field after graduation. From an employer's perspective, a good intern performs useful work at

---

29. *See* U.S. Dep't of Labor, *O*NET OnLine*, "Summary Report for: 29-2041.00 – Emergency Medical Technicians and Paramedics," ONETONLINE.ORG (updated 2019), https://www.onet online.org/link/summary/29-2041.00.

30. *See, e.g.*, 29 C.F.R. § 553.105.

less than the cost of a full-time employee. Interns also can form a pool from which to seek new employees in the future.

Internships may be paid or unpaid. Public employers (unlike private employers) have a choice with respect to interns. They may freely avail themselves of the services of "interns" if they treat them as volunteers and do not pay them any more than reimbursement of direct expenses or a *de minimis* token of appreciation. Or they may treat them as employees and pay them at least minimum wage (and maybe overtime). A public employer may not pay "interns" a stipend that amounts to less than the minimum wage. If a public employer wishes to pay an intern a stipend, then the intern becomes a temporary employee, subject to minimum wage and all of the other applicable requirements of the FLSA.[31]

Consider the following two "internships."

> *Tim is a twenty-year-old college student majoring in accounting. He expresses interest in an internship with the city's finance department over the summer. Chris, a high school athlete, applies for a position as an intern working in the city's summer camp program. The city offers both students the internships. Tim is offered a stipend of $2,500 for ten weeks of full-time work. Chris is told he will not be paid at all.*

It may come as a surprise, but in paying Tim a stipend of $2,500, the city is violating the FLSA. In not paying Chris anything, the city is complying with the FLSA. How can this be?

Neither the FLSA nor its regulations make mention of interns or internships.[32] For this reason, many employers assume that internship arrangements are not affected by the FLSA. The fact that internships are not addressed by the FLSA, however, means something very different. *It means that the FLSA does not recognize the internship arrangement as an exception to its requirement that a worker must be paid at least the minimum wage as well as overtime compensation once he or she has worked forty hours in a single workweek.*

Paying an Intern a Stipend

Let's return to Tim. He is working what is a full-time schedule for the city—forty hours per week—for the ten weeks of his summer break from college. He is being paid the lump sum of $2,500. That works out to $6.26 per hour, a full $1.00 per hour less than the federal minimum wage. "What's wrong with that?", many may think. After all, Tim is a college student. He hasn't earned his degree yet and has no previous experience working in a municipal finance office. Whatever Tim learns over the

---

31. Private employers do not have the same choice. They must pay an intern at least minimum wage, unless the internship is part of an experience for which the intern is receiving academic credit. See the sidebar on page 195, *infra*.

32. Except for one mention of "Congressional interns" and another of medical interns who have already received their medical degrees.

summer and however proficient he becomes at the particular duties he is assigned will be of no ongoing benefit to the city because Tim will go back to school when his internship is over. Moreover, as explained more fully below, the city could have lawfully offered him an unpaid internship.

How Private-Sector Internships Are Different

Public employers should be aware that DOL has developed a six-part test for determining whether the use of unpaid interns by private employers is lawful. Any private employer that does not meet each of the six requirements must pay its interns minimum wage. Unlike their public counterparts, private employers do not have the option of treating interns as volunteers. The latest articulation of this test may be found in a publication created by DOL's Wage and Hour Division, *Fact Sheet #71: Internship Programs Under the Fair Labor Standards Act* (remember, internships are not mentioned as a stand-alone category in the FLSA regulations).[a] Under this test, the use of unpaid interns by **private employers** is unlawful unless the internship arrangement meets **all** of the following requirements:

1. The internship, even though it includes actual operation of the facilities of the employer, is similar to training which would be provided in an educational environment.

2. The internship experience is for the benefit of the intern.

3. The intern does not displace regular employees but, rather, works under close supervision of existing staff.

4. The employer providing the training derives no immediate advantage from the activities of the intern and, on occasion, its operations may actually be impeded by that training/those activities.

5. The intern is not necessarily entitled to a job at the conclusion of the internship.

6. The employer and the intern both understand that the intern is not entitled to wages for the time spent in the internship.

The Second, Ninth, and Eleventh Circuits have rejected the DOL test in favor of a more flexible "primary beneficiary test" that includes some—but not all—of the DOL factors and looks at the totality of the circumstances.[b]

a. *See* note 34, *infra*.
b. *See* Glatt v. Fox Searchlight Pictures, Inc., 811 F.3d 528, 537 (2d Cir. 2016); Benjamin v. B & H Educ., Inc., 877 F.3d 1139, 1147 (9th Cir. 2017); Schumann v. Collier Anesthesia, P.A., 803 F.3d 1199, 1211 (11th Cir. 2015).

However reasonable it may seem to pay him a stipend of $2,500, as long as Tim is doing work for the city, he is "employed" within the meaning of the Fair Labor Standards Act. That is, he is "suffered or permitted to work."[33] Under those circumstances,

33. *See* 29 U.S.C. § 203(g).

Tim is an employee and, as such, he must be paid the minimum wage. This rule generally applies to internships in both the public and private sectors.

Unpaid Public-Sector Internships

Chris's situation is altogether different. In providing services for the city's summer camp without expectation of compensation, Chris is a volunteer, a term and concept which is addressed at length in the FLSA regulations. As discussed in the preceding section, under the FLSA, an individual may voluntarily perform services for a public agency for civic, charitable, or humanitarian reasons without promise, expectation, or receipt of compensation for services rendered if the services are provided freely and without coercion from an employer. Here, Chris receives no compensation for his camp counselor activities and has offered them to the city of his own accord. He is not employed by the city. He and the city may call his position an internship for the purposes of building Chris's resume and giving his experience working with the camp's children a more impressive title, but as a legal matter, Chris is a volunteer.[34]

Reimbursing Public-Sector Interns for Expenses

Could Chris be paid something and still maintain his volunteer status? As explained earlier in this chapter, the answer to this question is "yes." A volunteer may be paid expenses, reasonable benefits, a nominal fee, or a combination of the three without losing his or her status as a volunteer. For example, if the city requires its camp counselors to wear Carolina-blue colored t-shirts every day, it may give Chris and its other volunteer counselors a uniform allowance to cover the cost of five t-shirts. If Chris's duties involve coaching softball at the camp and all of his pants end up covered in dust or ripped at the knee, the city may reimburse him for reasonable cleaning expenses or for wear and tear. The city may also reimburse Chris for out-of-pocket expenses incurred while working as a camp volunteer, such as payment for the cost of meals or transportation expenses. The bottom line is that (1) reimbursements must be of actual expenses and (2) no amount paid to a volunteer may be based on productivity or hours of service.

Let's look at Tim's situation again. He could have volunteered his services to the finance department. The city could have paid him nothing. As in Chris's case, he and

---

34. In footnote 1 of its *Fact Sheet #71: Internship Programs Under the Fair Labor Standards Act*, DOL's Wage and Hour Division (WHD) acknowledges the existence of the internship dilemma in the public sector and says,

> The FLSA exempts certain people who volunteer to perform services for a state or local government agency or who volunteer for humanitarian purposes for non-profit food banks. WHD also recognizes an exception for individuals who volunteer their time, freely and without anticipation of compensation, for religious, charitable, civic, or humanitarian purposes to non-profit organizations. Unpaid internships for public sector and non-profit charitable organizations, where the intern volunteers without expectation of compensation, are generally permissible.

See https://www.dol.gov/whd/regs/compliance/whdfs71.pdf.

the city could call his service an internship if they so choose. But as far as compensation goes, the city has a clear choice to make: it can either (1) pay Tim the minimum wage for all hours worked up to forty hours per week and time-and-one-half overtime pay for any hour over forty or (2) treat him as a volunteer, paying him nothing and, at its discretion, reimburse him for any reasonable expenses. Paying him a stipend of $2,500 (equivalent to $6.25 per hour) satisfies neither alternative requirement and violates the FLSA.

Interns as Independent Contractors?

Public employers that wish to pay their interns a stipend that is more than a nominal fee but less than the equivalent of minimum wage may be tempted to treat the interns as "independent contractors." As the following sections make clear, this is not an alternative. Independent contractors perform work for employers without supervision and with minimal guidance. They are truly "independent" in a way that interns are not. In the public sector, interns can be true volunteers or they can be employees. There is no in-between legal status for an "intern." Independent contractor status does not provide a solution to this problem.

Independent Contractors

Government employers sometimes turn to independent contractors (sometimes inappropriately referred to as "contract employees") to perform work traditionally done by regular employees. Some of the advantages that employers see in this arrangement are listed below.

- *No overtime pay.* Only nonexempt employees are entitled to overtime.
- *No benefits.* Independent contractors are not generally eligible for participation in benefit plans such as health insurance or participation in a state retirement system.
- *No withholding, no FICA contribution.* Employers do not have to withhold federal, state, or local income taxes, or Social Security and Medicare taxes (FICA taxes) from their payments to independent contractors, nor are they required to make an employer FICA contribution for an independent contractor.
- *No workers' comp.* Independent contractors are not covered by the North Carolina Workers' Compensation Act.

The difference between the amount of total compensation (wages plus benefits) paid to an employee and that paid to an independent contractor doing the same work can be substantial. Classifying a group of workers as independent contractors, rather than as employees, can result in significant savings for an employer. But it also involves significant risk. Misclassifying an employee as an independent contractor can prove very expensive. Not least among the potential liabilities is liability for back overtime compensation for each employee mistakenly classified as an independent contractor going back for a period of two years. As the following sections show, a worker over whom an employer exercises control hardly ever meets the legal test for independent contractor status. Most of the time an employer's workers are, as a legal matter, employees.

A Beginning Hypothetical

Paradise County needs an additional sanitation worker in its public works department, an additional visiting nurse in its health department, and an additional accounts payable clerk in its finance department. In each case, the new position would have the same job duties as already-existing positions. The county commissioners do not think it will be possible to fund all three requests, but rather than choose among them, they allocate enough money for each of the three departments to add an additional worker on what the commissioners call an "independent contractor" basis: the workers are to be paid at an hourly rate but will not be paid overtime or receive any benefits from the county. The public works, health, and finance departments advertise for and hire workers, who sign agreements stating that they understand they are being hired as independent contractors and that, as such, they will not receive overtime premium pay or benefits.

After the new workers have been on the job for several months, one of them approaches the county payroll office and complains that she often works more than forty hours per week but does not receive overtime pay. The payroll office tells the worker that because she was classified as an independent contractor, she is not covered by the FLSA and is not entitled to overtime. Dissatisfied with this answer, the worker complains to her supervisor. The supervisor reminds her that she agreed to work as an independent contractor and tells her that if she doesn't like it, she can quit. The worker files a complaint with DOL, which begins an investigation into Paradise County's worker classifications.

Agreement to Work as an Independent Contractor Has No Legal Significance

The Paradise County hypothetical illustrates one of the most common misconceptions about who is and is not an independent contractor. Many employers believe that so long as a worker wants or agrees to be paid as an independent contractor, the employer is not responsible for paying overtime or for withholding taxes for that worker. That simply is not so. The three workers that Paradise County has hired as "independent contractors" are—as far as the law is concerned—employees.

Independent contractor is a distinct legal status determined by factors that go beyond the employer's and employee's mutual desire to contract for work on this basis. DOL has a test for determining whether a worker is an employee or an independent contractor for FLSA purposes. (The Internal Revenue Service, which oversees not only the withholding of federal income taxes but of Social Security and Medicare contributions as well, has its own test. Other statutes, such as anti-discrimination laws or state statutes governing who qualifies for unemployment benefits, use still other tests for determining a worker's status.)

Although the various tests for determining whether a worker is an employee or an independent contractor go by different names, they differ only slightly. All are variants of the common-law test for determining whether or not someone is an employee. Thus, the tests share common principles. Under all of the tests, the essence of the relationship between a hiring organization and an *independent contractor* is the agreement by the independent contractor to do a discrete job according to the independent contractor's own judgment and methods, without supervision by the hiring organization. The hiring organization retains approval only as to the results of the work. In contrast, an employer may require an *employee* to perform his or her duties in particular ways using particular methods at particular times even if, in fact, the employer gives assignments only occasionally. An employee may be disciplined—even discharged—for failing to follow the employer's instructions about how to perform a task.

The Fair Labor Standards Act Economic Reality Test

The FLSA defines "employee" broadly as "any individual employed by an employer."[35] It defines "employer" as "any person acting directly or indirectly in the interest of an employer in relation to an employee,"[36] while to "employ" someone under the statute means "to suffer or permit [them] to work."[37] On its face, it is hard to see what sort of worker would not fall within the FLSA's definition of employee—it would seem to cover everybody. DOL and the courts nevertheless recognize that there are people who perform work who simply cannot be called employees of the organization. To determine whether or not a worker is an employee for FLSA purposes, courts have developed what is called an *economic reality test.*

The economic reality test looks at whether a worker is economically dependent upon the organization for which he or she renders services.[38] To put it another way, the courts ask whether a worker depends upon an "employer" for the opportunity to render service or whether the worker is in business for himself or herself. To make this determination, the courts use a six-factor, question-based test.

1. What is the nature and degree of control that the hiring organization has over the way in which the worker is to perform the work? The more control the hiring organization has over the worker, the more likely it is that the worker is an employee.
2. Does the worker have an opportunity to make a profit or sustain a loss? The chance for profit or loss on a job is the hallmark of an independent contractor.
3. Does the worker have an investment in the materials, equipment, or other personnel required to perform the work? When a worker supplies the

---

35. 29 U.S.C. § 203(e)(1).
36. 29 U.S.C. § 203(d).
37. 29 U.S.C. § 203(g).
38. *See* Rutherford Food Corp. v. McComb, 331 U.S. 722, 726–28, 730 (1947).

materials or equipment needed for the job or directly hires others to assist him or her in performing the work, this factor will weigh heavily in favor of independent contractor status.

4. Does the work require skill and independent initiative? Independent contractors usually have a special skill and exercise initiative in seeking out assignments or clients.

5. What is the expected duration of the working relationship? The independent contractor relationship is usually for a limited duration. Where a hiring organization engages a worker indefinitely, or where the worker has performed services for the hiring organization for a long period of time, the courts are more likely to find that the worker is an employee.

6. To what extent is the work an integral part of the hiring organization's operations? Independent contractors usually perform work that is peripheral to the hiring organization's operations. Where a worker is doing a job that is essential to the organization's operations, this factor will weigh in favor of employee status.

No single factor is dispositive in making the determination of independent contractor versus employee, and some of them overlap. Each situation is evaluated in light of all of the circumstances of the hiring organization–worker relationship.[39]

The Internal Revenue Service's Right-to-Control Test

The Internal Revenue Service also has an interest in seeing that employers who classify workers as independent contractors (or, incorrectly, "contract employees") are legally entitled to do so. Under the Internal Revenue Code (the "Code"), an employer is required to withhold estimated federal income taxes from an employee's wage payments. In addition, the Code imposes Social Security and Medicare taxes on the wages of employees, both of which must be remitted by the employer to the IRS through payroll deduction. Employers themselves also pay Social Security and Medicare taxes (FICA taxes) on each person they employ.

In contrast, an organization is not required to withhold income or FICA taxes from its payments to an independent contractor, nor does it pay any Social Security or Medicare taxes on the independent contractor's fee. A hiring organization's legal responsibilities end with the filing of annual information returns (Form 1099) with both the worker and the IRS that show the money paid to the contractor during the

---

39. *See* McFeeley v. Jackson St. Entm't, LLC, 825 F.3d 235, 241 (4th Cir. 2016); Chao v. Mid-Atl. Installation Servs., Inc., 16 F. App'x 104, 106 (4th Cir. 2001); Dubois v. Sec'y of Def., 161 F.3d 2, *1 (4th Cir. 1998) (unpublished disposition); Donovan v. DialAm. Mktg., Inc., 757 F.2d 1376, 1382–83 (3d Cir.), *cert. denied*, 474 U.S. 919 (1985); Brock v. Superior Care, Inc., 840 F.2d 1054, 1059 (2d Cir. 1988). *See also* U.S. Dep't of Labor, Emp't Standards Admin., Wage & Hour Div., Wage & Hour Opinion Letter, FLSA 2019-6 (Apr. 29, 2019), https://www.dol.gov/whd/opinion/FLSA/2019/2019_04_29_06_FLSA.pdf (service providers for virtual marketplace companies are independent contractors).

tax year. An independent contractor is responsible for directly paying both income and FICA taxes directly to the IRS.[40]

In a 1987 Revenue Ruling, the IRS compiled a list of twenty factors that the courts had considered over the years in determining whether a worker was an independent contractor or an employee for tax purposes. These factors are referred to collectively as the right-to-control test. The twenty factors are as follows: (1) whether the worker must comply with another person's instructions about the work being performed; (2) whether the worker requires training in order to do the work; (3) whether the work performed by the worker is integrated into the hiring organization's operations; (4) whether the worker must perform the services personally; (5) who hires, supervises, and pays the worker's assistants, if any; (6) whether the worker and hiring organization have a continuing relationship; (7) whether the work must be performed during set hours; (8) whether the worker must devote most of his or her time to the work for the hiring organization; (9) whether the work must be performed on the employer's premises or can be done elsewhere; (10) whether the worker must perform services in an order or sequence set by the hiring organization; (11) whether the worker must submit reports about the work; (12) whether the worker is paid by the hour, week, or month; (13) whether the worker's business or traveling expenses are paid by the hiring organization; (14) whether the worker furnished the tools, materials, and equipment needed to perform the work; (15) whether the worker has a significant investment in facilities needed to do the work; (16) whether the worker can make a profit or suffer a loss as a result of performing the services for the hiring organization; (17) whether the worker can work for more than one firm at a time; (18) whether the worker makes his or her services available to the general public; (19) whether the hiring organization can discharge the worker; and (20) whether the worker has the right to terminate the relationship with the hiring organization.[41]

---

40. The IRS has stepped up its efforts to identify employees incorrectly classified as independent contractors in recent years. Independent contractors tend to understate their incomes— sometimes erroneously, sometimes consciously resulting in revenue loss for the federal government from underpayment of both federal income and employment taxes. Thus, when an employer is both withholding an employee's share and contributing its own share, federal tax revenues are both greater and more predictable.

41. *See* Rev. Rul. 87-41, 1987-1 C.B. 296, 1987 WL 419174. Most of these factors appear in the summary of the common-law test set forth by the United States Supreme Court in *Nationwide Mutual Insurance Co. v. Darden*, 503 U.S. 318, 323–24 (1992) (applying common-law test to determine who qualifies as an employee under Employee Retirement Income Security Act (ERISA)), and *Community for Creative Non-Violence v. Reid*, 490 U.S. 730, 751–52 (1989) (applying common-law test to determine who is an employee for purposes of the Copyright Act). *See also* Clackamas Gastroenterology Assocs., P.C. v. Wells, 538 U.S. 440 (2003) (Equal Employment Opportunity Commission focus on common-law test is appropriate for determining who is "employee" for purposes of Americans with Disabilities Act).

The Economic Reality Test versus the Right-to-Control Test

Because DOL and the IRS use nominally different tests to determine worker status, it is theoretically possible that in a particular case a worker could be found to be an employee under one test and an independent contractor under the other—that is, it is possible that the same worker could be an employee for FLSA purposes and an independent contractor for tax purposes, or vice-versa. But the two tests by and large look to the same factors and, in reality, a worker under the control of a hiring organization is likely also one who is economically dependent upon the hiring organization. Research for this book has uncovered no fact pattern in case law, DOL Wage and Hour Opinion Letters, or IRS Revenue Rulings that would lead to different conclusions under the two tests. The factors indicative of worker status under both the FLSA economic-reality test and the IRS right-to-control test will therefore be discussed together in the following sections. Failure to satisfy one test virtually always indicates failure to satisfy the other.

Determining Worker Status under Other Employment Statutes

The question of worker status as employee or independent contractor often arises in the context of overtime and tax withholding. But it can arise in other contexts as well. What happens when a worker suffers sexual harassment, for example? Sexual harassment is a form of gender discrimination prohibited by Title VII of the Civil Rights Act of 1964, but Title VII's protections extend only to "employees."

What happens when a worker is injured on the job? The North Carolina Workers' Compensation Act covers "employees" but not independent contractors. A worker who is dismissed from a job typically seeks unemployment benefits, but the North Carolina Employment Security Act makes benefits available only to "employees." Finally, what of the worker who grows too old to work? A worker who has worked as an "independent contractor" for a single public employer for as many as ten or even twenty years would not be eligible to draw benefits from either the Teachers' and State Employees' Retirement System or the Local Governmental Employees' Retirement System, since only "employees" are entitled to participate in these plans. To understand how work status is determined under each of the statutory schemes governing these programs, see Diane M. Juffras, *Independent Contractor or Employee? The Legal Distinction and Its Consequences*, Public Employment Law Bulletin No. 32, at 18–20 (UNC School of Government, May 2005), https://www.sog.unc.edu/sites/www.sog.unc.edu/files/reports/pelb32.pdf.

Factors Determinative of Worker Status as Independent Contractor or Employee

Imagine that a city wants to build a swimming pool. City officials have opinions about what features they want in a swimming pool, but they do not know how to construct a swimming pool, and no one in the city's regular employ has experience in swimming-pool construction. So, the city engages a swimming-pool contractor to construct the pool. This is a classic example of the independent contractor relationship.

The city will tell the swimming-pool contractor what result it wants: a swimming pool of a particular size, in a particular layout, with specified depths, complete with certain accessories like diving boards, stairs, and ladders. The city and the contractor will agree upon a price for the final product. While the city may negotiate with the contractor—and even have a price above which it will not go—the city will not be able to set the price unilaterally. The contractor, who will supply all of the materials, equipment, and workers needed to construct the swimming pool, will estimate how much time it will take to construct the pool and how much it will cost. It will then determine how much or how little profit it is willing to make to take this job.

Contrast this with the Paradise County hypothetical on page 194. In none of the three instances described in the hypothetical did the county set out to hire someone with specialized skills for a discrete job. What each department head had originally asked for was funding to hire one additional employee. What each got was permission to engage someone to perform the job functions of an employee under an alternate compensation arrangement.

Is there a way to legally classify the three new Paradise County workers as independent contractors? For FLSA purposes, the issue is whether the sanitation worker, the visiting nurse, and the accounts payable clerk are each, as a matter of "economic reality," workers dependent on the county with respect to the services they provide or whether they are in business for themselves. For Internal Revenue Code purposes, the issue is whether the county has the right to control the work of the sanitation worker, the visiting nurse, and the accounts payable clerk. A close look at the factors that comprise the economic reality and right-to-control tests makes clear that these workers cannot be classified as independent contractors for either FLSA or Internal Revenue Code purposes. They must be classified as employees.

The more control the hiring party has over a worker, the more likely it is that the worker is an employee. A hiring party has control over a worker when it has *the right* to unilaterally assign the worker a task or to require something of the worker at any given time. The hiring party does not have to actually exercise that right to have control over the worker for that worker to be an employee as a matter of law.[42] Where a hiring party may change a given worker's job duties or reassign duties among several workers, it has supervisory control over a worker.[43]

A hiring party is considered to have control over its workers when it sets the workers' schedules, prohibits workers from switching shifts, or disciplines workers who deviate from an assigned schedule or take unscheduled breaks. In a case where the status of house cleaners as employees or independent contractors was at issue, the fact that the owners of the company that matched the cleaners with cleaning jobs

---

42. *See* 26 C.F.R. § 31.3401(c)-1(b) (employment tax regulations); Weber v. Comm'r of Internal Revenue Serv., 60 F.3d 1104, 1110 (4th Cir. 1995).

43. *See* Mathis v. Hous. Auth. of Umatilla Cty., 242 F. Supp. 2d 777, 783 (D. Or. 2002) (Section 8 housing coordinator was subject to housing authority's control where she worked at housing authority offices, was subject to direction of executive director, and housing authority reserved right to change or reassign job duties).

dictated which cleaning products the cleaners could use, the methods they could use (hands and knees, mops versus no mops), and the specific order in which they were to complete tasks made clear that the cleaners were subject to a high degree of control and were thus employees.[44]

In a case brought under the FLSA on behalf of seasonal farm workers, DOL successfully argued that farm workers are employees rather than independent contractors in circumstances where the workers did not hold other full-time jobs and the farm owner scheduled the length of each worker's shift and the total length of time the workers would be employed.[45] In a New York case, the court found that HVAC installers were employees where the owner of a company that provided installation services to customers set the installers' schedules and directed their work each day. The company also required the installers to wear company t-shirts, hats, and sweaters and to use the equipment and materials that the company provided.[46]

Training in Required Methods

A hiring party makes clear that it wants services performed in a particular way when it provides training in the actual methods the worker is to use or, more generally, in the hiring party's policies and procedures. Training of this kind is indicative of an employment relationship. In one federal Fourth Circuit Court of Appeals case, where an architect was required to follow the procedures and directives in the hiring organization's handbook, could not exceed a set budget, and had his hours, leave, and pay set by the hiring organization, the court found that (1) the hiring organization had the right to control the architect's activities and (2) the architect was an employee for tax purposes.[47] Similarly, the IRS held that a park attendant hired on a seasonal basis by a government agency was an employee, in part because the agency provided training and instructions on methods to be used and set specific hours.[48] In a case involving a nurse-staffing service, the court noted that although nurses are skilled professionals not generally in need of close supervision, the fact that the staffing service required its newly hired nurses to undergo training on medical confidentiality, the use of ventilators and oxygen, and on other medical subjects weighed heavily in

---

44. *See* Perez v. Super Maid, LLC, 55 F. Supp. 3d 1065, 1077 (N.D. Ill. 2014).

45. *See* Perez v. Howes, 7 F. Supp. 3d 715, 723–27 (W.D. Mich. 2014).

46. *See* Kalloo v. United Mech. Co. of N.Y., Inc., 977 F. Supp. 2d 187, 202 (E.D.N.Y. 2013).

47. *See* Eren v. Comm'r of Internal Revenue, 180 F.3d 594, 597 (4th Cir. 1999).

48. *See* I.R.S. Priv. Ltr. Rul. 200323023 (Feb. 24, 2003), https://www.irs.gov/pub/irs-wd/0323023.pdf. *See also* Rev. Rul. 66-274, 1966-2 C.B. 446, 1966 WL 15365 (in the context of medical professionals, the right of a hiring organization to require a physician to comply with its general policies turns on whether or not the physician is subject to the direction and control of a chief of staff, medical director, or some other authority; a physician director of a hospital pathology department was not subject to the direction and control of any hospital representative, such as a chief of staff, and thus was an independent contractor). *See also* Rev. Rul. 73-417, 1973-2 C.B. 332, 1973 WL 33009 (physician director of hospital laboratory was an employee, in part because he was obligated to comply with all rules and regulations of hospital).

favor of employee status, as did the fact that the staffing company required the nurses to participate in ongoing on-site training four to five hours each month.[49]

Similarly, if the hiring party requires that services must be performed personally by the named worker, the presumption is that the hiring party is interested in the methods used to accomplish the work, rather than in the results alone. Thus, a requirement that the services be performed personally by the worker indicates an employment, rather than an independent contractor, relationship.[50]

Generally, where the hiring party has rules governing the worker's personal conduct, it is considered to be exercising control over the worker.[51] Nevertheless, providing safety training and requiring drug testing of individuals performing particular services or working at a particular job site does not in and of itself indicate control that would weigh in favor of employee status. In one federal Fifth Circuit Court of Appeals case, for example, the court found that the need for a safe oil-drilling site made safety training and drug testing a reasonable requirement for both employees and independent contractors because independent contractors who engaged in unsafe work practices would endanger the hiring party's employees in violation of a mandate from the Occupational Safety and Health Administration (OSHA) that employers "furnish a place of employment free from hazards likely to cause death or physical harm to employees."[52]

Monitoring Worker Performance

A hiring party does not have to "check up" on a worker's performance or conduct on a daily basis in order to exercise the level of control over the worker required for the worker's status to be "employee." To some extent, the degree of supervision needed is a function of the skills required to perform the work. Some workers perform their duties off-site where, as a practical matter, their performance cannot be monitored on a daily basis. For example, where off-duty police officers performing traffic and security work for a private company usually sat in cars for long periods of time,

---

49. See Gayle v. Harry's Nurses Registry, Inc., 594 F. App'x 714, 717 (2d Cir. 2014).

50. See Rev. Rul. 55-695, 1955-2 C.B. 410, 1955 WL 9366 (retired employee who was retained as a "consultant" by her former employer on a retainer-fee basis for the purpose of training her replacement was an employee). See also I.R.S. Priv. Ltr. Rul. 8937039 (Sept. 15, 1989), 1989 WL 596203 (psychologists required to perform services personally were employees); I.R.S. Priv. Ltr. Rul. 9326015 (Mar. 31, 1993), 1993 WL 238477 (physician employed in university health clinic was required to perform services personally and was an employee). See also Gayle, 594 F. App'x at 717.

51. See Richardson v. Genesee Cty. Cmty. Mental Health Servs., 45 F. Supp. 2d 610, 614 (E.D. Mich. 1999) (employing agency that provided nurses with patient-care guidelines, as well as with work rules governing "employee conduct," exercised supervisory control for purposes of determining whether nurses were "employees" within the meaning of the FLSA). See also U.S. Dep't of Labor, Emp't Standards Admin., Wage & Hour Div., Wage & Hour Opinion Letter, FLSA (Aug. 24, 1999), 1999 WL 1788146 (hospital is likely joint employer with nurse registry of private-duty nurses).

52. Parrish v. Premier Directional Drilling, L.P., 917 F.3d 369, 382 (5th Cir. 2019), citing 29 U.S.C. § 654.

only periodic supervision was called for—lack of supervision did not weigh against employee status in this case.[53] Even in circumstances where a representative of a hiring organization visits a job site as infrequently as once or twice a month, the courts have deemed the organization to be exercising control over workers at the site.[54]

A hiring organization might track a worker's performance of services by requiring that the worker submit written or oral reports. These may be reports of time spent on certain tasks or on a certain project as a whole. The worker may be required to give a detailed description of the work performed or of clients or patients seen in a given time period. The requirement that a worker submit reports is evidence that the worker is an employee.[55]

Regular Wages

Closely related to the requirement that a worker submit time reports to the hiring party is the practice of paying the worker a regular wage based on the amount of time spent performing services. Payment of any kind of regular wage—by the hour, week or month—even where the wage is not directly linked to the actual amount of time spent working during the pay period (as is the case with exempt salaried employees) generally indicates that the worker is an employee. In contrast, payment by the job or on a commission basis is evidence of an independent contractor relationship. However, if a worker is paid a regular wage merely as a convenience—that is, as a way of spreading out the payment of a lump sum that has been agreed upon as the cost of a job—then this practice would not be evidence of employee status.[56] Courts

---

53. *See* Acosta v. Off Duty Police Servs., Inc., 915 F.3d 1050, 1061 (6th Cir. 2019). *See also* Perez v. Howes, 7 F. Supp. 3d 715, 723–27 (W.D. Mich. 2014).

54. *See* Brock v. Superior Care, Inc., 840 F.2d 1054, 1057, 1060 (2d Cir. 1988) (where nurses worked off-site with individual patients needing home or specialized care, where the employer visited job sites (even as infrequently as once or twice a month) and required the nurses to keep and submit to it patient-care notes required by federal and state law, the employer was found to be exercising control and supervision over the nurses). *See also* Donovan v. DialAm. Mktg., Inc., 757 F.2d 1376, 1383–84 (3d Cir.), *cert. denied*, 474 U.S. 919 (1985); Mathis v. Hous. Auth. of Umatilla Cty., 242 F. Supp. 2d 777, 783 (D. Or. 2002). On the IRS side, *cf.* Weber v. Comm'r of Internal Revenue Serv., 60 F.3d 1104, 1110 (4th Cir. 1995).

55. *See Gayle*, 594 F. App'x at 717 (requirement that at completion of each shift nurse complete a comprehensive patient assessment weighed in favor of employee status); Kentfield Med. Hosp. Corp. v. United States, 215 F. Supp. 2d 1064, 1070 (N.D. Cal. 2002) (hospital psychologists required to submit daily reports of their work were employees); Rev. Rul. 73-591, 1973-2 C.B. 337, 1973 WL 33465 (beautician required to submit daily work reports to owner of salon was an employee); Rev. Rul. 70-309, 1970-1 C.B. 199, 1970 WL 20862 (oil-well pumpers who worked in field seldom saw employing corporation's agents but were nonetheless employees, in part because they had to submit written reports on a regular basis). See also the following IRS private letter rulings: Priv. Ltr. Rul. 9326015, *supra* note 50 (physician in university health clinic was an employee); Priv. Ltr. Rul. 9320038, 1993 WL 168902 (Feb. 22, 1993) (department of corrections medical director required to submit time reports was an employee); Priv. Ltr. Rul. 200323023, *supra* note 48 (seasonal park attendant required to keep logbook was an employee).

56. *See* I.R.S. Priv. Ltr. Rul. 9320038, *supra* note 55 (department of corrections medical director paid an hourly rate was an employee). See also the following IRS private letter rulings: Priv. Ltr.

consider the fact that the hiring party has unilaterally set a worker's hourly wage as evidence that the hiring party controls the worker.[57]

Thus, in two Fourth Circuit Internal Revenue Code cases, the fact that an architect and a minister, respectively, were paid on a salaried basis weighed in favor of employee status for each.[58] In two contrasting Revenue Rulings, the IRS found that a hospital physician whose compensation consisted *solely* of a percentage of his department's gross receipts was an independent contractor, while a hospital physician whose compensation was also a percentage of charges attributable to his department but who was also *guaranteed a minimum salary* was an employee.[59]

Paradise County's Control over Its New Workers

Think again about the hypothetical involving the construction of the city swimming pool. While the city will no doubt be curious about how the work is progressing, and while city officials may well visit the job site, the city will not be telling the contractor how to excavate the earth or what method to use in mixing concrete. Nor does the city have the right to tell the contractor that when the contractor is done with this swimming pool, the city has another one for him to construct at the same price on the other side of town (although the city and the contractor may well come to some agreement on a second job). The city may worry that the contractor is not working fast enough, but until the contractor misses a contractual deadline, the city must bite its tongue.

Now think about Paradise County's so-called "independent contractors." The sanitation worker, visiting nurse, and accounts payable clerk would each work under the supervision of another county employee. The sanitation worker will not choose his own routes, but he will have routes, a truck, and co-workers assigned to him by a supervisor. The visiting nurse will have to follow the health department's patient-care guidelines and will be required by the county to adhere to applicable state and federal regulations governing the treatment and billing of patients—all of which are

---

Rul. 200339006, 2003 WL 22222471 (June 9, 2003) (accounting technician paid an hourly wage was an employee); Priv. Ltr. Rul. 9728013, 1997 WL 381983 (Apr. 9, 1997) (part-time lifeguard paid an hourly wage was an employee); Priv. Ltr. Rul. 9326015, *supra* note 50 (physician in university health clinic was an employee); Priv. Ltr. Rul. 8937039, *supra* note 50 (psychologists treating patients for professional firm were employees).

57. *See Brock*, 840 F.2d at 1060. *See also* U.S. DEP'T OF LABOR, EMP'T STANDARDS ADMIN., WAGE & HOUR DIV., WAGE & HOUR OPINION LETTER, FLSA (Dec. 7, 2000), 2000 WL 33126542 (fact that company controlled rate at which package-delivery drivers were compensated was factor leading to conclusion that drivers were employees rather than independent contractors). *See also* Eren v. Comm'r of Internal Revenue, 180 F.3d 594, 597 (4th Cir. 1999) (architect whose pay and leave were set by hiring party was an employee).

58. *See Eren*, 180 F.3d at 597; *Weber*, 60 F.3d at 1111.

59. *See* Rev. Rul. 66-274, *supra* note 48 (independent contractor); Rev. Rul. 73-417, *supra* note 48 (employee).

indicia of employer control.[60] The accounts payable clerk will be told how the county tracks and records accounts payable and will have to use a software program already in place.[61]

All three workers will have to abide by county work rules governing personal behavior. All three will be expected to work scheduled hours. They will not be allowed to take care of personal or other business while working for Paradise County. They will be held to the same workplace standards for job performance and personal conduct as employees working for the county.

The conditions under which Paradise County's "independent contractors" work make clear that, in each case, the county has the right to control the performance of their work. Their working conditions are in marked contrast to those at issue in *Chao v. Mid-Atlantic Installation Services, Inc.*,[62] a Fourth Circuit FLSA case in which the court held that cable installers were independent contractors rather than employees. In *Mid-Atlantic*, the fact that the defendant company assigned daily routes to cable installers and required them to report in to a dispatcher on a regular basis did not establish employer control. The installers were free to complete the assigned jobs in whatever order they chose and were allowed to attend to personal affairs and to conduct other business during the day. They were also permitted to hire and manage other workers to help them complete their daily assigned installations. This freedom to complete their work whenever (during the day) and howsoever they chose weighed heavily in the court's determination that they were independent contractors.[63]

Control over Professional Employees

The degree of control necessary to find employee status varies in accordance with the nature of the services the worker provides. Professionals such as physicians, certified public accountants, lawyers, dentists, registered nurses, and building and electrical contractors (to name just a few examples) require specialized skills to do their work. The methods these skilled professionals use are frequently dictated by the standards of their individual professions rather than by their hiring organizations. The high level of knowledge and skill needed to perform their respective services often precludes direct supervision of their work. Nevertheless, when skilled workers such as these are hired under conditions in which they are paid a set salary and are required

---

60. *See* U.S. Dep't of Labor, Wage & Hour Opinion Letter, FLSA (Aug. 24, 1999), *supra* note 51 (hospital was likely joint employer with nurse registry of private-duty nurses).

61. *See* I.R.S. Priv. Ltr. Rul. 200339006, *supra* note 56 (accounting technician who was paid an hourly wage; given all necessary supplies, equipment, and materials needed to perform her services; and who received assignments from a supervisor who determined the methods by which the services were to be performed was an employee rather than an independent contractor); I.R.S. Priv. Ltr. Rul. 200222005 (Feb. 15, 2002), 2002 WL 1174253 (clerical worker, who was hired because she submitted the lowest bid but who worked under similar conditions to the accounting technician above her in the hiring organization's structure, was an employee).

62. 16 F. App'x 104 (4th Cir. 2001).

63. *Id.* at 106.

to follow prescribed routines during set hours, they lose some of the independence that characterizes the practice of their professions and their usual status as independent contractors and they become employees.[64]

Such is the situation of Paradise County's new visiting nurse. Registered nurses (RNs) are considered skilled professionals, and the IRS generally recognizes them as independent contractors when they perform private-duty nursing services for individual patients. In a private-duty nursing setting, nurses typically have full discretion in administering their professional services and are not subject to enough direction and control by the hiring party (usually the patient or the patient's family member) to establish an employment relationship. But when RNs are part of a medical staff of a hiring organization, they are usually subject to the control of a physician or another nurse. Under these conditions, an RN is an employee. The IRS makes a distinction between RNs on one hand, and licensed practical nurses (LPNs), nurses' aides, and home health aides on the other: LPNs and aides who assist patients with personal and domestic care do not generally render professional care and are usually subject to almost complete direction and control by hiring parties, regardless of the setting in which they perform their services; they are almost always employees.[65]

The Right to Discharge the Worker

One of the ways an employer exercises control over an employee is through the power of dismissal. Because an employee may be dismissed, he or she is inclined to obey the employer's instructions. A true independent contractor, however, cannot be fired so long as he or she produces a result that meets the hiring party's specifications. So, a hiring party's right to fire a worker is usually treated as evidence that the worker is an employee rather than an independent contractor. In one situation considered by the IRS, a medical staffing corporation argued that the workers it supplied to medical practices and hospitals were independent contractors rather than employees of the corporation. But, because the corporation had the right to direct the performance

---

64. *See* Eren v. Comm'r of Internal Revenue, 180 F.3d 594, 596 (4th Cir. 1999) (architect); Weber v. Comm'r of Internal Revenue Serv., 60 F.3d 1104, 1111 (4th Cir. 1995) (minister); Kentfield Med. Hosp. Corp. v. United States, 215 F. Supp. 2d 1064, 1070 (N.D. Cal. 2002) (psychologists). *See also* Rev. Rul. 87-41, *supra* note 43 (discussing the IRS' twenty-factor list for determining worker status); Rev. Rul. 58-268, 1958-1 C.B. 353, 1958 WL 10763 (dental hygienist); I.R.S. Priv. Ltr. Rul. 9323013 (Mar. 11, 1993), 1993 WL 198849 (psychiatrist at state psychiatric facility who served as court-appointed examiner charged with examining individuals who had been involuntarily committed to the facility was an employee; I.R.S. Priv. Ltr. Rul. 9201033 (Jan. 3, 1992), 1992 WL 800793 (x-ray technician).

65. *See* Rev. Rul. 61-196, 1961-2 C.B. 155. The finding in this ruling is similar to the distinction made by the Department of Labor in its regulations governing the classification of exempt and nonexempt employees: RNs may be classified as exempt professionals, while LPNs may not. *See* 29 C.F.R. § 541.301(e)(2).

of the workers' services for its clients and to fire the workers if they did not perform services to the satisfaction of clients, the IRS found the workers to be employees.[66]

The right of the *worker* to terminate his or her services at any time without incurring any liability is also characteristic of an employment relationship. As a general matter, an employee may simply quit. In contrast, an independent contractor who quits without completing the job might have to forfeit some of the contract price. The hiring party could also sue the independent contractor either for specific performance (an order from the court to do the work agreed upon) or for breach of contract, provided the hiring party can show damages.[67]

Opportunity for Profit or Loss

Where a worker has the opportunity to make a profit or faces the possibility of taking a loss on a job—by completing it faster or more slowly than anticipated, or at greater or lesser cost than estimated—the courts are more likely to find that the worker is an independent contractor. Employees almost never face a profit or loss: they are usually paid a straight salary or an hourly wage. Courts do not consider an increase in an hourly worker's take-home pay to be an instance of making a profit when that increase is merely the result of working a greater number of hours.[68] Conversely, the federal Fourth Circuit Court of Appeals has made clear that for purposes of determining independent contractor status, there is no opportunity for a worker to suffer a loss where the only possible loss a worker faces is the failure of the hiring organization to pay him or her.[69]

---

66. *See Weber*, 60 F.3d at 1111, 1113 (although a minister could not be fired at will, his failure to follow the Book of Discipline could have resulted in termination by fellow members of the clergy); Rev. Rul. 75-41, 1975-1 C.B. 323, 1975 WL 34829 (physicians working for a physician services corp. who could be fired at will were employees); I.R.S. Priv. Ltr. Rul. 9320038, *supra* note 55 (medical director who could be fired with thirty days' notice was an employee).

67. *See* Rev. Rul. 70-309, *supra* note 55 (oil-well pumpers could quit at any time); I.R.S. Priv. Ltr. Rul. 9320038, *supra* note 55 (department of corrections medical director who could be fired with thirty days' notice and who could quit at any time was an employee); I.R.S. Priv. Ltr. Rul. 200339006, *supra* note 56 (accounting technician who could quit without incurring liability or penalty was an employee).

68. *See* Richardson v. Genesee Cty. Cmty. Mental Health Servs., 45 F. Supp. 2d 610, 614 (E.D. Mich. 1999) (FLSA case; nurses at mental-health crisis clinic who had no opportunity for profit or loss were employees); Acosta v. Off Duty Police Servs., Inc., 915 F.3d 1050, 1059 (6th Cir. 2019) (no opportunity for profit or loss where workers worked a set schedule and were paid an hourly wage); Randolph v. Powercomm Constr., Inc., 309 F.R.D. 349, 357 (D. Md. 2015) (same); *Eren*, 180 F.3d at 597 (Internal Revenue Code (IRC) case; salaried architect who was not paid commission or percentage of profits had no opportunity for profit or loss); *Weber*, 60 F.3d at 1111 (IRC case; minister who was paid a salary and provided with a parsonage, a utility expense allowance, and a travel allowance had no opportunity for profit or loss). *See also* U.S. DEP'T OF LABOR, EMP'T STANDARDS ADMIN., WAGE & HOUR DIV., WAGE & HOUR OPINION LETTER, FLSA 2019-6 (Apr. 29, 2019), https://www.dol.gov/whd/opinion/FLSA/2019/2019_04_29_06_FLSA.pdf.

69. *See Eren*, 180 F.3d at 597.

In the *Mid-Atlantic* case discussed on page 204, *supra*, the cable installers' opportunity for profit or loss manifested itself in a number of ways. First, the hiring company could charge the installers if they failed to comply with either the technical requirements of an installation or with local ordinances regulating cable installation. Second, the fact that the installers supplied their own trucks and tools and were responsible for their own liability and automobile insurance showed that the installers incurred expenses of a type (1) not normally borne by employees and (2) that affected the amount they ultimately earned from a set of jobs. So, too, did the fact that the installers were responsible for paying any assistants they hired and for reporting payments made to those assistants to the IRS.[70] Similarly, in a federal Eighth Circuit Court of Appeals case, the court found that process servers were independent contractors because they were paid a flat rate for each job, which could take anywhere from a quarter of an hour to several hours. The process servers, the court found, could make a profit, or at least more money, by managing assignments more efficiently and completing more of them.[71]

In contrast, nurses paid an hourly wage by a staffing agency have been found to have had no opportunity for profit or loss whatsoever. As the court put it, they had "no downside exposure." The staffing agency paid the nurses promptly regardless of whether the agency had been reimbursed by patients' insurance companies.[72]

Returning to the Paradise County hypothetical, the compensation of the county's new sanitation worker, visiting nurse, and accounts payable clerk would be entirely a function of the number of hours worked by the particular worker. Each worker has no opportunity for profit and loss. This factor weighs strongly in favor of employee status in each of their cases.[73]

Worker Investment

Whether a worker has made an investment in the materials, equipment, or additional workers needed for a job is an issue that is closely related to the question of whether the worker has an opportunity for profit or loss. The two questions are sometimes analyzed as one, since purchasing supplies and equipment and hiring assistants are both forms of investments, and a worker who has no investment in the work cannot incur a loss or make a profit.[74]

---

70. *See* Chao v. Mid-Atl. Installation Servs., Inc., 16 F. App'x 104, 107 (4th Cir. 2001).

71. *See* Karlson v. Action Process Servs. & Private Investigations, LLC, 860 F.3d 1089, 1094 (8th Cir. 2017).

72. *See* Gayle v. Harry's Nurses Registry, Inc., 594 F. App'x 714, 717–18 (2d Cir. 2014).

73. *See* I.R.S. Priv. Ltr. Rul. 200339006, *supra* note 56 (accounting technician who was paid by the hour and could not hire assistants or substitutes had no opportunity for profit or loss).

74. *See* Rev. Rul. 70-309, *supra* note 55 (oil-well pumpers who worked in the field and who assumed no business risks were employees). *See also* I.R.S. Priv. Ltr. Rul. 9251032 (Sept. 21, 1992), 1992 WL 371564 (nurse in state tuberculosis outreach program who assumed no risk of profit or loss was an employee).

Where a worker supplies materials or equipment or directly hires others to assist him or her in completing a job, the courts will weigh this factor in favor of independent contractor status. Where the hiring party supplies materials, equipment, and personnel, it is evidence of an employment relationship.[75] For example, when a hospital provided psychologists with staff, office space, and all of the supplies necessary for them to see patients, a court found that the psychologists were employees, not independent contractors. Similarly, when a church provided a minister with an office, a court found that this factor weighed in favor of employee status. The minister had argued that the fact that he used his home computer for church business gave him an investment in "the business," but the court rejected that argument, finding that he chose to work at home for his own convenience.[76]

The mere fact that a worker supplies some small piece(s) of equipment to assist in the job does not in and of itself weigh in favor of independent contractor status. Where traffic flaggers provided their own protective gear—hard hats, glasses, ear protection, vests, and steel-toed boots—a court deemed their investment insignificant in comparison with the pick-up trucks, paddles, cones, and walkie-talkies the employer provided.[77]

Consider again the example of the construction of the city swimming pool. The contractor will come to work having already purchased everything that is needed to do the job. The city is unlikely to supply anything. Since the construction of a pool certainly requires more labor than a single worker, the contractor will supply and pay his or her own assistants. The contractor will factor the cost of the material, the equipment, and the helpers into the price of the job. Whether the contractor accurately assesses these direct and indirect costs impacts whether he or she makes a profit or takes a loss on the job.

Similarly, in the *Mid-Atlantic* case discussed on page 206, *supra*, factors weighing heavily in the court's conclusion that the cable installers were independent contractors were the fact that they invested in and brought with them to each job their

---

75. *See* U.S. Dep't of Labor, Wage & Hour Opinion Letter, FLSA 2019-6, *supra* note 68. *See also* Weber v. Comm'r of Internal Revenue Serv., 60 F.3d 1104, 1111 (4th Cir. 1995) (when the church provided him with an office, the fact that a minister used his own computer at home for church work did not mean that he had an investment in the equipment used for his work; he chose to work at home for his own convenience); Kentfield Med. Hosp. Corp. v. United States, 215 F. Supp. 2d 1064, 1070 (N.D. Cal. 2002) (where psychologists were provided with staff, office space, and all of the tools and equipment necessary for their work, and where the psychologists performed their work at the hiring party hospital, this factor weighed in favor of employee status); Rev. Rul. 71-524, 1971-2 C.B. 346, 1971 WL 26811 (drivers of tractor-trailer rigs were employees of a truck-leasing company that supplied rigs and drivers to a common carrier, where the truck-leasing company owned the rigs; furnished major repairs, tires, and license plates; generated all jobs; and bore major expenses and financial risks); I.R.S. Priv. Ltr. Rul. 9320038, *supra* note 55 (department of corrections medical director who was provided with all necessary supplies and equipment was an employee).

76. *See Weber*, 60 F.3d at 1111.

77. *See Randolph* v. Powercomm Constr., Inc., 309 F.R.D. 349, 358 (D. Md. 2015).

own tools, trucks, and assistants and that they paid for the insurance that covered the various aspects of their work.[78] In contrast, in *Richardson v. Genesee County Community Mental Health Services*, nurses working at a crisis clinic at an hourly rate who supplied nothing beyond their own expertise were found not to have any investment in their work.[79]

In the Paradise County hypothetical, neither the sanitation worker, the visiting nurse, nor the accounts payable clerk will bring tools of the trade to work (notwith-standing that the nurse may bring her own stethoscope). They will each use the employer's supplies and equipment. To the extent that the work requires collabora-tion, they will each work with other workers hired by the employer, rather than going out and seeking assistants themselves. Their individual lack of investment in the resources needed to perform their respective jobs also weighs in favor of employee status for each of these workers.

Work Requiring Special Skills and Initiative/Offering Services to Others

Independent contractors usually have special skills and exercise initiative in seeking out assignments or clients. For example, electricians, carpenters, and engineers, like swimming pool contractors, have specials skills.[80] Registered nurses are also skilled workers.[81] But the mere fact of having a special skill is not in and of itself indicative of independent contractor status. What counts is whether the worker exercises sig-nificant initiative in locating work opportunities or clients.[82] Thus, electricians and carpenters who service the needs of a single hiring organization over a long period of time will likely be found to be employees rather than independent contractors.[83] But when a worker advertises his or her services to the public on a regular and consistent

---

78. *See* Chao v. Mid-Atl. Installation Servs., Inc., 16 F. App'x 104, 107 (4th Cir. 2001). *See also* U.S. DEP'T OF LABOR, EMP'T STANDARDS ADMIN., WAGE & HOUR DIV., WAGE & HOUR OPINION LETTER, FLSA (Sept. 5, 2002), 2002 WL 32406602.

79. *See* 45 F. Supp. 2d 610, 614 (E.D. Mich. 1999).

80. *See Mid-Atl.*, 16 F. App'x at 107.

81. *See Richardson*, 45 F. Supp. 2d at 614.

82. *See* Hobbs v. Petroplex Pipe & Constr., Inc., 360 F. Supp. 3d 571 (W.D. Tex. 2019) (although pipe welding requires specialized skills, plaintiffs had limited opportunities to display initiative in the performance of their jobs, as they were given work assignments with strict specifica-tions); *Richardson*, 45 F. Supp. 2d at 614 (nurses working after regularly scheduled hours at crisis clinic run by same employer not considered to be locating clients independently), *citing* Brock v. Superior Care, Inc., 840 F.2d 1054, 1060 (2d Cir. 1988) (where nurses are paid hourly rate by employing organization rather than directly by patient, they are likely to be employees). *See also Mathis* v. Hous. Auth. of Umatilla Cty., 242 F. Supp. 2d 777, 784 (D. Or. 2002) (special skills factor weighs toward employee status where Section 8 housing coordinator's work and client contact took place at housing authority during regular business hours; coordinator did not use skills in any independent way).

83. Where a job does not require any special skills but requires only initiative for success, this factor will not weigh strongly in either direction. *See* Thomas v. Global Home Prods., Inc., 617 F. Supp. 526, 535 (W.D.N.C. 1985) (local distributor for cookie and candy company is employee), *aff'd in part, modified and remanded*, 810 F.2d 448 (4th Cir. 1987).

basis and performs services for a number of unrelated persons or businesses at the same time, that fact generally indicates that the worker is an independent contractor. Performing services for two or more persons or businesses simultaneously, however, is not dispositive evidence of independent contractor status; a person can work for two organizations or persons as an employee of each.[84]

In the Paradise County hypothetical, neither the job of sanitation worker nor accounts payable clerk require any special skills or initiative. Individual sanitation workers do not generally offer their services to the public; trash collection is usually a municipal service or one provided by a company under contract. If an accounts payable clerk provided services to a variety of different clients at the same time, the clerk could be an independent contractor. In this situation, however, the fact that the clerk works a regular forty-hour week for the county under direct supervision argues against such status.

The visiting nurse does have a special skill. This factor will not weigh heavily in favor of independent contractor status, however, because the nurse does not seek out client service opportunities on her own but is assigned patients by the health department and is paid by the county, rather than by the patient.

Duration of the Relationship

Although it is possible for an independent contractor to have a long-term relationship with an employer, the typical independent contractor relationship is for a limited duration.[85] The swimming pool contractor is a case in point: the relationship between the city and the contractor lasts only as long as it takes to construct the pool; once payment is made for the finished product, the relationship ends.

A continuing relationship, on the other hand, is strong evidence of employee status. Employers should note that for FLSA and Internal Revenue Code purposes, a continuing relationship can exist where work is performed at frequently recurring, but nonetheless irregular, intervals, such as when a person works on an on-call basis. One example of such a relationship would be that of a physician who sees patients at a clinic only when needed.[86]

---

84. *See* Rev. Rul. 70-572, 1970-2 C.B. 221, 1970 WL 20593 (race-horse jockey who offered services to the horse-racing public was an independent contractor). *Cf.* I.R.S. Priv. Ltr. Rul. 9251032, *supra* note 74 (nurse for state tuberculosis outreach program did not represent herself as offering services to the public and was thus an employee).

85. *See Mid-Atl.*, 16 F. App'x at 107 (fact that many cable installers had worked with hiring organization for a number of years was a neutral factor in independent contractor analysis, since it is possible for independent contractors to have a long-term relationship with an employer. *See also Brock*, 840 F.2d at 1060 (nurses were employees, even though most nurses received referrals from other sources and a few had continuing relationships with the defendant). *See also* U.S. Dep't of Labor, Wage & Hour Opinion Letter, FLSA 2019-6, *supra* note 68.

86. *See* United States v. Silk, 331 U.S. 704 (1947); Eren v. Comm'r of Internal Revenue, 180 F.3d 594, 597 (4th Cir. 1999) (worker who had performed services for hiring party exclusively for more than twenty years was employee rather than independent contractor); Weber v. Comm'r of Internal Revenue Serv., 60 F.3d 1104, 1113 (4th Cir. 1995) (minister's relationship with the church

The projected continuing relationship of Paradise County with its three newest workers further indicates that these workers should be classified as employees.

Integral Part of the Employer's Business

Where the activity that a worker performs is an integral part of the employer's operation, the worker is more likely to be found to be an employee than an independent contractor.[87] How do the courts measure whether a specific job is integral to an organization? One measure is whether the worker provides services that the employing organization exists to provide. Workers who perform the mission work of an agency are an integral part of the employer's business.[88] For example, nurses hired by a crisis clinic to provide mental-health crisis intervention and referral services to the public were found to be an integral part of the clinic's operation.[89] Similarly, a Section 8 housing coordinator who supervised one of three programs administered by the employer housing authority was considered to be an integral part of the housing authority's organization.[90] And a minister's work was clearly part of the regular work of the United Methodist Church, just as treating patients was an integral part of the professional practice of a group of psychologists.[91] None of the positions in these examples were entitled to independent contractor status; all of the workers were employees.

Another question that courts may ask in determining a worker's status is whether the worker performs the same work as others who are classified as employees. Where "independent contractors" perform the same work as employees, they are considered integrated into the employer's hierarchy and more likely to be found to be employees.[92] Similarly, where workers are independent contractors "after hours" for their regular employers but perform the same job duties as they do during "regular hours," they are most certainly going to be determined to be employees for all of the hours worked.[93] Indeed, for FLSA purposes, even where regular employees are hired to

---

was clearly envisioned as permanent where church paid salaries to ministers even when there were no positions available locally); Kentfield Med. Hosp. Corp. v. United States, 215 F. Supp. 2d 1064, 1070 (N.D. Cal. 2002) (psychologists were required to work forty-eight weeks per year and had ongoing relationships with hospital); I.R.S. Priv. Ltr. Rul. 9326015, *supra* note 50 (physician in university health clinic had continuing relationship with clinic despite the fact that he only worked there when needed). *See also* I.R.S. Priv. Ltr. Rul. 9320038, *supra* note 55 (department of corrections medical director was position with continuing relationship with hiring party).

87. *See Thomas*, 617 F. Supp. at 535. *See also* U.S. Dep't of Labor, Wage & Hour Opinion Letter, FLSA 2019-6, *supra* note 68.

88. *See* chapter 2, pages 20 through 21.

89. *See* Richardson v. Genesee Cty. Cmty. Mental Health Servs., 45 F. Supp. 2d 610, 614 (E.D. Mich. 1999). *See also* U.S. Dep't of Labor, Wage & Hour Opinion Letter, FLSA, *supra* note 51 (hospital was likely joint employer with nurse registry of private-duty nurses).

90. *See* Mathis v. Hous. Auth. of Umatilla Cty., 242 F. Supp. 2d 777, 785 (D. Or. 2002).

91. *See Weber*, 60 F.3d at 1112 (minister); I.R.S. Priv. Ltr. Rul. 9320038 (Feb. 22, 1993), 1993 WL 168902 (psychologists).

92. *See* Brock v. Superior Care, Inc., 840 F.2d 1054, 1057–58 (2d Cir. 1988); *Mathis*, 242 F. Supp. 2d at 785.

93. *See Richardson*, 45 F. Supp. 2d at 614.

perform different jobs after hours, they almost always must be treated as employees. As DOL advised one company that desired to hire an employee (the lead designer of its monthly magazine) as an independent contractor (to do the typesetting and laying out of books) through her private business:

> [I]t is our opinion that the graphic designer when performing work for your company in her freelance graphic design capacity would also be an employee of your company and not an independent contractor. This is so even though the work that she would perform as a freelance artist would be different than her normal job responsibilities at the company. *It has long been the position of the Wage and Hour Division that it is unrealistic to assume that an employment and "independent contractor relationship" may exist concurrently between the same parties in the same workweek.*[94]

In the case of the swimming pool contractor, it is clear that the contractor does not provide services that are basic to the employer's mission (because even if providing recreational services is basic to a city's business, building swimming pools is not). Nor does the contractor do work similar to that done by employees—indeed, the whole point of bringing in the swimming-pool contractor was to tap into expertise and experience that is both lacking in the city's workforce and unlikely to be needed again.

The situation of the hypothetical Paradise County workers is markedly different. Two perform some of the "mission work" of the county (sanitation work, provision of public health services), while one performs work essential to the county's business operations (paying its bills). All three perform the same work as others hired as employees. A court would likely find all three to be an integral part of the county's operations. This factor weighs heavily in favor of employee status.

Summing Up: Paradise County Has Three New Employees

In engaging the services of the sanitation worker, the visiting nurse, and the accounts payable clerk, Paradise County has taken on three new employees, notwithstanding how the county or the workers describe the relationship. Why is that the case? Because Paradise County

- has retained the right to control the work of the sanitation worker, the visiting nurse, and the accounts payable clerk;
- has the right to fire each of these workers; and
- has not provided the workers with the opportunity to make a profit or suffer a loss.

The workers, for their part,

---

94. U.S. Dep't of Labor, Wage & Hour Opinion Letter, FLSA (July 5, 2000), 2000 WL 33126569 (emphasis added).

- have not individually invested in the performance of their services for the county and
- do not seek out client opportunities on their own.

Finally, with respect to each of the workers,

- both Paradise County and the worker envision a continuing relationship and
- the work done is an integral part of the business of county government.

As a matter of law, all three workers are employees, not independent contractors.

What Happens When a Worker Desires to Be an Independent Contractor?

Sometimes a worker will want to be classified as an independent contractor rather than as an employee. The worker may be willing to "waive" the right to overtime, Social Security contributions, and other benefits to which an employee would be entitled. This will not work. The worker's desire to be classified as an independent contractor is irrelevant to a determination of his or her appropriate legal status. A worker cannot waive his or her status as an "employee" for either FLSA or Internal Revenue Code purposes. If a worker is, as a matter of economic reality, dependent upon the hiring party, or if the hiring party has the right to control the worker, the fact that the parties have called the worker an independent contractor will not alter the worker's legal status as an employee.[95]

Some Hard Cases

Positions Funded Through Grants

Almost all North Carolina government employers—state agencies, local governments, community colleges, and four-year colleges—have positions with salaries that are funded through grants from federal or private sources. Because these positions are generally created outside of the organization's usual classification and budgeting process, employers may be tempted to engage the workers as independent contractors. An IRS Revenue Ruling on the status of a professor and a clerical worker whose salaries were funded through a grant to a college makes clear that for *all* grant-funded positions, employers should continue to do economic reality and right-to-control analyses. The ruling shows that most workers hired to fill grant-funded positions will be employees rather than independent contractors.

In Revenue Ruling 55-583, the IRS found that a state college professor who was responsible for conducting research and supervising support staff under a grant from

---

95. *See* Thomas v. Global Home Prods., Inc., 617 F. Supp. 526, 534 (W.D.N.C. 1985), *citing* Robichaux v. Radcliff Material, Inc., 697 F.2d 662, 667 (5th Cir. 1983), *and* Real v. Driscoll Strawberry Assocs., Inc., 603 F.2d 748 (9th Cir. 1979) (both FLSA cases). *See also Mathis*, 242 F. Supp. 2d at 786 (Section 8 housing coordinator's request to be treated as an independent contractor did not alter the "economic reality" that she was a housing authority employee) (FLSA). See also *Weber*, 60 F.3d at 1113 (Internal Revenue Code).

a private foundation to the college was an employee of the college with respect to both that portion of his salary that was paid out of the college's budget *and* the portion paid out of grant funds. Although the professor had discretion with respect to the means and methods of performing the research, as well as authority over the hours of the research work, the college had broad general supervision over the way the grant money was spent and had a right to exercise direction and control. The professor had hired a clerical assistant to work exclusively on grant-related research, and her salary was also paid from grant funds. The IRS found that she had been hired with the implied consent of the college and held that where one employee (here, the professor) hires other individuals (the assistant) in connection with the first employee's work with either the express or implied consent of the employer, those other individuals are also employees of the employer.[96]

Two points are worth emphasizing here. First, except perhaps in the case of certain kinds of scientific research, most grants are made to the organization—sometimes to the individual who will carry out the project *and* the organization jointly—and only rarely to the individual alone. This means that the hiring organization will usually have the right to exercise direction and control over the activities funded by the grant. As explained above, the right to control a worker's activities weighs heavily in favor of employee status, even where the hiring organization does not exercise that right.

Second, the individual in charge of administering a grant may well prefer that workers hired under the grant not receive the benefits paid to other employees in the organization. This may be because the positions are for a defined, short-term duration or because the grant money is not sufficient to cover the cost of the benefits. Even if grant-funded workers do not receive benefits, they are likely to be found to be employees if the organization or an employee of the organization is directing them in the performance of their duties. While a short work relationship is a factor inclining toward independent contractor status, the mere fact that a job is temporary will not turn the worker into an independent contractor where other factors weigh in favor of employee status.

Adjunct or Part-Time Instructors in Colleges, Recreation and Parks Departments, or Employee Training and Development Programs

Educational institutions make the greatest and most obvious use of adjunct or part-time instructors, but they are not the only ones that do so. Local government recreation and parks departments also frequently hire part-time workers to teach physical education and activity classes and other subjects. Similarly, employers offering employee training and development programs are likely to make use of outside, adjunct workers to lead training sessions. For the following reasons, use of adjunct

---

96. *See* Rev. Ruling 55-583, 1955-2 C.B. 405, 1955 WL 9362.

instructors such as these would, on its face, appear to be a textbook example of the proper classification of workers as independent contractors:

- adjunct instructors are engaged for a limited duration to do a defined job;
- adjunct instructors typically have a particular expertise for which they are hired and typically perform similar or related services for other organizations or individuals;
- for colleges and local government recreation programs, the hiring organization charges a fixed fee for the courses or sessions that adjunct instructors teach and typically pay the instructors some percentage of that as a fixed fee for their services.

The IRS, however, takes a different view. In a series of revenue rulings, private letter rulings, and technical advice memoranda, the IRS has held that part-time instructors are employees where the hiring organization

- determines the courses that are offered,
- determines the content and hours of each course,
- enrolls the students, and
- provides the facilities at which the instruction is offered,

and where the instructor

- is required to perform his or her services personally;
- has no investment in the facilities; and
- does not bear a risk of profit or loss (that is, the instructor is paid the same amount whether or not tuition and fee payments cover the hiring organization's expenses).

The IRS takes this position even when an instructor provides teaching services or services related to the subject of expertise to others and may devote only a small percentage of work time to the instruction performed for the hiring organization.[97] The IRS analysis focuses on the fact that the hiring organization controls everything about the way in which the "teaching services" are performed—that is, in each of the cases the IRS considered, the hiring organization controlled everything except the actual delivery of the material.

Would the FLSA economic-reality test provide a different result? Probably not. As discussed above, the economic-reality test and the IRS right-to-control test consider essentially the same factors. Research for this book has not revealed any cases that address the issue of an adjunct instructor's status as employee or independent contractor under the FLSA. This lack of case law is not surprising. Most instructors would have little reason to bring an FLSA claim. Many instructors would qualify as FLSA-exempt professionals, and few nonexempt part-time instructors are likely to work in excess of forty hours, so overtime is probably not going to be an issue.

---

97. *See* Rev. Ruling 70-308, 1970-1 C.B. 199, 1970 WL 20861; Tech. Adv. Mem. 91-05-007 (Feb. 1, 1991); I.R.S. Tech. Adv. Mem. 89-25-001 (June 23, 1989); I.R.S. Priv. Ltr. Rul. 8728022 (Apr. 10, 1987), 1987 WL 421922.

Physicians

Correctly classifying (as employees or independent contractors) physicians hired to staff health clinics, on-site occupational-health offices, or public hospitals presents some of the same challenges as classifying registered nurses, discussed above in the section on professionals. Given their very high level of specialized training, physicians generally exercise almost complete discretion in their treatment of patients and are subject to relatively little day-to-day supervision. Where there is such supervision, it is generally provided by another physician.

As discussed earlier, an important factor in determining whether a worker is an employee or independent contractor is the extent to which the worker's services are an integral part of the organization's regular business. As the IRS has noted in Revenue Ruling 66-274,[98] a hiring organization that engages a physician usually does so because providing medical services is necessary to its operation. More important than the question of whether a physician's services are integral to an organization is the way the services of the physician are integrated into the hiring organization. Significant factors are (1) the manner in which the physician is paid for his or her services—that is, whether the physician is paid on a percentage basis, a salary basis, or a percentage basis with a guaranteed minimum; (2) whether the physician is permitted to employ associate physicians or to engage substitutes when he or she is absent from work; (3) if the physician is permitted to engage substitutes, whether the physician or the hiring organization is responsible for compensating them; and (4) whether the physician is permitted to engage in the outside private practice of medicine or to perform professional services for others.[99] In other words, in the case of physicians, the right to control is a less important set of factors for IRS purposes than is the extent to which the physician is economically independent of the hiring organization.

Applying these factors, the IRS found that a physician director of a hospital pathology department was an independent contractor where the physician received a percentage of the department's gross receipts as his only compensation; personally paid his associates or substitutes; was permitted to engage in the private practice of medicine; and was not subject to the direction and control of any hospital representative, such as a chief of staff.[100] But in a different case, a physician director of a hospital laboratory was found to be an employee where he was guaranteed a minimum salary in addition to a specified percentage of charges attributable to his department and he could not pursue outside business or provide pathology services to others without written consent.[101]

---

98. *See supra* note 48.

99. *See id. See also Weber,* 60 F.3d at 1112 (minister's work clearly part of regular work of United Methodist Church); I.R.S. Priv. Ltr. Rul. 9320038 (Feb. 22, 1993) (dep't of corrections medical director paid hourly rate is employee); I.R.S. Priv. Ltr. Rul. 8937039 (Sept. 15, 1989) (psychologists treating patients for professional firm are employees).

100. *See* Rev. Rul. 66-274, *supra* note 48.

101. *See* Rev. Rul. 73-417, *supra* note 48.

Penalties: A Price to Pay

Most people performing services for a public-sector organization are "employees" within the common-law definition of that term. True independent contractors are few. As set forth in more detail below, when a government employer misclassifies an employee as an independent contractor, it can unwittingly accrue substantial unfunded liabilities in the form of unpaid overtime, unpaid employer FICA contributions, and penalties for violating the FLSA and the Internal Revenue Code. The penalties that employers face for misclassification of an employee as an independent contractor make illusory those projected savings that tempt employers to engage workers as independent contractors in the first place. For this reason, it is crucial that each public employer establish a procedure for reviewing any proposed relationship with a worker it plans to engage on an independent contractor basis. Few will so qualify. A model checklist to assist employers in analyzing worker status may be found at the end of this chapter.

FLSA

Suppose that an employer misclassifies a worker as an independent contractor when the FLSA's economic-reality test shows that the worker ought to be classified as an employee. If the worker is a nonexempt employee and has worked in excess of forty hours in any workweek, the employer is in violation of the FLSA. The employer certainly will not have been paying overtime. In such an instance, the worker will have a claim to unpaid overtime compensation. Employer liability for violations of the FLSA's overtime provisions include the full amount of unpaid overtime going back for a period of two years and an additional amount equal to the amount of the unpaid overtime as liquidated damages.[102] That's the penalty when the violation was not willful. Where the violation is willful—that is, where the employing organization has been put on notice of its noncompliance with the FLSA by DOL or otherwise has reason to know that it is noncompliant, or where it shows a reckless disregard for the provisions of the FLSA—then the liability of the employer for unpaid overtime compensation extends back for a period of three years and it will be responsible for an equal amount in liquidated damages.[103]

---

102. *See* 29 U.S.C. §§ 216(b), 255(a).

103. *See* 29 U.S.C. § 255(a); *Brock* v. *Superior Care, Inc.,* 840 F.2d 1054, 1061 (2d Cir. 1988). Note that conduct that is merely unreasonable or negligent with respect to ascertaining an employer's obligations under the FLSA is not considered to be willful. *See* McLaughlin v. Richland Shoe Co., 486 U.S. 128, 131, 133–35 (1988), *overruling* Donovan v. Bel-Loc Diner, Inc., 780 F.2d. 1113 (4th Cir. 1985). *See also* Troutt v. Stavola Bros., Inc., 905 F. Supp. 295, 302 (M.D.N.C. 1995) (mere failure to seek legal advice, standing alone, is insufficient to establish willfulness where there is no pattern of complaints to the employer or in the industry that could establish knowledge or recklessness on part of employer), *aff'd,* 107 F.3d 1104 (4th Cir. 1997). But an employer's failure to investigate whether its policies violate the FLSA where employees have questioned those policies would be reckless. *See* Davis v. Charoen Pokphand (USA), Inc., 302 F. Supp. 2d 1314, 1327 (M.D. Ala. 2004); LaPorte v. Gen. Elec. Plastics, 838 F. Supp. 549, 558 (M.D. Ala. 1993). In the Fourth Circuit, the determination of whether a violation was willful or not under 29 U.S.C. § 255(a), and thus whether the employer's liability for back overtime extends back three or merely two years,

Internal Revenue Code

When the Internal Revenue Service determines that a worker has not met the requirements of the right-to-control test and has been erroneously classified as an independent contractor, the employer will (1) be liable for a percentage of the worker's federal income tax liability, for both the employer's own share of the worker's FICA tax liability and a percentage of the worker's share, and (2) potentially be liable for interest on the underwithheld amounts and penalties. Where the employer has *unintentionally* misclassified the worker but has at least filed a Form 1099 showing the amounts paid to the worker each tax year, the employer will be liable for only 1.5 percent of the worker's federal income tax liability and up to 20 percent of the worker's missing FICA contribution. The employer's liability increases to 3 percent of the worker's income tax liability and up to 40 percent of the worker's missing FICA contribution if it has failed to file a Form 1099. If the IRS finds that the employer *intentionally* misclassified the worker, the employer may be liable for the worker's entire federal income tax liability and for the worker's entire FICA contribution. The employer may not seek reimbursement from the worker for taxes, penalties, or fines imposed by the IRS.[104]

> **When Workers Sue for Lost Benefits**
>
> In several private-sector cases, workers engaged as independent contractors have sued their hiring organizations, claiming that they were in fact employees and that they were therefore entitled to participate in the hiring organization's employee benefit plans. In some cases, the employees have sought the value of benefits retrospectively. For a discussion of whether such a suit would be successful against a North Carolina public employer, see Diane M. Juffras, *Independent Contractor or Employee? The Legal Distinction and Its Consequences*, Public Employment Law Bulletin No. 32, 20–25 (UNC School of Government, May 2005), https://www.sog.unc.edu/sites/www.sog.unc.edu/files/reports/pelb32.pdf.

Joint Employment

An employee might work for two different employers. When the two employers have no relationship with one another, the situation is uncomplicated. But when the employers do have a relationship, the FLSA's rules on "joint employment" may be implicated. Generally speaking, joint employment is the sharing and control of an employee by two separate organizations. Joint employers are jointly and separately liable for the wages, straight-time and overtime, of workers in whose performance

---

will be determined by a jury. *See* Fowler v. Land Mgmt. Grp., Inc., 978 F.2d 158, 162–63 (4th Cir. 1992); Soto v. McLean, 20 F. Supp. 2d 901, 913 (E.D.N.C. 1998) (denying defendants' motion for summary judgment).

104. *See* 26 U.S.C. §§ 3509, 6601, 6651, 6662, 6721.

they share an interest if certain conditions are met. Organizations that use a staffing agency to find needed workers may be joint employers of those workers with the staffing agency. When a local government brings in an outside company to perform work on its premises—a construction company, for example, or a plumbing contractor or landscaping company—it could be a joint employer of those workers together with the company with whom it contracts. There is no general legal definition of *joint employment*. Each employment statute has its own standards for imposing joint liability for violation of an employee's rights under the statute, although the standards are similar.

For FLSA purposes, there are two categories of joint employment. In the first, there is one employer but another organization benefits from an employee's work. This is the most common type of joint employment. It arises where there is a single employer (a staffing agency and/or a contractor) and another organization with which that employer contracts (say, a city, county, or state agency) benefits from the work of the staffing agency's or contractor's employee's work.[105] The second FLSA category of joint employment occurs far less frequently in the public sector. It occurs when two employers are said to be "significantly associated." This section will discuss the first and most familiar type of joint employment first. A brief discussion of "significantly associated" will follow.

Using a Staffing Agency: Joint Employment Where the Work of Another Organization's Employee Benefits a Public Entity

Here's what the FLSA regulations, specifically, Section 791.2 of Title 29 of the Code of Federal Regulations (C.F.R.), say about DOL's first category of joint employers:

> . . . the employee has an employer who suffers, permits, or otherwise employs the employee to work . . . but another person simultaneously benefits from that work. The other person is the employee's joint employer only if that person is acting directly or indirectly in the interest of the employer in relation to the employee.[106]

Where a local government engages the services of a staffing agency or has brought in a contractor with its own employees for a specific purpose, the local government is not the primary employer. The staffing agency or contractor is. The public entity hopes to benefit from the contractor's employees' work—otherwise it is not getting what it is paying for! But what does it mean for a city or county or the state to be—in the words of Section 791.2(a)(1)—"acting directly or indirectly in the interest of" the contractor that it has hired, that is, in the interest of the staffing agency or contractor? It is an odd notion.

---

105. *See* 29 C.F.R. § 791.2.
106. 29 C.F.R. § 791.2(a)(1).

The Four-Factor Test

For a public agency to be a joint employer with a company with whom it contracts, the public entity must

1. hire or fire the employee, and/or
2. supervise and control the employee's work schedule or conditions of employment, and/or
3. determine the employee's rate and method of payment, and/or
4. maintain the employee's employment records.

These are the four factors that DOL will take into consideration in determining whether a second organization (in this case, the public entity) is also an employer of a worker and liable for its straight-time and overtime wages. No one factor is determinative. The second entity (that is, the public organization) does not have to satisfy all four factors to be a joint employer. The factors are considered in the totality of the circumstances.[107]

This is a boiled-down, elementary version of the right-to-control test, similar to the economic-reality test used by DOL and the twenty-factor right-to-control test used by the IRS in evaluating whether an individual worker is an employee or independent contractor. There are, however, important differences. First of all, the second organization—the city, county, or state agency—must **actually exercise** one or more of these four indications of control for the public entity to be considered a joint employer. It isn't enough that its agreement with the primary employer gives it **the right** to give instructions to the employee or to fire the employee if he or she is incompetent or untrustworthy.[108] The second organization must actually exercise those rights. Conversely, if the government organization's agreement with the primary employer doesn't give it the right to control the employee in any of these ways but the reality is that it does, then it may be a joint employer.[109]

Second, the economic dependence of the employee on the work it does for the public entity, the employee's opportunity to make a profit or loss, and whether or not the employee uses the public organization's supplies or brings his or her own is irrelevant to the joint-employer analysis. Those are key features of the FLSA and IRS independent contractor tests, but they are *not* part of the joint-employment test.[110]

---

107. *See id.*

108. In the tests used for determining independent contractor vs. employee status, a hiring organization need only have the right to control the worker for it to count toward employee status. Evidence that the hiring organization actually exercised the right is not required.

109. *See* 29 C.F.R. § 791.2(a)(3)(i). The four-factor test is similar to that used for determining joint-employer status under federal anti-discrimination laws such as Title VII, the Age Discrimination in Employment Act, and the Americans with Disabilities Act. *See, e.g.,* Butler v. Drive Auto. Indus. of Am., Inc., 793 F.3d 404, 408 (4th Cir. 2015) (Title VII).

110. *See* 29 C.F.R. § 791.2(c).

When Two Employers Are "Significantly Associated": Another Type of Joint Employment

In the second type of joint employment relationship, there are two separate employers of a single individual. Frequently, one employer hires an employee for a certain number of hours each week and another employer hires the same employee for a different set of hours each week. Most of the time, this is not joint employment because the employers are acting independently of one another. Indeed, they may not even know that the other employer exists at the time of hiring. But occasionally, the two employers are "significantly associated" in such a way that DOL considers them joint employers.[111] This sort of joint employment is relatively rare in the public sector.

The Meaning of "Significantly Associated"

DOL gives three instances in which it will consider two separate entities to be *significantly associated* with respect to the hiring by each entity of the same employee. The first is where two employers agree to share the services of the same employee.[112] In the public sector, this situation is most likely to occur when a city and a county have a combined department, such as a city-county planning department or a combined 911 operation. In this case, the city and the county are jointly the employers of employees of the combined department. This arrangement is different from one in which a city or county contracts out a service to another local government entity, such as when a municipality contracts with a county for 911 emergency service.

Another type of "significant association" occurs when two employers have hired the very same person but one employer is acting in the interest of the other employer, either directly or indirectly.[113] An obvious example of this in the private sector would be where one employer company owns a second employer company or where both employers are subsidiaries of the same holding company. In the public sector, it is possible that the relationship between a tourism board and a city or county could fall into this category, as could, perhaps, the relationship between a housing authority and a city or county. Whether a relationship between two public employers falls into this category depends upon the details of the underlying arrangement.[114]

---

111. *See* 29 C.F.R. §§ 791.2(e)(1), (2)(i).

112. *See* 29 C.F.R. § 791.2(e)(2)(i). This is similar to the first category of joint employment relationship, discussed above, except that in the first category there is a single formal employer, whereas here two entities have hired the same employee. The same four-factor test applies.

113. *See* 29 C.F.R. § 791.2(e)(2)(ii).

114. Still another example of "significant association" is where the two employers share control of an employee because one employer controls the other or is under common control with the other employer. *See* 29 C.F.R. § 791.2(e)(2)(iii).

Determining Whether There Is a Joint-Employer Relationship

In its FLSA regulations, DOL has included a number of examples of how the joint-employer rule is to be applied. Four of the examples are especially relevant to public entities. These are presented below, translated into the public employment context.

> The City of Paradise hires a janitorial services company to clean its buildings after hours. The city agrees to pay the janitorial company a fixed fee for these services and reserves the right to supervise the janitorial employees in their performance of those cleaning services. But the city does not set the janitorial employees' pay rates or individual schedules and does not in fact supervise the workers' performance of their duties in any way. Is the city a joint employer of the janitorial employees?

As DOL explains, the public employer in this situation would not be a joint employer of the janitorial employees because it does not hire or fire the employees, determine their rate or method of payment, or exercise control over their conditions of employment. The city's reserved contractual right to control the employee's conditions of employment is not enough to turn it into a joint employer where it does not exercise that right in practice.[115]

Here's the next fact pattern:

> A county contracts with a landscaping company to maintain its public golf course. The contract does not give the county authority to hire or fire landscaping employees or to supervise their work. In practice, a county employee oversees landscaping employees by sporadically assigning them tasks throughout each workweek, providing them with periodic instructions during each workday, and keeping intermittent records of their work. At the county's direction, the landscaping company agreed to terminate a worker for failure to follow the county employee's instructions. Is the county a joint employer of the landscaping employees?

Here, the county **is a joint employer** of the landscaping employees. Why? Because the county exercises sufficient control, both direct and indirect, over the terms and conditions of their employment. It directly supervises the landscaping employees' work and determines their schedules on what amounts to a regular basis. The county indirectly controls the employees because it had the landscaping company fire one of the employees for not following the directions of a county employee.[116]

Consider a third fact pattern.

---

115. *See* 29 C.F.R. §§ 791.2(g)(3)(i), (ii).
116. *See* 29 C.F.R. §§ 791.2(g)(i), (ii).

A county department requests certain types of workers from a staffing agency on a daily basis. The staffing agency determines each worker's hourly rate of pay, but the county department supervises each one's work continuously adjusts the number of workers it requests and the specific hours for each worker, sending workers home depending on workload. Is the county department a joint employer of the staffing agency's employees?

Yes, this is another example of joint employment. The county department is a joint employer of the staffing agency's employees because it exercises sufficient control over their terms and conditions of employment by supervising their work, and controlling their work schedules.[117]

Below is the last example.

The Association of North Carolina Local Governments provides optional group health coverage to cities and counties to offer to their employees. Both the City of Paradise and Paradise County provide the Association's optional group health coverage to their respective employees. The employees of both the city and the county choose to opt in to the health plans. Does the participation of the City of Paradise and Paradise County in the Association's health plan make the Association a joint employer of the city's and the county's employees? Are the city and the county joint employers of each other's employees?

The answer to each of these questions is a resounding "no." The Association is not a joint employer of the city's or the county's employees and the city and the county are not joint employers of each other's employees. Participation in the Association's optional plans does not involve any control by the Association, direct or indirect, over the city's or the county's employees. And while the city and the county independently offer the same plans to their respective employees, there is no indication that they are coordinating, directly or indirectly, to control the other's employees.[118]

Bottom Line on Joint Employment

If a governmental employer chooses reliable staffing agencies or contractors that pay employees in full and on time, it will be unlikely to find itself liable for the straight-time and overtime wages of that company's workers. Public employers should nevertheless steer clear of exercising direction or control over the employees of other organizations unless they have affirmatively decided to do so. Cities and counties who use staffing agencies are likely to exercise control over the workers whose services they obtain in this manner, but they should be aware that such an arrangement is not risk-free. As for companies that do work on the employer's premises, a public employer should refrain from directing the work of such a company's employees.

---

117. *See* 29 C.F.R. §§ 791.2(g)(6)(i), (ii).
118. *See* 29 C.F.R. §§ 791.2(g)(8)(i), (ii).

Appendix A. Model Checklist to Help Determine Independent Contractor or Employee Status

Employers should modify this checklist, as appropriate, to align with the nature of their organization as a whole or to meet the needs of a particular department. Every proposal to engage a worker as an independent contractor must be assessed individually. Whether that worker legally qualifies as an independent contractor will depend on the facts and circumstances of the individual situation.

PART I. The answer "yes" indicates that the factor weighs in favor of employee status, while the answer "no" indicates that the factor weighs in favor of independent contractor status.

	Factor	Yes	No
1.	Does the hiring organization have the **right** to control (a) when, where, and how the worker will do the job or (b) the order and sequence in which the worker will perform services? (Check "yes" even if the organization does not intend to exercise that right.)		
2.	Does the hiring organization set the worker's hours and schedule?		
3.	Must the work be performed personally by the worker (as opposed to the worker subcontracting it out or furnishing his or her own substitute)?		
4.	Is the hiring organization providing training of any kind?		
5.	Does the hiring organization provide the worker with the tools, supplies, and/or equipment needed to do the job (as opposed to requiring the worker to bring his or her own tools, equipment, and supplies)?		
6.	Does an employee of the hiring organization supervise the worker?		
7.	Does the worker have to submit written, or deliver oral, reports?		
8.	Is the work performed on the hiring organization's premises or at a site controlled or designated by the hiring organization?		
9.	If the worker is performing services off-site, does the hiring organization have the right to send supervisors to the site to check up on the worker? (Check "yes" even if the organization has no intention of exercising that right.)		
10.	Can the worker be fired at the will of the hiring organization?		
11.	Can the worker quit the job at will without incurring any liability?		
12.	Will the hiring organization hire, fire, and pay the worker's assistants?		
13.	Will the worker be paid by the hour, week, or month (as opposed to being paid for the successful completion of the job or piece)?		
14.	Has the hiring organization unilaterally set the worker's rate of pay?		
15.	Does the hiring organization reimburse the worker for expenses and travel?		

PART I, *cont'd*

	Factor	Yes	No
16.	Is the relationship between the hiring organization and the worker going to be a continuing relationship?		
17.	Does anyone working for the organization as an employee perform the same or similar services as those to be performed by the worker?		
18.	Are the services performed by the worker part of the core or day-to-day operations of the hiring organization?		
19.	Is the worker a current employee in another capacity?		
20.	Was the worker an employee at any time during the past year? If so, did the worker provide the same or similar services as an employee that he or she will be providing now?		

PART II. Here, the answer "yes" indicates that the factor weighs in favor of independent contractor status, while the answer "no" indicates that the factor weighs in favor of employee status.

	Factor	Yes	No
21.	Does the worker perform similar services for others as an independent contractor?		
22.	Does the worker advertise his or her services to the public?		
23.	Has the worker made any investment in facilities or equipment needed to do the work?		
24.	Does the arrangement between the hiring organization and the worker allow the worker to make a profit or suffer a loss?		

Subject Index

www.ingramcontent.com/pod-product-compliance
Lightning Source LLC
Chambersburg PA
CBHW050039220326
41599CB00044B/7226